WHAT
REALLY
HAPPENS
IN
VEGAS

A list of titles by James Patterson appears
at the back of this book

WHAT REALLY HAPPENS IN VEGAS

JAMES PATTERSON

with MARK SEAL

C

CENTURY

1 3 5 7 9 10 8 6 4 2

Century
20 Vauxhall Bridge Road
London SW1V 2SA

Century is part of the Penguin Random House group of companies
whose addresses can be found at global.penguinrandomhouse.com.

First published by Century in 2023

www.penguin.co.uk

A CIP catalogue record for this book is available from the British Library.

ISBN: 9781529136739 (hardback)
ISBN: 9781529136746 (trade paperback)

Interior book design by Marie Mundaca

Printed and bound in Great Britain by Clays Ltd, Elcograf S.p.A.

The authorised representative in the EEA is Penguin Random House Ireland,
Morrison Chambers, 32 Nassau Street, Dublin D02 YH68

www.greenpenguin.co.uk

MIX
Paper | Supporting
responsible forestry
FSC® C018179
www.fsc.org

Penguin Random House is committed to a
sustainable future for our business, our readers
and our planet. This book is made from Forest
Stewardship Council® certified paper.

CONTENTS

INTRODUCTION: "LUCK BE A LADY…"   3

1   WELCOME TO LAS VEGAS   13
    Harry Reid International Airport

2   THE RIDE   19
    Wayne Newton Boulevard

3   THE ARRIVAL   31
    The Wynn

4   THE VIP HOST   43
    The VIP Wing of a Major Las Vegas Resort

5   WHEEL OF FORTUNE!   55
    Harry Reid International Airport

6   THE WEDDING QUEEN OF THE WEST   61
    A Little White Wedding Chapel

7   FROM VILLAIN TO VISIONARY   77
    The Mob Museum

8   THE HEALER AMONG THE HUSTLERS   95
    The Sapphire Las Vegas Pool and Dayclub

9   WHAT HAPPENS HERE, STAYS HERE   109
    R&R Partners Advertising Agency

10 THE QUEEN OF LAS VEGAS   131
    The Strip

CONTENTS

11 UNMASKING THE JACKPOT WINNER
OF THE MASK 157
Treasure Island

12 RISK CITY 173
The STRAT

13 THE INVASION OF THE SUPERCHEFS! 185
Spago Las Vegas

14 MAGIC 209
The Mirage

15 THE GREATEST SHOW ON EARTH 229
The "O" Theater

16 THE TRIUMPH OF THE OPERATIC TENOR 249
The MGM Grand Garden Arena

17 EARNING A NAME AT THE PALMS 261
N9NE Steakhouse

18 THE GHOST OF ELVIS PRESLEY 281
Cruising the Strip

19 THE HABITAT OF THE WHALES 295
The Cosmopolitan Reserve

20 THE HUSTLER 305
The Wild Side of Town

21 HERE COMES THE SUN 321
Circa Resort and Casino, and the Wynn

22 THE VALLEY OF FIRE 341
The Mojave Desert

ACKNOWLEDGMENTS 355

"LUCK BE A LADY..."

IT'S 5:30 A.M. in the city of overnight fortunes and broken dreams.

Beneath the glittering marble halls and jangling slot machines, behind a pair of massive steel doors, twenty-five dive-certified men and women begin their workday. Some pull on scuba gear; others don blue fire-retardant work clothes, with their names embroidered on patches over their chests. It's a secret underground world, a vast clandestine warehouse filled with giant machines, rows of tools, half-disassembled robots, and spare parts. The crew calls it the Bat Cave.

They're a tight-knit group. A former rock 'n' roll technician for the Stones and AC/DC. A few military vets, engineers, and mechanics. Assorted refugees from blue-collar jobs and the corporate world. Led by manager Victoria

Rios, they form a band of brothers and sisters, united in the service of something bigger than themselves.

"Hope you finally caught some sleep last night," says one.

"Barely," answers another. "Up all night, thinking about the faults."

The first man shrugs. *The faults.* There are always faults, something amiss. That's what they're here for: to fix the faults, in a city practically founded on faults. "We'll get it taken care of today," the man says.

By 6 a.m., the crew is aboard a barge in a finger of lake that extends into the Bat Cave, sailing in battle-ground solemnity into a crystal-blue expanse filled with twenty-two million gallons of the single most precious commodity for a city in the middle of the desert: water.

The lake, located in the heart of Las Vegas, encom-passes eight and a half acres. Beneath its surface, ready to emerge at the appointed time, lies a complex network of equipment: pipes, valves, pumps, lights, motors, manifolds, sensors. The crew inspects every inch of it. Divers float through the water, using pressure gauges to search for leaks in the miles of metal tubing. They hover over com-puterized electronics arrayed in gigantic concentric circles. The circles are composed of robotic machinery equipped with 1,214 water jets in escalating calibers. Some are the size of a person; others are as large as a small automobile. All are capable of spraying water with industrial force and acrobatic precision. The smallest and most numerous, the 798 jets known as minishooters, can send plumes of water shooting one hundred twenty feet skyward. More powerful ones, the 192 supershooters, can reach two hundred forty-four feet. In the central ring are the monsters—the 16 extreme shooters—whose blasts soar four hundred sixty feet.

Out on the surface of the artificial lake, the team moves across the water slowly, in search of problems. The sun has yet to rise over the city, but the water is already almost as warm as blood, bathed in a brighter-than-daylight glow from the signs that encircle it. In any system this size, things go wrong. But this one—state-of-the-art when it was installed—is now twenty-five years old, and requires significant maintenance. Lines get snagged, limiting their range of motion. Hardwired programs must be manually plugged into a central computer. If there's a fault, the crew will need to drag the defective part back to the Bat Cave, to repair the damage or swap in a spare. "Think of it as a twenty-five-year-old car—only more complicated," explains a member of the team.

The individuals who tend to the equipment seem to be both in love and obsessed with their historic charge. On good days, the machinery confers a sense of majesty. "When I was single, girls would flock here just to watch us work," one worker recalls.

"Twenty-two million gallons of water going up in the air every day and night," says another.

"I cared about it so much that it kept me up at night," says one team member of the sleeplessness that comes with the responsibility for a massive mechanical assembly that sprawls across so many acres and so many imaginations, tended to by a crew determined to do whatever it takes to make it run absolutely right.

After six and a half hours of repairs, adjustments, and cleaning, the crew is finally done for the day. It's half past noon as they make their way back to the Bat Cave. The sun is high in the Las Vegas sky, and sweat and sunblock drip from their faces. In summer, the mercury soars well above one hundred ten; in winter, it often plunges to just above freezing. But whatever the temperature, they have done their job. Their dream machine is ready to perform.

The Fountains of Bellagio show is about to begin.

Every weekday at 3 p.m.—and weekends at noon—the fountain's enormous apparatus of rings and shooters rises before each performance via hydraulic arms from its resting place beneath the lake like some futuristic mechanical beast. The two hundred eight oarsmen (the fountain's only water jets whose directions can vary) point their nimble mechanical arms skyward, preparing to erupt in a dizzy, dancing array of aquatic acrobatics. On some days, fog pours from the manifolds and crawls across the surface of the lake; at other times, the lake appears to be boiling, from a hidden apparatus below. Then comes the music, mournful and intimate, blasting from two hundred thirteen hidden speakers in and around the lake.

They call you Lady Luck…

It's Frank Sinatra, singing "Luck Be a Lady," one of the city's many anthems. And with the music comes the water, so much water that it defies imagination. Millions of gallons shoot into the air with incredible precision, a majestic spray as symphonic as the song, maybe even more so: water dancing, water shimmying, water swaying, water waving daintily like fingers curled in beckoning. And most impressively, water *shooting,* as high as the edifice behind it, the looming towers of the Bellagio Resort and Casino.

With each word Frank Sinatra sings to Lady Luck, the water responds. Staccato horns punctuate the lyrics, each brassy burst accompanied by an upward stab from the minishooters.

The water drops, the fountain is still for a beat, and then the nozzles fire at full blast as Sinatra and the big band roar, *Luck be a lady tonight!*

The oarsmen unleash slinky tendrils, evoking Lady Luck striding across the casino floor, her eyes wandering toward the other gamblers she might take up with for the night.

The fountain's jets fire off in unison like a high-kicking chorus line, then gently spiral outward like an unfurling flower, to accompany the tender pleading in Sinatra's voice. With the final repetition of the chorus comes the big finish, the raw power of the extreme shooters harmonizing with the delicate sprays of the minishooters.

When it's over, and the fountain falls silent, a

thunderous roar rises from the spectators that have gathered to watch the show. They're cheering both the melancholy defiance of the music and the breathtaking majesty of the fountain, the lake that can make water dance.

From now until midnight, the Fountains of Bellagio will perform up to four times an hour—on weekends and holidays, as many as thirty-three times over the course of a day and night. Since its debut in 1998, it's a spectacle that has become the iconic image of a city built on image, replacing the symbols that came before it: the WELCOME TO FABULOUS LAS VEGAS sign erected as a neon welcome at the edge of town in 1959; Vegas Vickie, the neon cowgirl who kicked up her bootheels above the Glitter Gulch strip club; or her "husband," Vegas Vic, the neon cowboy who still stands in front of the old Pioneer Club. But all of those were mere *signs,* now rendered tired and tame by comparison to the dancing waters, which have been called the eighth wonder of the world.

The idea was dreamed up over dinner one night at the palatial home of the Bellagio's creator, Steve Wynn, back when the resort was still in the process of being born.

"What are the characteristics of all great gathering places in Europe?" someone who was at the meeting recalls Wynn asking the executive team he had assembled. Was it sculpture? Art? The views? The people watching?

Fountains.

From Paris to Madrid to Vienna to Rome, the great piazzas of Europe all feature fountains.

From there the concept grew from a mere fountain into one of the world's most colossal spectacle machines, free to everyone in Vegas, from the high rollers in their mansion-sized supersuites to the down-and-outs hoping for a turn of fortune. But the best view is from the Strip itself, where some fifty thousand people stop to watch the fountain each day, gathering at the railing around the lake to revel in the towering spumes of spray.

As the sun sets and the Strip is swathed in a neon glow, the Fountains of Bellagio dress for the evening, adding 4,792 underwater lights to their display, choreographed to an ever-changing lineup of thirty-five songs such as Andrea Bocelli's "Con te Partirò," Lady Gaga's "Bad Romance," and Elvis Presley's "Viva Las Vegas." A miracle of mechanics and magic for a city once dismissed as a folly, forever determined to prove its worth to the world.

In advance of the final season of *Game of Thrones,* for one night only in 2019, the fountain is where holograms of flying dragons were projected onto the spray and mist while real flames flickered on the surface of the lake. At the end of *Ocean's 11,* George Clooney's charming gang of thieves—Brad Pitt, Matt Damon, and the rest—gathered at the fountain on the night after their big heist and leaned on the railing, enthralled by the waters dancing to Debussy's "Clair de Lune" as the camera panned across their faces. Céline Dion performed a special televised rendition of "My Heart Will Go On" on a floating replica of the *Titanic* bowsprit alongside comedian and

TV host James Corden, before dropping a replica of the film's famous Heart of the Sea necklace into the lake's crystal-blue waters.

The crew found that necklace. Just as the four-person, dive-certified "clean team" finds almost everything else when they scour the bottom of the lake between shows, the collective hope and despair of a gambler's town: real jewelry, cast into the fountain for luck or flung in rage; empty bottles of booze; discarded clothes, cell phones, and cameras; and an estimated two tons of coins per year, each token an unspoken wish, and every cent donated to charity.

At the heart of the fountain, as in most attractions of Las Vegas, is fantasy. And while the city was built on fantasy, fantasies must be created, and every act of creation requires skill and coordination and hard work, the unseen toiling of armies of personnel.

Behind the curtain of water and music and magic lies a clandestine world of grit and gumption—the daily, hidden work required to conjure up the desert mirage of Las Vegas. Like the Fountains of Bellagio, the city's attractions require a complex network of labor to run. The endless battalions who build, service, and maintain the perpetually expanding facilities; the dealers and croupiers who run the games; the international superchefs, cocktail wizards, and servers who fortify the multitudes; the dazzling superstars of stage, screen, nightclub, and stripper pole; the pilots, limo drivers, and cabbies who keep the city on the move.

All of this effort produces something greater than the sum of its infinite parts: a sense of fantasy and escape, perhaps the greatest fantasy and escape machine on Earth, everything working together as a whole to create an illusion, a spectacle as seductive, and, for some, as fleeting, as a mirage—the experience of Las Vegas, Nevada.

Chapter 1

WELCOME TO LAS VEGAS

HARRY REID INTERNATIONAL AIRPORT

THE CITY BEGINS casting its spell at the airport.

Harry Reid International isn't just a portal to the city, the place where one million visitors arrive and depart every week from around the world. It's the opening act, the master of ceremonies, designed to seduce new arrivals with a shimmering display of slot machines, shopping, dining, advertising, and glitz. Set on one of the largest footprints in southern Nevada, covering 4.4 square miles, the airport's glass-sheathed towers shimmer by day in the desert sun and glow in the neon-lit night.

In an office tucked behind a Starbucks and a TSA security checkpoint sits the airport's director, Rosemary

Vassiliadis. Under her watchful eye, the airport runs twenty-two hours a day, pausing only for two hours just before daybreak. "We never lock our doors," says Vassiliadis. There are nearly one thousand flights every day, with more than one hundred direct routes from big cities like New York and Los Angeles and London as well as towns like Bozeman, Fort Collins, and Humboldt. On many Sundays and Mondays, Harry Reid has served more people than any other airport in America.

So many visitors pass through the terminals every day, as many as 52 million in one year, that the airport has its own police and fire departments. The single biggest carrier, Southwest Airlines, has commandeered an entire concourse—Concourse C, in the ever-expanding Terminal 1—shuffling 1.5 million arriving and departing passengers in November 2022 alone, according to one published report. Many of the larger casinos, from Caesars Palace to the MGM Grand, operate their own charters for elite customers at the adjacent private air terminals at the airport, and private helicopters can be seen taking off for aerial tours of the Grand Canyon.

Travelers arriving at one of the one hundred ten gates are met with a blast of air conditioning that belies the summer heat, which regularly rises above one hundred degrees. These dreamers and schemers arrive wearing slick suits and skimpy dresses, formal tuxedos and wedding gowns, cargo shorts and flip-flops—"things they don't wear at home," says Vassiliadis. They come for love and lust, superstar concerts and trade conventions, magic shows and boxing matches, and, threading through it all, *action*. They have practiced their bets during their flights, reading how-to books that promise secrets for beating the house. What many don't realize is that the house begins here, at Harry Reid International Airport.

"Give them Vegas as soon as that jet-bridge door opens," Vassiliadis likes to say, "and keep Vegas going until it shuts."

It's a creed reflected in the airport's every detail. From the moment passengers disembark, rowdy and ready for fun, Vegas begins its seduction. At the airport, the hours are set to Luxury Standard Time: every clock, in every terminal, is a Rolex. Even the floor, which Vassiliadis had first seen in the Disney Store at Caesars Palace, is designed to induce awe: a swirling terrazzo, glittering with bright shards of broken mirrors. Here, the fancy floors announce, money is no object, glories abound, and wonders never cease.

"A lot of bling," Vassiliadis says of her airport. "A lot of bling, and branding *everywhere*."

Arrivals are eager for the action, giddy with anticipation. "They get off the plane and they're ready to go," says one airport official. "They want to get into their cab. Get to the hotel, get to the casino, get to the action. They want to get on their way. They're yelling, 'Vegas, baby!' and things like that. They're getting the party started before they even leave the airport."

Slot machines are ubiquitous. There are more than one thousand one-armed bandits throughout the airport, strategically arranged in mazes outside each gate and in enticing lines next to the baggage claim carousels. The machines were first installed in 1968, and the numbers grew throughout the 1970s. Originally they were coin-operated slots, but today the entire collection is digital, with constantly upgraded contraptions that offer ever-mounting jackpots. In almost every terminal, the blaring Wheel of Fortune slot is a main attraction.

"Our surveys let us know that our visitors want to *hear* the slot machines," says Vassiliadis, who ensures that the volume on the slots is turned up loud. "It's not noise to them—it's music, it's attraction. That's why they come here. Only two airports in the nation have slots—us and Reno."

The jangling din of the slot machines tends to obscure the actual music, the soundtrack pouring from unseen speakers throughout the airport—the legendary music of Las Vegas, a nonstop playlist featuring the artists and songs most associated with the city. Elvis's "Viva Las Vegas," Barry Manilow's "Here's to Las Vegas," and Frank Sinatra's "Luck Be a Lady" along with tunes by Céline Dion, Sammy Davis Jr., Gwen Stefani, and the Killers.

"We have customized our overhead terminal music to the entertainers who made their careers in Las Vegas—the Rat Pack, Elvis—along with modern-day entertainers with residencies here, and, of course, songs about Las Vegas," says Vassiliadis.

Vegas is surely one of the most marketing-driven cities in the world. Thanks to the Las Vegas Convention and Visitor Authority's massive marketing and surveying operations, even before passengers land at the airport, Vegas knows the purpose for their visit, the number of nights they'll stay, their "gaming behavior and budget," what they plan to do and see, and more. Everything at the airport is scaled to reflect a grandiose vision of bigger, better, *more*—the mammoth terminals with their skyscraping ceilings, their soaring escalators, and their endless vistas of slots and shops and restaurants.

Past the vast concourses of temptation lies a centerpiece of the airport. Known as the Poker Chip, the custom-made floor mosaic in the baggage claim area celebrates the skylines of old and new Las Vegas. On one side of the Poker Chip is the past: long-gone resorts like the Dunes, the Landmark, and the Desert Inn, where billionaire hermit Howard Hughes once holed up. On the other side is the present: the towering Stratosphere spire, the Bellagio, the Wynn, the volcano at the Mirage.

Once the passengers descend into the baggage claim area, they find the Liquor Library, a megastore selling every conceivable spirit that claims to be the only non-duty-free liquor store in an airport baggage claim area in America. "Vegas starts at the Liquor Library," a sign boasts, inviting visitors to stock up on booze while they're waiting for their luggage. "We know why you come to Las Vegas and the Liquor Library is here to help."

From there, the skyline of the Strip beckons, shimmering in the distance like a mirage. It's so close, only three short miles from the airport, that some people believe they can run to it—and some, fortified by spirits from the flight or provisions from the Liquor Library, are probably tempted to try.

Chapter 2

THE RIDE

WAYNE NEWTON BOULEVARD

OUTSIDE THE AIRPORT terminal, on Wayne Newton Boulevard, passengers catch a lift to the Strip. It's fitting that the street ushering visitors into Vegas is named for Mr. Las Vegas himself, the city's resident entertainer for more than six decades. A high school dropout originally from Virginia, Newton, like most who come to Vegas, arrived from somewhere else. It was 1959, when he first performed in what was to be a two-week "tryout" at the old Fremont Hotel and Casino. It instead lasted forty-six weeks, and Wayne Newton never really left. Today, on the boulevard that bears his name, taxis and limos and car services line up to whisk the new arrivals to the visions of glory that have drawn them to Las Vegas, just as they drew the teenaged Wayne Newton.

Chauffeur Raymond Torres is waiting for his first ride of the day. Suit, tie, starched white shirt, leather shoes, black leather gloves, and his signature sunglasses—everything spotless. "I'm like a fireman," he says. "Once the phone rings, I get suited and booted, and I'm ready to go."

Out in the airport parking garage, his jet-black Rolls-Royce Ghost awaits. Torres stands outside baggage claim with an iPad bearing the name of his client. If it were one of the celebrities he has chauffeured in the past—Mariah Carey, Warren Buffett, Christina Aguilera, Brad Pitt, or Ryan Seacrest—he would be waiting across the tarmac at one of the airport's private jet terminals. "A lot of times you don't even know who you're picking up until they're in the car," Torres says. "Most of the celebrities have code names. Like Nicolas Cage. He lived here when I drove him and I'd take him out on the town. But his security would only give me the code name on the paperwork, because they don't want you calling someone and saying 'Hey, I'm picking up so-and-so.'"

"Everybody becomes their true selves in Las Vegas," Torres says. He sees it happening every day in his rearview mirror: the trophy wife who becomes a high-rolling gambler, the straitlaced executive who becomes a reckless ladies' man, the schoolteacher who takes a temporary job as an exotic dancer. This morning, Torres is waiting for Toby, one of his top clients. Back home, Toby's built a career in financial consulting. But in Vegas, he reinvents himself as a renegade gambler, a high roller going by the nickname Thunderboom. He comes to the city for months at a stretch, living in the high-end resorts on the Strip while he tries his luck at the casinos.

Torres is affiliated with a group of seven chauffeurs known as the Untouchables, who have access to a sizable fleet of luxury vehicles. But for clients like Toby, only Torres himself will do—because, says Toby, "he's so trustworthy."

Torres, in a sense, is emblematic of Vegas, a city with a criminal past and a corporate present. Today, he's a chauffeur for the stars. Once, he was accused of stealing from one of them.

If passengers are interested, Torres tells them his story of growing up in Las Vegas, where kids grow up fast. His father, who owned a roofing company, took him to his first strip club, Crazy Horse, when he was around sixteen. To help him gain entry, his dad took some tar and painted a moustache on his face. Before long, young Ray was embroiled in a life of crime, as a thief and a drug dealer. Vegas being Vegas, there was always plenty to steal, and plenty to deal.

In 1995, when he was only twenty-six, Torres played a central role in a high-profile art scam. He ended up with between two and three million dollars' worth of paintings by the likes of Dalí, Matisse, and Renoir in his possession. But the stolen artworks, which he'd planned to fence on the black market, didn't belong to just anybody. They belonged to Mr. Las Vegas himself, Wayne Newton.

Torres tried to sell the paintings to Colombian drug

dealers in exchange for one hundred ten pounds of cocaine. But the drug dealers were working as informants for the FBI and the Drug Enforcement Administration. A sting operation closed in, and Torres was convicted and sentenced to nineteen years and seven months in federal ·prison. When he was released after eighteen years—his sentence shortened for good behavior—he converted his criminal past into a shiny new future. One of his former associates had landed a job in a casino and arranged a job interview for Torres at a limousine service. The manager of the company asked Torres about his years in prison, then posed a pivotal question.

"How's your driving record?" he asked.

"I haven't had a ticket in eighteen years," Torres replied.

The manager laughed, and Torres was hired.

Ray Torres is summoned to the airport this morning via a text on his cell phone. He calls the phone his office because he doesn't have an office, and his phone is forever pinging with calls and texts and emails. Being a chauffeur in Vegas means doing more than just driving. "If somebody wants a helicopter," Torres says, "if somebody wants a jet, if somebody wants tickets at the fifty-yard line or bottle service at a club, if somebody wants restaurant reservations or designer clothes or some company for the evening, whatever somebody wants—just about *anything*—I can provide for them. Except anything illegal."

The text he got from Toby last night was simple: **Vegas, baby, 8 a.m. pickup. Ready to rock and roll.**

Now his client—bearded, middle-aged, his business suit traded for a red hoodie and baseball cap—is sitting in the back of the Rolls, headed to Resorts World, which he'll call home for the next month, maybe longer. When Toby's in town, Torres is on call, driving him everywhere: to the grocery store, to a restaurant or the casinos, on all-night club crawls. "Ray responds immediately," Toby says. "I trust him with my life. If it's midnight and I call him and say, 'I'm bored, me and my friends wanna go to a strip club,' he's on his way."

As they roll out of the airport, Toby is ready to indulge in everything Vegas has to offer. But first comes the ride, a preview of the coming attractions, starting with the line of gigantic billboards advertising shows, spectacles, resorts, or restaurants, each bigger and grander than the last. The front side of the billboards—the ones facing visitors heading into the city—feature seductive come-ons for Lady Gaga at the Park MGM or the magician Shin Lim at the Mandalay Bay or Thunder from Down Under, the all-male strip revue at the Excalibur. The back side of the billboards—the ones seen by those leaving Las Vegas—feature ads for personal injury lawyers or FOR LEASE signs, or nothing at all.

Nobody's selling to anyone leaving Las Vegas.

Turning off the street named for the entertainer whose stolen paintings sent him to federal prison, Torres merges right onto Paradise Road and takes a left onto Tropicana

West, taking the longer, more scenic route into town. In the distance, he can see the Mandalay Bay Resort and Casino on the Strip's southern edge, next to the massive glass pyramid of the Luxor. Straight ahead and to the left are the pointed castle towers of the Excalibur, and the Tropicana, built in the late 1950s and updated as a gleaming ivory tower. On the right is the sprawling, emerald-green MGM Grand, with its fifty-ton bronze lion, its 171,500 square feet of gaming space, and its hidden high-roller resort and private casino, the Mansion, reserved for the biggest players. "I've driven clients there who are sitting in the front seat next to me with bags full of money," says Torres. "Billionaires. I'm talking, like, Louis Vuitton *bags* full of money. Staying at the Mansion MGM Grand for, like, a week."

"Those villas are nice," says Toby, who sometimes stays at the Mansion himself. "Speedy Lee used to stay there and play baccarat in their high-roller room." Speedy Lee is the nickname of a legendary gambler. "Speedy Lee has eight girls with him in long red dresses, like his harem. He plays on two tables at the same time, hooked up to an oxygen tank so he can play for seventy-two hours straight, three hundred fifty thousand dollars a hand on each table, the girls just sitting behind him, watching. And everything has to be feng shui in the room. They spray this special spray in the air to clear the energy, because he's very superstitious. When I saw him, I was like, *How small am I playing in my life? Speedy Lee is going all out!*"

"When Speedy Lee was at the Mansion, he had limos waiting twenty-four-seven," Torres recalls. "I was one of the drivers waiting to pick him up, to take him whenever he needed to go. But sometimes he'd have drivers waiting and he never came out. Sometimes you wouldn't see him for hours or days, but there would always be a line of limos waiting for him, both a day shift and a night shift. And every time he got in the car, he always tipped at least a few hundred bucks."

Torres takes a right onto Las Vegas Boulevard, and passes New York–New York, with its replicas of the Chrysler and Empire State buildings. The ultrahip Cosmopolitan ("Just the Right Amount of Wrong"). Planet Hollywood. The Eiffel Tower and Arc de Triomphe of the Paris Hotel and Casino, which commands the skyline across from the Bellagio. Each has its particular come-on: to gamble, eat, drink, dance, and revel in almost anything that money can buy. Each one prompts a memory.

Torres remembers a husband and wife he used to ferry from the airport. "Wholesome family, kids and everything," he says. "The husband would come every once in a while by himself, and I'd take him to a strip club. Then next trip, he'd come with his family. One time, I picked him up from the private airport and he looked like crap. Obviously drunk, in shorts and flip-flops. I'm like, 'You all right?' And he says, 'Nah. I'm getting a divorce.'"

Toby leans forward. He's gone through a divorce of his own. "And afterwards I went on a Vegas rampage to make up for the lost time."

"The guy goes, 'It was my fault,'" Torres continues. "He said that him and his wife used to come to Vegas and stay at a hotel together. They came to an agreement where he would go play around, she would go play around, and they'd come back and share their experiences." For the wife, though, one of those experiences turned out to be more than just a playdate. She met somebody she really liked, and she left her husband.

"She ended up staying with the other guy," says Torres.

"Very dumb," says Toby. He recounts his own story of coming to Vegas after his divorce. It was a few years ago, he says, when the Patriots were playing Atlanta in the Super Bowl. He had a reservation to watch the game with a friend at Sapphire, which bills itself as "the World's Largest Gentlemen's Club." Before long, the manager came over to their table.

"You guys need anything?" the manager asked.

"Yeah," Toby told him. Soon a dancer was at his table, helping him forget about his ex-wife. "After my divorce," he explains, "I was like, I'm just gonna enjoy my life."

Which is exactly what he's come to Vegas to do.

They pass the Bellagio, the Italianesque monolith rising behind its enormous lake with its famous Fountains of Bellagio. The sight triggers a new story from Torres, this one about Andrea Bocelli, the blind Italian operatic tenor superstar.

"Andrea Bocelli is one of the nicest guys," says Torres. "When I drive him, I'm always invited stage side to enjoy his concert."

Bocelli is fascinated by Las Vegas, even though he can't see it. He sits in the front seat, next to Torres, attuned to everything around him.

"Ray, what kind of car is this?" he'll ask, according to Torres.

"It's a Cadillac Escalade," Torres will say.

"What year?" asks Bocelli.

When Torres tells him, Bocelli reaches out and turns on the radio, knowing exactly where to press the touch screen.

"It's amazing," says Torres. "Then he'll roll down the window and he'll just *listen* to the city as we're going down Las Vegas Boulevard. He doesn't speak much in the car, but sometimes he'll sing. Last time, a Christian song came on and he started singing along with it. But most of the time he'll just roll down the window and listen."

And feel the red-hot energy of the town, palpable even to someone who can't actually see it.

Passing the white expanse of Caesars Palace brings to mind another musician. "I drove for Elton John when he was in a residency at Caesars," Torres says, referring to the common practice in Vegas of having a performer appear in a resort showroom for an extended period, often months or years at a time. "Another driver and I would pull right into the garage connected to his dressing room, where his butler and chef would be waiting to serve us food and drinks while we watched the concert from a big-screen monitor in the dressing-room lounge." Next is the Mirage, where Torres says he once picked up Brad Pitt. "My job was to take him to Signature Flight Support, which is a private airport," he recalls. "He had a meeting in LA just to sign some papers, and he was gonna fly straight back.

It's only a forty-five-minute flight, but I wound up waiting at the airport for a few hours for him to return from LA. When I dropped him off back at the hotel, the security guard tipped me out. I didn't even look how much it was. But I waited because I saw Brad saying something to the bodyguard. Before I pulled off, the guard tapped at the window and said, 'Wait, give me back that thirty dollars.' Then he handed me a hundred. Brad must have asked him how much he gave me, and told him to give me a hundred bucks."

Farther along are the shimmering golden towers of the Wynn, home to one of the city's most exclusive night-spots: a supper club called Delilah. "Clients will call and say, 'Ray, we wanna go skydiving, off-roading, hiking, we wanna go see a show, have dinner at a certain place,'" says Torres. "Delilah is the hot new restaurant. Last time I checked, they were booked for the entire year. You couldn't even get in unless you knew somebody."

"Yeah, you got me into Delilah," Toby interjects. "That's the newest, hottest place in town."

"A lot of celebrities go there, a lot of socialites," says Torres. "I was there once with a major comedian and he was so taken with Delilah that he pulled out his cell phone to take a photo. I'm like, *Man, what are you doing?*"

Torres got an autograph for his daughter from Ryan Seacrest once, when *American Idol* was being filmed at the Wynn. Toby's stayed there, too. "Right on the golf course," he says. "Steve Wynn used to have the last villa, a three-story villa. If you were playing golf, you could see his artwork through the glass walls. He had that one that was just painted red and that was like fifty million dollars, and you could see it from the golf course."

Las Vegas Boulevard continues north, and soon, they arrive at Resorts World, the first new major resort to be built in Vegas since the Cosmopolitan in 2010, and the most expensive at $4.3 billion. Its 59-story tower is home to three hotels and a casino that encompasses 117,000 square feet—which architect Paul Steelman designed to create an illusion of not merely inhabiting another world, but becoming another person:

"The key to a successful casino design is to imbue visitors with a feeling of being the suave and sophisticated James Bond," says Steelman. "The casino's interior is carefully orchestrated to create a profound sense of empowerment, drawing patrons into a realm where they feel extraordinary. Noticeably lower ceilings help foster a more intimate and exclusive atmosphere, while warm and flattering lighting enhances the allure of the space, making everyone appear and feel their best. Curiously, you won't find any mirrors adorning the walls, for looking into one would only shatter the illusion of being a debonair secret agent."

This is where Toby will be spending the next month—or longer, if the cards are kind. He'll be up for the next twenty-four hours but won't start gambling until after midnight.

"I play better after midnight," he says as he steps out of the Rolls. "My brain relaxes then, and I go into a theta brainwave state, like a Buddhist monk who has been meditating for thirty years. Only I'm at the baccarat table in Vegas."

Torres is already standing by, handing Toby his luggage, offering him a ride anywhere he wants to go.

"When you pick me up later," Toby says, "I'll have more stories for you."

His very own Las Vegas residency is about to begin.

Chapter 3

THE ARRIVAL

THE WYNN

FOUR MIDDLE-AGED MEN from Atlanta are in a taxi headed to the Wynn, a forty-five-story, copper-colored curved building resembling a cupped, welcoming hand. This is the last—and most spectacular—resort built by the Las Vegas impresario Steve Wynn, who reinvented the city with his colossal resorts. The men from Atlanta have stayed in most of them. The Golden Nugget, the first luxury resort downtown. The Mirage, with its South Sea islands theme. Treasure Island, with its full-scale pirate battle raging out front. The Bellagio, an Italian lake resort on steroids. And now, Wynn's pièce de résistance. The one he named after himself. The one that tops them all.

Back home, Damon Raque—who serves as both cheerleader and guide for the men from Atlanta—is the owner of a wine storage and tasting lounge called Bottle Bank. But in Las Vegas, he becomes the ultimate thrill seeker: every trip is an attempt to top the one before with new extravagant activities that will, as he says, "make my buddies say 'Wow,' or 'What an experience,' or 'Man, that was amazing!'"

Raque's first stays in Vegas as a bachelor in the 1990s were at the Palms, whose young owners "really brought the nightlife wave to Las Vegas" with their Playboy Club and Playboy Suite, complete with a replica of Hugh Hefner's circular bed. Then Raque moved on to the raging pool parties at the Hard Rock, where noon was the new midnight and the champagne flowed like water. He has sampled every hot new nightspot in town, swum with the dolphins at the Mirage, raced Baja trucks in the desert, done the skydiving and the rock climbing, taken master classes in fine wine at the Rio and prepared truffle risotto in a cooking class with Frank Sinatra's granddaughter at the Wynn. Whatever money can buy in Las Vegas, Raque has done it. *Been there, spent that.* But of all his visits, staying at the Wynn has always been the pinnacle experience. "Because it's the best," he says. "The first time I came into the Wynn, I said: This is the place that God would have built if he had money."

In the late 1980s through the mid-2000s in Las Vegas, the man with the money was, of course, Steve Wynn. "After what Steve Wynn did for Las Vegas, there should be a statue of him under the WELCOME TO FABULOUS LAS VEGAS sign," says Marc Schorr, former chief operating officer of

Wynn Resorts. And while there is no statue of Wynn, who left Las Vegas in 2018, the monuments he built remain: the Towers at the Golden Nugget, the Mirage, Treasure Island, the Bellagio, and the Wynn.

As a connoisseur of Vegas, Raque knows precisely who is responsible for helping Steve Wynn make the Wynn look and feel so great. He invokes the name with reverence, as if referring to a deity.

"Roger Thomas," he whispers.

For years, Thomas was the interior designer who took Wynn's wildest dreams and turned them into reality. Now in his seventies, Thomas has semiretired to Italy after a long and illustrious career, but even while no longer at the Wynn in person, his presence is felt in every extravagant inch.

Roger Thomas knows Las Vegas because he is a son of Las Vegas. His father, E. Parry Thomas, was a mentor, as close as a second father, to Steve Wynn. As president of Valley Bank of Nevada, Parry Thomas helped steer the city away from mob money and into conventional financing. Roger Thomas similarly helped lead Las Vegas out of the era when, as he told *The New Yorker* in 2012, borrowing a line he had long heard, "every casino looked as if it had been designed by two hookers and a pit boss."

"With the Bellagio, Steve asked me to give to him the most beautiful, most elegant hotel on planet Earth," says Thomas, whose own elegant appearance *The New Yorker* described as "so relentlessly well-groomed that even his rare forays into scruffiness have an air of deliberation." The designer rose to the challenge, creating the most luxurious and audacious resort Vegas had ever seen, a palace whose lobby ceiling is covered by two thousand hand-blown glass flowers designed by the glass artist Dale Chihuly, at a cost of $3.5 million. Then, in 2000, Wynn once again turned to Thomas and asked him to create the greatest hotel on Earth.

"If I would have known you were going to ask me to do that again," Thomas famously told Wynn, "I wouldn't have tried so hard the first time."

Wynn gave him a clear mandate for the new resort that would bear his name. "If you appeal to the very most sophisticated, well-traveled, most finely educated of your guests," the resort magnate told him, "if you satisfy *them*, everybody else is going to be happy."

That mandate was delivered in the dramatic voice of a showman. "He was very commanding," says Wynn's longtime associate Marc Schorr. "He always stole whatever room he was in. When Steve talked everyone listened. Being a bingo operator, Steve's father taught him public speaking. Because a person who calls bingo is a speaker. You have to have rhythm calling the numbers. *B-3!* and *N-35!* He taught Steve how to do that, and Steve used that talent in telling his stories."

"Steve told me that if you want someone to *really* remember something, you pause before you say it, and you pause after saying it," says Roger Thomas.

What Wynn told Thomas next required long pauses on both ends:

"He said he wanted the Wynn to be something that no one had ever seen before, completely original."

The result was an immense resort set on 217 verdant acres, initially with 2,716 rooms, twelve restaurants, two ballrooms, an eighteen-hole golf course, the giant Lake of Dreams, a shopping mall, an enormous spa and fitness center, five swimming pools, and, in the beginning, a Ferrari dealership.

"I'm a Ferrari collector. Steve's an art collector, and we put his art collection in the Wynn so people could see it," says Marc Schorr. "I said, 'Steve, there are more people who would rather look at a red Ferrari than look at a Picasso.' He said, 'You may be right.' I said, 'There's no Ferrari dealership in Nevada. Let's see if we can become a dealership.' So we got the Ferrari-Maserati dealership at the Wynn, and we had upwards of one thousand people a day."

"I want people to be transported by the hotel," Wynn told *Vanity Fair* magazine in 2005. "I'm thinking: What is it that would make people be delighted and amazed?" The resort's brochure was even less modest. "It took Michelangelo four years to complete the ceiling of the Sistine Chapel," visitors were informed. "Your room took five."

The grandeur begins on the street, before guests even enter the hotel. "We had always put what Steve called a hook in the front yard," Thomas recalls. "At the Mirage it's a volcano. At Treasure Island it's sinking pirate ships. At Bellagio it's the fountain. But that, we learned, was a mistake. The best view of the fountain at Bellagio was not from Bellagio. It was from the restaurants across the street. We determined to never do that again."

At the Wynn, the hook is as imposing as it is unmissable: a mountain rising eight stories tall, covered with towering pine trees and what seems like every species of greenery known to nature. "It's a KEEP OUT sign on the front lawn," Thomas explains. "It's the mountain built in front, so you would have to come inside to see what we have."

Past the mountain, Damon Raque and the men from Atlanta exit their taxi beneath the hotel's porte cochere. Guiding them past two massive foo dogs—Chinese symbols of luck and wealth—Raque ushers his group through the hotel's revolving doors, and into another world.

The lobby alone always stops the men in their tracks. Walking into the Wynn is like entering some surreal primeval forest, with its gigantic ficus trees covered in twinkling lights, from which hang enormous, multicolored flower-covered ornaments, and its extravagant marble floor inlaid with brightly colored floral motifs and glass mosaics, gleaming with natural light. Even the air here is different—fresher, more inviting somehow, instilling a fleeting moment of serenity before the senses are overwhelmed.

"I wanted, as you entered the front door, for you to have a moment of exhale," says Thomas—the sense of relief after a long journey. "Then the next thing I wanted was for you to gasp—to inhale in awe. If you are not creating things that have never been seen before—if you are not being more dramatic, more romantic, more joyful, more mysterious, just *more*—then why bother? We never tried to create any fantasy except that you had *arrived*—that term in its most literary sense."

The grandeur of the Wynn struck Damon Raque so profoundly on his first visit that he had to commune with the resort alone. "I wanted to be by myself," he says. "It's like going to a museum. It's not fun to go with people. You have to go at your own pace." Now, even though he has spent dozens of nights here, Raque is experiencing the resort anew, just as Thomas had envisioned. "People tend to take on the characteristics of a room," Thomas told *The New Yorker.* "They feel glamorous in a glamorous space and rich in a rich space. And who doesn't want to feel rich?"

The men from Atlanta are feeling pretty rich right now. Only a few steps inside the Wynn and they're ready to empty their wallets, on, well, everything: the cocktail lounges, the pool services, the boutiques, the eateries. Together with its adjacent sister hotel, Encore, the resort offers more four-star award-winning restaurants than any resort in North America, its website proclaims. Before Wynn came along, Las Vegas was driven by the business concept known as *loss leader.* "You made money in the casino," as Thomas puts it, "and you kind of almost gave away everything else."

"You can experience things in Las Vegas differently than you can anywhere else in the world because of economics," Raque says of the megaresorts that line the Strip. "Because the casinos are basically ATM machines for the resorts. You'll walk into a restaurant, and they've spent twenty million dollars building out the space, right? You couldn't spend twenty million dollars building out a restaurant anywhere else because you couldn't make the math work on the revenue side. You'd have to charge eighty bucks for a baked potato. But when it's part of a four-billion-dollar resort, twenty million dollars is nothing. So, the scale of what's available—everything from the moldings and the marble and the fixtures to the restaurants, spas, and nightclubs—is just remarkable. The casinos make so much money it allows them to do things unlike anywhere else."

Wynn recognized that every aspect of a resort—the restaurants, the shops, the rooms, the entertainment—could contribute as much to the bottom line as the gambling. If he offered the best of everything, from the biggest and most luxurious rooms to five-star meals, he'd make money before the guests even made it to the casino floor.

The Bellagio cost $1.6 billion to build, but the investment was quickly repaid. "Per guest room, the resort generated four times as much revenue as the Las Vegas average," *The New Yorker* reported. In a desert town once known for its cheap buffets and lower-end strip clubs, the approach was nothing short of revolutionary. Wynn and Thomas "remade the architecture of gaming itself," according to *The New Yorker,* "creating spaces that allow people to enjoy the act of losing money, thus encouraging them to lose even more."

Every facet of the Wynn's ambiance has been carefully

calculated to seduce. The vast space is lit to resemble candlelight, "because candlelight is the most flattering light to all complexions," says Thomas. Even the air, pumped through a massive air conditioning system, triggers a subtle sense memory. "You have to pay attention to the scent that's in the air," Thomas explains. "It has to smell fresh and kind of sweet. DeRuyter Butler, the architect of Steve's resorts, always designed the air systems to exchange the air more often than anybody else did. Wynn resorts never smelled smoky. The Mirage had a floral scent. Bellagio was kind of a floral spicy scent. For the Wynn, the scent we asked for was 'new mowed grass.' It was designed by a scent developer. It had a tiny bit of lemongrass in it. It smelled like the best air on a spring day."

Scent was first introduced by Wynn Resorts at the Mirage via a system called Aromasys. "We interjected a Piña Colada aroma at the Mirage," says DeRuyter Butler. "Because when you go on vacation you like to lie on the beach with a drink, and Piña Colada is a vacation favorite. We wanted to appeal to all five senses. Most resorts appeal to three at most. But they neglect the all-important fifth sense of smell."

The men from Atlanta are inhaling the Wynn's intoxicating air now. Nothing as mundane as luggage is allowed to break the spell. Their suitcases and golf bags have been collected at the front door and transported by conveyor system, like the luggage of most every other guest, to the mezzanine, where the mechanics of the hotel check-in—bellhops, carts, and a baggage room—are stationed. "I always wanted guests to feel like they could be a little more dramatic," Thomas says. "I wanted them to feel like they could make the romantic gesture, they could say the romantic line. I wanted people to feel they were in a really good movie."

Just past the entrance garden, the Bar Parasol contains an interpretation of the famous umbrella painting by the Belgian surrealist René Magritte—eighteen giant parasols, in a swirl of colors, subtly moving up and down in what Thomas once described as a dreamlike ballet. Beyond the ballet of the parasols is the Wynn's showpiece: the Lake of Dreams, three acres of crystal-blue water, under a fifty-three-foot-high waterfall, bubbling and shimmering in an ever-shifting display of delights. Sometimes the lake transforms itself into a rainbow. Sometimes it froths like the world's largest glass of champagne. Sometimes surprises rise up from its depths. For many years, colored balls—one pink, one blue—magically chased each other around the lake before being joined by a little baby ball that pops up from the depths, a comic ending to a flirtatious pas de deux.

Once, when country music superstar Garth Brooks was celebrating his birthday at the SW Steakhouse overlooking the lake, a twenty-five-foot animatronic frog wearing a cowboy hat arose from the water and serenaded him with a twangy "Happy Birthday." The frog, created for the Wynn by a Disney alumnus, was said to have been designed to help persuade Brooks to emerge from his retirement and perform once more on the Wynn's main stage. The frog—along with a big paycheck, transportation by private jet, and most importantly, "his personal 'testing' of the

Encore theater for its acoustics and amenities," says DeRuyter Butler, the resort's architect—sealed the deal.

To ensure that every guest has a stunning view of the lake, an expensive solution was devised. Instead of installing conventional, straight-line escalators, which had blocked the view of the fountain at the Bellagio, they purchased two of what were then the few existing curved Mitsubishi escalators in the United States, which now cost around six million dollars each.

"It's the *wow!* moment," says Damon Raque, who revels in the sight of the Wynn's lake on each visit. "Because the escalators are curved, you look out and see the entire Lake of Dreams. It always makes me want to work harder at home to be able to come here, while also forcing me to slow down and appreciate the moment. It's inspiring. It sets the tone."

Now, even before going to their rooms, the men from Atlanta are ready to hit the casino, where they can hear the jangle of slot machines. There, Thomas had yet another mind-bending innovation. "We wanted to make the gamblers feel they are playing at *their* blackjack table, *their* roulette table, *their* craps table," he says. "Steve always asked me to think of intimacy. But making a large place feel intimate and personal is a great challenge."

On the surface, the solution Thomas came up with seemed simple: placing chandeliers over every table in the Wynn's cavernous casinos. The problem was, the chandeliers blocked "the eye in the sky," the high-tech array of cameras the casino's security team monitors to catch cheaters and card counters. "Steve allowed me to spend a fair amount of time and money developing a chandelier equipped with integral cameras, and we were able to prove that they not only provided the view prescribed by the Nevada Gaming Control Board, they improved it," Thomas recalls. The Wynn patented the devices, but thus far, no other casino has tried to copy the idea. "No one else understood that having a chandelier over a gambling table makes you instantly relate to your dining table or your kitchen table in your home."

"There will never be another Steve Wynn, who would take the time and spend the money for the right resort," says Marc Schorr. "Today the Wynn stands above all other resorts and is still the number one resort in Las Vegas in occupancy and revenue."

For Raque, the Wynn is a cathedral of inspiration. Even after all his years coming to Vegas, all the wild days and crazy nights and high-priced thrills, he's still looking for a way to do the seemingly undoable, still in search of something new and radically different than anything he has done before. The Wynn makes him want to top himself, just as the resort topped what Wynn, Thomas, and their associates had achieved with the Bellagio.

"It makes me determined to commit to excellence in my own life," Raque says. "To create a Vegas experience as beautiful and impactful and memorable as the hotel."

By the time he enters his room, high in the Wynn Tower Suites, overlooking the golf course and the mountains and desert beyond, his audacious new idea to top all he has done in Vegas before has arrived.

Chapter 4

THE VIP HOST

THE VIP WING OF A MAJOR LAS VEGAS RESORT

THE GAMBLER IS prepared to spend a fortune.

He's a mystery man from overseas, a roulette player. Eddie, a VIP host, gets a call from the man's associate, stating that the gambler plans to "post"—meaning place money on deposit in the casino—around one million dollars in checks.

Eddie is paid a sizable salary to field calls like this. As a VIP host, his job is not only to fulfill the needs of every guest, no matter how last-minute or outlandish, but also to handle minor setbacks and full-blown crises with an equal measure of courtesy and calm—especially when a gambler is prepared to post a million in his resort.

As he speaks to the associate, Eddie does a quick online search of the gambler's name. The guy looks legit:

he's an international businessman, so his checks should be good. "We always have to verify the checks," Eddie explains, "to be sure there's no holds or stops on them."

But there's one snag: the gambler needs transportation from Los Angeles. Can the resort send its jet to pick him up?

Now Eddie is the one who has to gamble. The flight is less than an hour from Los Angeles to Las Vegas. But sending the resort's jet won't be cheap. It's "a beautiful plane," Eddie says, and the round-trip flight will cost the resort around twenty thousand dollars.

It's a white-knuckle moment for the VIP host. Is the gambler good for the money? Is he a whale? Or a wannabe?

Time is of the essence. The associate has already sent the checks to the casino, and the credit department has begun the process of trying to confirm them. The gambler is waiting for an answer.

The VIP host checks with his boss, but it's really just a formality. Eddie is a very experienced host. He's come through with major players in the past, and his boss trusts him implicitly. It's pretty much his call.

Eddie sends the plane and awaits the verdict.

Standing at his post in the luxurious VIP area of the resort and casino that is his second home, Eddie could be part of the resort's opulent design. From every aspect of his ultra-hospitable demeanor to his friendly manners and copious charm, he serves as a best friend to well over a hundred regular clients. This morning began like every other: on the phone.

"I woke up and there were fifteen texts from people and a few phone calls," he says. "It's people just needing things. Because we live in a society where everyone is so last-minute. And I get it. They're on vacation. They have needs and wants, whether it be dinner reservations or a limo ride. There are a lot of last-minute details that need to be ironed out before their trips. And unfortunately, everyone waits until twenty-four hours before they come."

VIP hosts form a veritable army in Las Vegas, hundreds of men and women whose mission is to attend to the high rollers who flock to the most exclusive wings of the city's most exclusive resorts. Once these clients arrive, it's the job of the VIP hosts to keep them there, dining and drinking and gambling in the all-encompassing worlds that begin and end at the resort's VIP entrance. The hosts don't just arrange reservations at exclusive nightclubs or tickets to a Lady Gaga concert—they often accompany their clients when they go out at night, partying with the high rollers before ushering them safely back to their VIP accommodations.

Eddie has been attending to guests since he arrived in Las Vegas years ago. He had traveled a fair amount and wasn't looking to settle permanently, but a friend who was working in Vegas uttered the magic words: *Why don't you apply for a job here?* And, just like that, Eddie could envision his future.

He quickly realized that the real money and gratification wasn't in hotel management but in managing VIPs. His tremendous work ethic and easy smile quickly got him elevated to the VIP check-in desk at his first major resort. "That's where I met this amazing cast of characters," he says. "We got everybody—Tom Cruise, Nicole Kidman, Michael Jackson. Big, big, big celebrities."

And not just fame. There was money, and lots of it. "People would come with big bags full of cash," he says. "It was like something out of the movie *Casino*," the 1995 Martin Scorsese movie starring Robert De Niro and based on the life of Frank "Lefty" Rosenthal, who managed Vegas casinos for the Chicago mob.

There was also royalty. "It was the first time I saw a royal title on a credit card," Eddie says, recalling a certain aristocrat rolling up with her retinue in grand style.

Along the way, Eddie learned the fine art of anticipation, knowing what guests need "before they arrive at the hotel, or even think of it themselves." Whatever they desire—from sports or concert tickets to stocking their rooms with beverages, flowers, and other amenities—the veteran VIP host is there. "If they're celebrating a special occasion like a birthday, I arrange for theme cakes, and special tables at restaurants, along with shopping excursions at the stores where I know the salespeople," says Eddie. And there are the cars, a vast array, dispatched with chauffeur to ferry the chosen around town. He'll do anything and everything—except provide companionship for the evening. "I'm often asked, but politely decline to assist in that area," he says. "Because it's illegal." There *are* legalized brothels in rural Nevada, but not in Las Vegas.

As Eddie reminisces, his phone rings. It's always ringing. It's only nine in the morning, but he's already fielded a dozen calls. His phone is his command center, buzzing and pinging and lighting up around the clock, 365 days a year. He used to sleep with the thing, but then he couldn't sleep. Because his clients never do. "They need things," he says. "Always needing things."

And Eddie has learned never to say no to anything legal—no matter how bizarre or eccentric the request. "This is their recreation, and I'm the person who facilitates all of it for them. I'm important in their lives, because I'm their fun. This is their Disneyland. Disneyland for adults."

On the phone is a cherished client—meaning, above all, a big spender. "I would say, anywhere from fifty to a hundred a day. Thousand. Comes to gamble. Mostly slots."

But as Eddie listens, his seemingly perpetual smile vanishes. "Oh, no!" he says. "You're kidding? Oh, no! I'm *so* sorry to hear that."

His client is entangled in some sort of crisis.

"Oh, I'm sorry. Oh, boy! Yeah. Yeah. Yeah. Right. Sure, I'm the same way. I'm *so* sorry!"

He hangs up, wishing he could rush over and console his client. "I genuinely like people," he says. "And when they're in trouble I want to help them.

"You become friends with your clients, and that's the beautiful part of my job," Eddie says. "Because I find them fascinating, these people. They run big businesses, and I learn a lot from them. But they're also just nice people."

The tradition of providing guests with VIP hosts began like so many other Vegas innovations—back in the swinging, ring-a-ding-ding era of the 1950s and '60s Sands Hotel. Gamblers arriving on junkets from New York, Chicago, and Miami needed someone to get them reservations for dinners and shows. And the casino needed someone to set up the credit lines for the gamblers.

"The casino host was the top credit manager, taking care of VIP players," explains Ed Walters, who served as a pit boss at the Sands during the 1960s. "But we didn't want to say 'credit manager.' We wanted a word to say, 'We're here to help you with whatever you need.' The Sands was very service oriented. The floorman was watching the games. The pit boss was watching the pit, which was my job. And then you had someone who walked around everywhere—the restaurant, the casino. He was there to help our good players with whatever they needed. And that person came to be called the host."

The first to assume the host role at the Sands? "My father, Marty Goldberg," writes Anne Hodgdon, adding that Marty's uncle, Texas oilman Jake Freedman, was the president and principal owner of the legendary resort until his death in 1958. Freedman introduced the "eye in the sky" surveillance cameras that all casinos now use, and he imported gaming executives and others, including Marty Goldberg, from across America to serve his clientele. "Perhaps you could say my dad coined the 'host' identity in Las Vegas," says Hodgdon.

Goldberg first came to Las Vegas from Philadelphia to oversee the liquor operations at the Sands's Copa Lounge, a role that quickly expanded into something new. Red Norvo, a jazz musician who played the Copa Lounge, wrote a song called "Marty's Walk" to "pay tribute to the way my father walked all night, greeting people and making them feel important," says Hodgdon.

"His key role," she continues, "was to know 'who was who,' and to ensure they were recognized and treated like royalty while guests at the hotel."

The VIP hosts not only accommodate guests once they've arrived; they also bring VIPs into the resort. When Steve Wynn bought the Desert Inn Hotel and Casino, which would become the site of the Wynn, he put "his whole bankroll at risk," says the longtime Wynn associate Marc Schorr. "We didn't know it was going to be a success. We knew we had to make a destination hotel; we had to make it the place to be. Bellagio was surrounded by resorts with thousands of rooms. But the site of the Wynn had none of that; it had a closed Frontier across the street, a closed Stardust nearby. You had to build your customer base one customer at a time."

Having sold Mirage Resorts to MGM, Wynn was left without a customer base. "The new owners kept our customer base," says Schorr. "To build a new customer base, we fished where the fish were."

And those doing the fishing were the VIP hosts. "We'd go to the racetrack, where the people at the clubhouse were the customers we wanted," Schorr continues. "We'd have a Wynn table in the clubhouse. If one host couldn't hook the guy, we'd send another host to get him. Eventually we got them all. In the end, you've got to build a better mousetrap where the customer wants to be."

Today, gaining access to VIP hosts like Eddie and the VIP suites and towers that have been built in most of the major Las Vegas resorts—complete with their own private entrances and elaborately designed lobbies—is based on a gambler's "spend," a system of carefully calibrated tiers. "We rate customers based on their playing," says Eddie. "They start out at the casino rate. That's somebody you just want to encourage to come. You give them a little bit of a discount, say 10 to 15 percent off the room rate." The same discount applies to "guests of"—friends of established gamblers. "I put in the rooms at the casino rate, to give them a little discount," he continues. "But they still check in at the regular front desk."

To get to the VIP hosts and the VIP suites, guests must be prepared to spend serious money at the tables. "My guests start at five thousand dollars in play," Eddie says, meaning the amount a guest commits to playing during their stay. "That probably gets them a room comp." The next tier are the RFB players—meaning room, food, and beverages are all on the house. "RFB begins when they have a budget of ten thousand dollars, and they play to it," Eddie says. "You can't just have it sitting there. It has to be in action, whether at the tables or the slot machines."

The casino attempts to determine the precise level of play. Supervisors track the players' wagers at the tables, and loyalty cards, which players insert into slot machines, automatically show their level of play. This enables the players to be rated by the casino, although some players prefer to play in anonymity. However, being rated and being issued a loyalty card enables the gambler to earn complimentaries, or "comps." Once issued, the gambler takes the player's card to either the table or the slot machine, and their play is tracked. Hopefully, just a small percentage in cash, "because we don't want people taking the cash out of the casino and buying things," Eddie notes. "We want them to use it for gaming purposes only."

Most VIP hosts have to hustle to get their clientele. Not Eddie. "I do very little marketing," he says. "Since I became a host, most of my gamblers are established clients or come to me by referrals from other players. So it's just about fielding phone calls." They come from all over: from Venice to Vancouver, from Paris to Prague, from Minneapolis to Madagascar. "But I would say the majority of my people are within driving distance. Seventy-five percent are from California, Arizona, Colorado, and Texas."

The biggest gamblers have always come from the most lucrative industries, be it oil and gas or mining and manufacturing. In his younger days, Eddie would party with his clients. "But now that I'm older, I don't. And believe it or not, I'm not a gambler. I don't gamble one penny." Nowadays, he sticks to dinners, opulent affairs with his favorite whales. "I had a very high-high-high-high-end client," he says. "He had a very big personality. He'd come in with four hundred thousand dollars." They'd dine together at luxe French restaurants, where they'd drink Petrus, the most expensive Bordeaux, with every course, then rare Cognac with dessert—the bill sometimes running over ten thousand dollars.

His phone rings. "Hi, buddy. Did you miss your flight? Oh, okay." The client has left something valuable behind in his room, as they often do. "I'll run up there and get it. Do you want me to have it shipped to you? Or I can hold on to it if you're coming back soon. Yeah, I'll hold on to it. Oh, you're welcome. My pleasure! All right, have a safe trip home."

Eddie remembers how he once landed a client. "He was going to a blackjack tournament at another casino, but they sent an older plane to pick him up," he recalls. The guest was upset. "So he called me up."

Send your best private jet, the guest said, "and I'll be a customer for life."

It was early morning, and Eddie had to move fast. Was the jet available? Would it get to his guest in time to fly back to Vegas for the tournament? "I really had to scramble," Eddie said. "I was under the gun—there was a lot of pressure to do it."

The VIP host pulled it off. The guest opened a major line of credit. And he's been loyal ever since.

The plane is in the air, en route from Los Angeles. The gambler is on board, headed to Vegas. Throughout the flight, Eddie has been working with the credit department to confirm the checks. If there are any problems, then the VIP host is in trouble, along with the gambler.

Just before the plane touches down, word comes in that the gambler is good for the money. The checks will clear. Eddie rolls out the red carpet.

As soon as the gambler lands, the pampering begins: the limo from the private airport, the seamless arrival through the VIP entrance to the suites in the sky. The whale is dressed casually. He knows no one here, but his connection to Eddie is enough.

In the end, the guest doesn't turn out to be much work for the VIP host. He spends almost all his time in the casino, asking only for dinner reservations. He winds up playing "the full line," meaning he gambles his entire line of credit—all of which he loses.

But he loses it happily. "It was very quick, in and out," says Eddie. "He didn't even spend the night. We ended up flying him back that same day."

As the whale leaves for the airport, his associate turns to Eddie and says the words every VIP host longs to hear—especially when his gambler is leaving a loser.

"He had a great time," he says of the gambler. "We'll be back."

Chapter 5

WHEEL OF FORTUNE!

HARRY REID INTERNATIONAL AIRPORT

IT'S TEN MINUTES until boarding, and Megan Toole-Hall is about to become a big winner in an unlikely place.

An insurance agent, Toole-Hall has left her home in Flower Mound, Texas, for Las Vegas in the midst of a weeklong ice storm, accompanied by her husband, Darien, and her district manager and his wife, for a few days of gambling and fun. "I've got a large staff, I've got my cell phone," she assures her manager. "We'll be back after the weekend." She won't post anything on Facebook, so nobody will even know they're out of town.

Now it's 10:30 a.m., and Toole-Hall is sitting in Las Vegas's Harry Reid International Airport awaiting her flight home, ruing her losses and waiting for her plane to take off. Like many gamblers, Toole-Hall arrived in the city with no strategy for winning—only hope, always hope. They stayed at Aria, the megalopolis hotel rising up within a sprawling urban development on South Las Vegas Boulevard that is part of the largest privately financed construction project in the history of the United States. Built for approximately $9 billion in a joint venture between MGM Resorts and Dubai World, and opened and operated by MGM Resorts in 2009, the massive complex of hotels, casinos, restaurants, and the Crystals shopping mall encompasses eighteen million square feet. Two of the hotel casinos in the development, Aria and its adjacent sister hotel, Vdara, are now wholly owned by MGM Resorts.

Right off the bat, Toole-Hall hit the blackjack tables and won $500. Her zeal to gamble was limited only by the cash in her pocket—and by her district manager, whom she tasked with serving as her "accountability partner." He agreed to stand beside her at the tables and rein her in, forcing her to walk away before she blew any winnings or got too far down. At first, Toole-Hall was on a lucky streak: She followed up the $500 win from blackjack with another $920 in winnings at the slots. Then she cashed out and headed to the Yves Saint Laurent shop in Aria's megamall, where she bought a wallet in which to keep her winnings.

The money didn't stay in her new wallet long. Toole-Hall spent much of the trip at the roulette wheel—winning, losing, winning, losing—and drinking a vodka cocktail, her "go-to." Finally, emboldened by liquor or luck, she decided to go all in, pushing in $2,500 in chips on black.

The wheel spun and landed on red. She lost it all. By the time Toole-Hall headed to the airport for the flight home, her new YSL wallet was not only empty—she was down $3,600.

Except for three crisp $100 bills her husband had given her. *Not for gambling!* To pay their nanny, stuck in the ice back in Flower Mound, babysitting their three kids.

An announcement fills the terminal. *Southwest Airlines flight to Dallas will be boarding in ten minutes at gate twenty-five.* Passengers begin to gather their belongings, but something calls to Toole-Hall: one of the slot machines that stand like sentries all over the terminal. She decides to try her luck one last time. There are more than one thousand slot machines in the airport, strategically placed throughout each terminal, encircling every Starbucks and Quiznos and Jamba Juice and Lucky Streak bar. The one that calls to Toole-Hall is the loudest and gaudiest of all, a swirling phantasmagoria of light and color. A machine that sings with the sound of a crowd shouting the name of a TV game show that has entranced audiences for almost fifty years:

WHEEL! OF! FORTUNE!!!

With her husband and accountability partner waiting at the gate, Toole-Hall parks her pink carry-on suitcase beside her and sits on the cushioned seat before the slot machine. All she sees in front of her are the three swirling slot-machine wheels that, if lined up correctly, will give her a chance to unleash the jackpot blinking in lights at the top of the machine. Today's payoff stands at $302,000.

Toole-Hall pays no attention to the number. She's just looking for one last win, a thrill to end her getaway on a high. She takes one of the $100 bills out of her new wallet and slides it into the machine. *I'm just trying to make it spin,* she tells herself. If she lines up one WHEEL OF FORTUNE SPIN symbol, the big wheel at the top of the machine will spin, just like it does on the game show, and she'll pocket whatever amount it lands on.

She begins hitting the lighted buttons, followed by the 2x button to double her bet. *Nothing.* She punches away, over and over again, until her $100 is gone.

Only five minutes left before boarding. Toole-Hall is getting frustrated. She feeds another $100 into the machine and starts hitting the buttons. Up comes one WHEEL OF FORTUNE SPIN symbol.

The wheel at the top spins and starts chanting the TV game show's theme.

WHEEL! OF! FORTUNE!!!

The wheel stops at 75.

Seventy-five bucks! Toole-Hall thinks. *I've almost won my first $100 back.*

Then she realizes she's sitting at a quarter machine, not a dollar machine. Meaning she just won seventy-five quarters. A whopping $18.75.

Now Toole-Hall is seriously pissed off. *Hell,* she thinks. *At this rate, I'm never gonna win my money back.*

Inserting her last $100 bill into the machine, she

decides to stretch her money by punching the 1X button, meaning one quarter, wagering 25 cents at a time. But the clock is ticking. *The plane's about to take off,* she thinks. *I'm not gonna win anything—I better just play this out.*

She starts hitting MAX BET.

MAX BET. A loser.

MAX BET. Another loser.

MAX BET...

The first reel stops on the WHEEL OF FORTUNE logo.

The second reel stops. WHEEL OF FORTUNE.

The third reel starts spinning rapidly, making a noise that sounds like the engine of a revving racecar.

It's not going to hit, there's no way, Toole-Hall thinks.

But the third reel comes to a stop, and everything goes crazy:

WHEEL! OF! FORTUNE!!!

The slot machine begins screaming, every wheel spinning, every light flashing, a lurid frenzy unlike anything she's ever experienced in her life.

"I think I won!" Toole-Hall cries, happy to have recouped her losses with one last bet. "I think I won!"

The noise and lights draw a crowd. A woman approaches Toole-Hall and taps her on her shoulder.

"Ma'am, you did win," the woman tells her.

"What?" Toole-Hall says. "What did I win?"

"Look up! Look up!" the woman replies.

Toole-Hall looks up to the top of the machine. There, in dazzling lights, is a number.

$302,000!

Toole-Hall begins running around in circles, dancing and clapping, trying to grasp the impossible. "I won! I won!" she screams.

People close in on her. "Can I touch you?" they ask, hoping that some of her luck will rub off on them.

"It's an adrenaline rush," Toole-Hall recalls of the moment she won. "You just feel like you're out of your body." She feels herself levitating, floating above the scene like some celestial spectator.

Suddenly, she returns to reality. *My husband. Where is he?*

"Darien! Darien!" she screams.

Alerted by someone at the gate, Darien cuts through the crowd to join her.

"I just won $302,000!" she screams.

"Oh, my fuck," he says.

As they wait for an official to arrive and verify the win, Toole-Hall instructs her husband to play $100 on another Wheel of Fortune slot, hoping he can piggyback off her Max Bet luck. Dutifully, Darien does as he's told. He winds up winning another $2,400.

Now, even more people want to touch Megan Toole-Hall.

A dozen cell phones are hoisted high in the air, harvesting videos of the winner. After someone posts a video of the jackpot online, the airport win goes viral. Footage of the moment ends up on *The Tonight Show* that evening.

So much for sneaking off to Vegas during an ice storm.

Chapter 6

THE WEDDING QUEEN
OF THE WEST

A LITTLE WHITE WEDDING CHAPEL

"**WHAT IS LOVE** to you?" the Wedding Queen of the West asks the nervous couple standing before her.

Moments before, they had been sitting in the lobby, side by side, looking apprehensive.

Is this a good idea?

The groom was talking and texting on his phone. The bride was wide-eyed and jittery, wearing a dress that looked fancy compared to the groom's casual attire. Both seemed ready to bolt. Then Charolette Richards entered the lobby.

Then eighty-six, Richards is a small woman, but a giant in the business of love in Las Vegas.

She is the Vegas pioneer who invented the drive-through wedding. She helped put Las Vegas on the matrimonial map with the Elvis Pink Cadillac Ceremony, in which couples exchange their vows while sitting in or standing next to Richards's own long 1971 pink Cadillac. Its personalized plates proclaim 4ELVIS beneath a canopy emblazoned with the words THE TUNNEL OF LOVE flanked by two cartoon Cupids firing their arrows into the hot desert sky.

Ms. Charolette, as she is known, leans over the couple waiting in the lobby of her Little White Wedding Chapel. She looks into their eyes and smiles.

"How did you meet?" she asks.

"On a dating site," the bride says.

"Who's got the ring?" Richards asks.

"We don't have one," the woman replies. "Spur of the moment."

"The ceremony takes two hours," Richards warns.

"*Huh?*" the couple gasps, in unison.

"I'm joking," Richards says, laughing. "Ten minutes."

She points to one of her assistants. "She's going to start the music and you walk down the aisle," Richards tells the bride. Then she leads them into the little chapel adjacent to the lobby.

White twinkling lights. White flowers spilling from white vases. White chandeliers of giant intertwined wedding rings studded with tiny white lights. And twenty white tufted love seats. As if a vast congregation of witnesses is expected, instead of this single couple, about to sail into a new life absolutely alone.

"I've only done this fifty thousand times," Richards says, instructing the groom to stand beside her at the altar as his betrothed walks down the aisle. For many years, the musical accompaniment was provided by Rhoda Jones, the chapel's now retired, ninety-nine-year-old organist/accordionist. She would handle the wedding march with whatever song—or tempo—a soon-to-be-newlywed couple desired. These days, it's usually a recording.

"Here we go!" Richards adds, as if experiencing it all for the first time. "Here comes the bride!"

It's only a dozen steps to the altar, but it must seem like an eternity to the nervous bride. Her groom turns off his phone and stands fidgeting next to Richards, as if startled to suddenly find himself on the precipice of marriage.

"I just know you two are going to have a beautiful life together," Ms. Charolette begins. "Because God is here. I invited Him here."

There's no reaction. But Richards isn't worried. She knows how to reach them. Some couples ask if they can skip even the quickie ceremony and just pay for a marriage license. Others show up drunk, barely able to stagger down the aisle. But if people are too sloshed or impatient to say vows, Richards turns them away. To her, the marriage ceremony is sacred, even if it only takes ten minutes. It can't be disrespected. The couple standing before her has paid seventy-five dollars for the basic Little White Chapel Ceremony, which comes complete with music, a witness, and all document processing—not including a voluntary gratuity for the minister, who, at the Little White Wedding Chapel, is often Ms. Charolette herself.

Now the Wedding Queen of the West delivers her signature line:

"What is love to you?"

Love in Las Vegas, for Charolette Danielson Richards, began as a hurting thing. A long and lonely drive out west for a young bride from the sticks, with three young sons at her side. Wilson Wright, her wandering husband, had sent her one hundred dollars and instructed her to drive their old Ford—"a jalopy," as she calls it—from Sandy Hook, Kentucky (population five hundred), to Las Vegas, Nevada, a strange and glittering oasis in the desert, to meet him at the Stardust Hotel and Casino, the newest and grandest resort on the Strip.

On June 10, 1959, smack in the middle of a blistering heat wave—with a record-setting number of days without rain, and with the highest temperature reaching one hundred thirteen degrees—Charolette pulls into town and goes looking for her husband. She wears long pants and a stifling woolen sweater, which sticks to her skin in the sweltering heat. In her arms is her three-year-old son. Her two older boys trail behind in a lonely parade of woe.

The Strip is becoming the main thoroughfare of a town still experiencing growing pains, a place where mobsters rub shoulders with cowboys, and where many of the casinos have Wild West themes, evoking the area's frontier spirit. Elvis Presley is still in the army, Howard Hughes has yet to buy his first stretch of land in Las Vegas, and the mob is plowing its ill-gotten gains into new casinos at breakneck speed: the Flamingo, the Tropicana, Hotel Last Frontier, the Sands, the Desert Inn, and now the Stardust, its giant neon sign lighting up the sky. It's the largest hotel in the world at that point, with over one thousand rooms and a massive casino. Bob Hope tells jokes in the resort's showroom, and an array of other performers consider it their second home. It's where Charolette expects to find the father of her three children.

Wilson "Willy" Wright had swept her off her feet when she was only seventeen years old, dishing up sundaes in an ice cream parlor in Eugene, Oregon. He was said to be what was then called a "mechanic," a gambler who would prearrange the odds in his favor while he was at the table. Wright would saunter in to play in the card games upstairs, always taking the time to order a vanilla shake. Months of milkshakes led to a proposal, and Charolette became a teenage bride, married by the justice of the peace. Wright took her to live in a series of small towns, until finally, to lighten his load, he left his wife and kids at his parents' home in Kentucky, and took off. "Mr. Wright," Charolette Richards later says, "was Mr. Wrong."

Before long, an envelope arrived at the Sandy Hook post office, containing one hundred dollars in cash and instructions for Charolette to take the kids, drive across country, and meet her husband at the Stardust. But when she finally arrives and parks her beat-up Ford in the lot and enters the gleaming white resort, she finds...nothing.

No greeting. No explanation. No Wilson Wright.

Nobody at the Stardust has ever even heard of him.

And since children aren't allowed in casinos, Charolette and her kids are summarily given the boot.

Using her last dollars, she rents a cheap motel room and spends the days and nights walking the Strip with her children in tow, scanning the crowds for any sign of Wright. After a week of searching, her money is just about gone and the kids are screaming and there is no sign of her husband.

Then, just as she feels like she's about to fall to the pavement, sobbing and exhausted, a "very good-looking man" on the street stops and smiles at her.

"How come I see you here every morning?" he asks.

Charolette doesn't know what to say.

"Where is your husband?" asks the stranger.

"I don't know," she replies. "I'm looking for him."

Her tale comes pouring out in a torrent of tears. She pulls out her last dollar and a few cents. "This is all I've got left," she says. "I don't know what to do."

The man introduces himself: Merle Richards, a photographer and the owner of the Little Church of the West wedding chapel. He finds her a place to stay and a babysitter for her kids and gives her a job at his wedding chapel adjacent to the Algiers Hotel on South Las Vegas Boulevard. He picks her up every morning and drives her to work. There, inside the little chapel, Charolette makes herself indispensable: taking payments, calling the ministers to perform the ceremonies, keeping the books. In a few years, she'll open her own flower shop.

A few months after her arrival in Vegas, Wilson Wright reappears, hoping to reconcile. He hadn't intended to abandon her and the kids on the street, he explains. He'd just been unable to find them. But Charolette is ready to call it quits.

She hitches her star to Merle Richards and his wedding business. Both eventually formally divorce their respective spouses and marry each other. Her new husband isn't a gambler like Wright, but he has his own demons. Many nights, Charolette Richards closes up the wedding chapel and goes home alone. After ten years, her marriage to Merle is over.

Soon she is an ordained minister, ready to perform her first wedding. A couple arrives at the chapel, their names and marriage date lost to time. Before this point, Charolette Richards had been a mere "wedding hostess": she would bring couples into the church, fill out the paperwork, and hire the photographer, usually Merle. A reverend would then perform the ceremony. Not Charolette. Never Charolette.

But on that day, when the couple arrives, Richards puts on the robe and prepares to recite the immortal words that will join a husband and a wife.

"You're the first people I've married, so excuse me if I make a mistake," she tells the couple. Thus, Richards retrieves all of the love that she had lost to two errant husbands, transferring it to the strangers standing before her and infinite couples thereafter. "I was proud once I got through," she says, "and I started doing those weddings like they were candy."

Charolette Richards had found her calling, always beginning her ceremonies—ten minutes short, but powerful enough to last a lifetime—with what would become her trademark:

What is love to you?

Before long, another savior appears. Bert "Wingy" Grober, the casino host at Caesars Palace, has been coming to Richards's flower shop for the signature lucky carnations he wears in his lapel. He lends her fifty thousand dollars, which she uses to buy her own wedding chapel, a cute little cottage with white clapboard siding and a short steeple rising up into the desert sky. It's called A Little White Wedding Chapel. Now, she's not only a licensed, ordained minister but also a notary public, founding her own business on the very thing that had lured her to Las Vegas and broken her heart: love.

It's a Saturday in June, and the metal doors to the Little White Wedding Chapel, at 1301 South Las Vegas Boulevard, are as hot as a branding iron. But today, like every other day—365 days a year—the doors swing open every few minutes, welcoming a veritable parade of love, lust, and overnight devotion. Couples arrive either on their own or accompanied by friends and family. Some come by car, limo, or motorcycle. Others on foot, skates, or skateboards. Many change from street clothes into tuxedos and wedding gowns in the chapel's outdoor bathrooms, which serve as changing rooms.

"I used to do twenty-four hours a day," Richards says, recalling the days when her chapel was open around the clock. "In one day, I performed 124 weddings."

Now the hours are constrained only by those of the county marriage license bureau, which has taken to opening at 8 a.m. and closing at midnight. Still, some key elements from the old days of Las Vegas weddings remain. No blood tests. No waiting period. To get married in Las Vegas, all you need is a license and ten to fifteen minutes.

Richards used to practically live in her chapel, available whenever love came calling. "I never know when Cupid is going to strike," she says. So she waited—*love is patient, kind*—and they came in droves, rich and poor, famous and unknown: Joan Collins and her fourth husband, Peter Holm, in November 1985; Michael Jordan, wearing a red Polo shirt and arriving by taxi at 2:30 in the morning to marry his first wife, Juanita Vanoy, in September 1989.

Richards decorated the room for Frank Sinatra and Mia Farrow's wedding in July 1966 ("He was upset that she had cut her hair"). She arranged flowers for the weddings of Elvis Presley and Priscilla Beaulieu in the Aladdin Hotel in May 1967 ("I was his wedding coordinator," she told the *Herald* in Scotland. "I got the judge, the flowers, his cake, everything. And I made sure that everything ran well."), and for Wayne Newton and Elaine Okamura in June 1968 at the Little Church of the West. On November 21, 1987, she was summoned to a suite at the Golden Nugget to marry the actors Bruce Willis and Demi Moore. "I didn't know who they were," she tells *Vegas* Magazine. "When I pronounced them husband and wife, they were crying." Willis lifted Moore into the air, then gently lowered her until their lips met. "It was like a movie," she recalls.

She once married five couples at the same time. In another ceremony, she lined up twenty couples who had been married in her chapel and renewed their vows in a single go. The stars she has married are many, all standing with their beloveds before Richards or her emissaries. But celebrity matters little to her. "I'm not into stardom," she says. "I'm into God."

It took only six months for Charolette Richards to pay Wingy back. Slowly but surely, marriage by marriage, she transformed herself into the Wedding Queen of the West. After making the arrangements for Frank Sinatra's wedding, she found herself semi-famous in Las Vegas, sitting in the front row at the International, watching Elvis Presley perform. Then, like something out of a dream, Elvis leaned down...and drawled in a voice full of Memphis molasses, "Come here, honey." He reached down and grabbed her hand to bring her onstage, where she sat beside him as he serenaded her. It eventually gives her the idea for an Elvis impersonator wedding. It's an instant hit, and couples flock to the chapel.

"I love love," Richards tells everyone she meets, passing out cards printed with her Recipe for a Happy Marriage:

> *2 Hearts Full of Love*
> *2 Heaping Cups of Kindness*
> *4 Armfuls of Gentleness*
> *2 Cups of Friendship*
> *2 Cups of Joy*
> *2 Big Hearts Full of Forgiveness*
> *1 Lifetime of Togetherness*
> *2 Minds Full of Tenderness*
> *Stir Daily with Happiness, Humor and Patience. Serve with Warmth and Compassion, Respect and Loyalty.*

The big names keep coming to Richards's Little White Wedding Chapel: Sarah Michelle Gellar and Freddie Prinze Jr.; Natalie Maines of the Dixie Chicks; "Stone Cold" Steve Austin; Joe Jonas and Sophie Turner; and Ben Affleck and Jennifer Lopez, who write in an online post about the experience, "In the end, it was the best possible wedding we could have imagined."

"We've had people who got married here 50 years ago... and their kids and their grandkids are getting married here," Richards tells John Katsilometes, then of the *Las Vegas Sun*. "That's a wonderful history to have." They come from Africa, Asia, Europe, and Australia. But mostly they come from the state next door: California. Richards marries them wherever their heart desires. But mostly it's in her chapel or, for many years, in her chapel's own hot air balloon, which she emblazons with hearts and stars and the words A LITTLE WHITE CHAPEL IN THE SKY. One man, a doctor from Germany, asks Richards to perform a wedding ceremony on a small private plane. She boards the plane, only to discover that it's a stunt. After the jet takes off, high above the desert, the man pulls out a ring and proposes to her.

"Will you marry me?" he asks.

Then he gets up, opens the door, and leaps out of the plane.

Later, Richards learns that the German doctor was also a parachute developer. He had a parachute under his formal wedding dinner jacket, but it malfunctioned, and he plunged ten thousand feet to his death. She never found out why he wanted to marry her.

If Bugsy Siegel turned Vegas into the gambling capital of the world, it was Richards who found a way to capitalize on the gamble of love. Back when wedding licenses were available twenty-four hours a day, Richards would sleep in her chapel, emerging at all hours to perform weddings, which gave her another idea for innovation: to make weddings more convenient by sparing brides and grooms from even getting out of their vehicles to be wed. One of her sons broke down one of her wedding chapel's walls and installed a window—and just like that, the drive-through wedding was born.

The window opened on Valentine's Day, 1991. Couples pulled up in their cars, motorcycles, or mobile homes and pressed a buzzer. Richards would appear at the window, slide back the glass, and lean out, *USA Today* reported, "looking for the world as if she is ready to take their order."

The average cost of a wedding that year, according to *Modern Bride,* was $13,310. Couples at the drive-through window spent $25. "Some don't even unfasten their seatbelts in the car," reported *USA Today.*

By 2002, Richards owned five wedding chapels in Las Vegas, each with tuxedo rentals and florists and gift shops offering every possible wedding amenity. She had sixty-five employees and a fleet of fifteen limousines. Many came for the Elvis wedding, complete with an Elvis impersonator crooning "Love Me Tender" and done up as an Elvis from one of the various periods of the King's life: hip-swiveling rockabilly, smooth matinee idol, overweight Vegas showman.

In November 2022, Richards sold her chapel to the rival matrimony venue Vegas Weddings, marking the end of an era.

Over the course of sixty years, Richards figures she and her chapels have presided over more than five hundred thousand weddings. She tries not to judge anyone, but she worries about some of the couples. "Do you realize what you're doing?" she told Katsilometes in the *Las Vegas Sun* that she wants to ask them. "That this is forever? Never to part? That your hearts are going to belong to each other, and you're going to be as one?" And so she stands before the multitudes, hoping for the best.

One sweltering day, in a single twenty-four-hour period, Richard says, she and her crew performed more than 574 weddings, which is believed to be a record. Over and over, hour after hour, looking into the eyes of each new couple standing before her, Richards poses the same question at every ceremony.

"What is love to you?" the Wedding Queen of the West asks.

The nervous couple standing before her glance at each other, not knowing how to answer this personal question, this so-close-to-the-heart query from a woman they met only moments ago.

"Love is patient, kind, it's joy," says Richards. "Love never fails. God is love."

The bride begins to softly cry. The groom remains stoic.

"I want you to look into each other's eyes," Richards continues. "These are the eyes you will look into for the rest of your life. These are the eyes that will cry. These are the eyes that will laugh. These are the eyes that will wonder what to do."

They look into each other's eyes.

"What would you like to say to each other?" Richards asks.

Suddenly, something shifts between the couple. The room seems to spin. Richards's words have touched something deep inside them both. Seconds ago they were on two different planets. Now they are joined as one.

"I never thought I'd have somebody like you," the groom says, his facade cracking, his voice trembling, his eyes wet with tears.

"Oh, my God!" the bride gasps.

As if on cue, the music in the chapel swells and the twinkling white lights blaze. The Wedding Queen of the West, Cupid's emissary in the city of sin, has struck again.

"Your endless love starts right here," she tells the couple. "By the power vested in me by the state of Nevada…"

The couple's kiss goes on and on. They seem to have forgotten that they're in Las Vegas.

"Congratulations to you both!" Richards exclaims, beaming as if she's just performed her very first wedding. "Hooray! Hooray! Hooray!"

The newlyweds walk out of the chapel and into the heat of Las Vegas. For the first time, they gaze upon the city as a married couple.

The Wedding Queen of the West, once again triumphant, steps into her chapel's foyer.

"Okay," she asks her attendants, "who's next?"

Chapter 7

FROM VILLAIN TO VISIONARY

THE MOB MUSEUM

OSCAR GOODMAN HAS a dream.

It's June 28, 1999, and he has just been sworn in as mayor of Las Vegas, his victory an improbable, only-in-Vegas feat. After arriving in the city on August 28, 1964, as an ambitious young lawyer looking for work, Goodman became known as the go-to attorney for the mob. Over the years he represented everyone from lowly soldiers to the—as Oscar is always careful to emphasize—*allegedly* crooked kingpins who ran rampant in the town. He took on cases few others would accept, much less win, and usually received his payment in cash.

Now, as the city's new mayor, Goodman has once again

emerged triumphant. Just as he did when he defended Tony "the Ant" Spilotro, who served no time for any of the more than twenty murders the FBI claimed Spilotro committed. Or when he won an impossible acquittal for drug smuggler Jimmy Chagra, accused of hiring a hitman to kill a federal judge. Now, taking his place behind his desk in the mayor's office, on the tenth floor of City Hall, the first thing Goodman sees through the window is the U.S. Post Office and Courthouse, where he had tried and won his first federal case, representing the stepbrother of an—alleged—mobster.

The old federal courthouse, like much of downtown Vegas, is in sorry shape. Opened in 1933, it has stood empty for years, its stately neoclassical facade crumbling, its forty-two thousand square feet vacant and unloved. The site of so much history, it has become a daily reminder of the hard times that have befallen downtown Las Vegas, an eyesore in a city where image is everything.

Goodman has only been in office a matter of hours but immediately swings into action. Picking up the phone, he calls the General Services Agency in San Francisco, the branch of the federal government that owns the building. After introducing himself as the new mayor of Las Vegas, he gets right down to business.

"What's going on with our old courthouse?" he asks.

Absolutely nothing, he is told. The building is listed as surplus, an unnecessary and unwanted relic of the past. The city of Las Vegas is welcome to purchase it for a dollar, if the city will restore the courthouse to its original condition and use it as some sort of cultural attraction. "Like a museum," Goodman is told.

"We have a deal," the new mayor declares.

Then he hangs up, and returns to reality.

Las Vegas doesn't do museums, he thinks. *No one will come to our blighted downtown to see artworks or sculptures. They don't even visit the glistening galleries on the Strip.*

The historic courthouse he has just purchased for a buck occupies his thoughts all day. That night, after his customary three or four Bombay Sapphire with a jalapeño martinis, he has an epiphany.

Where did we come from? he asks himself. *We are unique. We were born from the mob.*

Goodman decides then and there that he will turn the old, decaying courthouse into a museum. A museum dedicated to the dark forces that built Las Vegas:

A mob museum.

There's only one problem with the idea.

Most people in Las Vegas hate it.

As Goodman presents his idea around town, he's met with a mixture of disbelief and outrage. A *mob* museum? The idea is considered so ridiculous, so far afield, that if he weren't mayor he might have been laughed right out of town. Throughout his years as a lawyer, Goodman had denied that the mob even existed. *Now he wants to build a mob museum? What's he going to do to our reputation?*

Which makes Goodman laugh. "Reputation?" he asks. "Sin City?"

Goodman meets with various civic groups, including a prominent Italian American organization, whose members are dead set against it. "How dare you demean us?" he remembers someone shouting.

"It got so bad I thought they were going to hurt me," says Goodman. "They were livid that I would even *suggest* a mob museum."

Ever the skilled attorney, Goodman defuses the tension with a joke. "I'm just kidding!" he tells the group. "I meant a *mop* museum. You know—mops, vacuums, brooms."

Goodman knows his idea is in trouble. How do you sell a city on spotlighting the very thing it has always consigned to the shadows? How do you save a derelict building in a town that prefers to blow up old buildings and replace them with something new and shiny?

Finally, he hits on an idea: he will seek the support of an old opponent, one he squared off against in court for so many years.

He reaches out to the FBI.

Special agent Ellen Knowlton is retiring after twenty-four years with the FBI, serving as special agent in charge of the Bureau's Las Vegas office since 2002. Her position didn't exactly endear her to Goodman and his clients. But now, to her surprise, he's coming to her with a proposition.

"Will you help me enlist the government's aid in building a mob museum?" he asks.

Knowlton has heard the naysayers, and the whispers that Goodman is building the museum as a tribute to his clients—and himself. But after years in front of skeptical juries, Goodman is a master of winning people over. The museum, he assures Knowlton, won't glorify criminals. It will present the true history of the mob *and* the story of the FBI's dogged fight against it. The "even handed" approach will even be highlighted in the new institution's formal name, inscribed at the very top of the old courthouse: the National Museum of Organized Crime and Law Enforcement.

Knowlton agrees to take the idea and a delegation of city officials to meet with the criminal division of the FBI at FBI headquarters in Washington, DC. "The meeting went well, and the members of the criminal division, who were responsible for the FBI's national organized crime program, pledged their support," says Knowlton, who had previously agreed to chair the museum's first board of directors.

With the FBI in his corner, Goodman feels sure he'll be able to get the city and state power brokers on board.

Now all he has to do is figure out how to build the damn thing.

♣

Dennis Barrie is at his desk in Cleveland when the phone rings. "Oscar Goodman's office calling," he's told.

Barrie is something of a legend for his ability to create museums devoted to seemingly unlikely subjects. He cocreated and served as the first executive director for the Rock and Roll Hall of Fame, which opened in 1995, a rousing testament to an original American art form. In 2002, he developed the International Spy Museum in Washington, DC, offering a total immersion in the history and intrigue of government espionage.

That's why Goodman is on the phone. The mayor of Las Vegas has just finished touring the spy museum, and he wants Barrie to create a similar experience in Las Vegas. With one notable difference: "It will focus on the mob," he tells Barrie.

The museum creator gives a one-word response: "Great."

Barrie heads to Vegas to meet with the mob-lawyer-turned-mayor. But the meeting doesn't go well. Goodman always trusts his gut when it comes to first impressions, and he takes one look at the bearded, intellectual museum creator and doesn't like what he sees.

"I made my feelings known," Goodman tells *Cleveland Magazine*. "I was cold, aloof, distant."

But the mayor soon discovers he has made a colossal error. One day, during a break in a televised baseball game "upon which I had a very substantial bet," Goodman starts flipping through channels, looking for something to pass the time. By chance, he lands on *Dirty Pictures*, a Golden Globe–winning TV movie from 2000 starring James Woods as none other than Dennis Barrie. The movie dramatizes Barrie's valiant fight as director of the Contemporary Arts Center in Cincinnati in 1990, when he was arrested and charged with "pandering obscenity" for presenting an exhibit of photographs by artist Robert Mapplethorpe, whose work had become a target of right-wing censors. After standing up to a vicious campaign of harassment and intimidation, Barrie was not only acquitted—he became a First Amendment hero.

Goodman immediately calls Barrie. "Boy, did I make a mistake in judgment," he admits. "I apologize. You're my man."

It doesn't take Barrie long to realize that, with the mob museum, he's got another bruising fight ahead of him. Some city boosters in Las Vegas are still opposed to the idea. And Goodman envisions the museum dedicating itself exclusively to the history of the mob in Las Vegas—along with the law enforcement history of fighting the mob in Las Vegas.

Focusing on Vegas as a city, Barrie knows, will limit the museum's allure, reducing it to the kind of "back in the old days" exhibit that only appeals to local history buffs. Back in their office in Cleveland, Dennis and his wife Kathy, the museum's codeveloper and curator, had a breakthrough: their research had shown that organized crime organizations in cities across America all had ties to Las Vegas. "It was like our own version of RICO (the Racketeer Influenced and Corrupt Organizations Act), which is all about illustrating a pattern of criminal activity throughout a criminal enterprise. We could see in the patterns from an earlier time in mob history that Las Vegas was the nexus."

It becomes clear that the mob's influence in Las Vegas had reverberations nationwide. "All the mobsters who came to Las Vegas came from somewhere else," says Dennis Barrie. "They could come to Las Vegas and not get busted like they had in Chicago and Kansas City and New York and Cleveland."

The Barries told Oscar Goodman and the museum's board members that the museum "really should be more than the Las Vegas story— it's the national story of organized crime in America."

"What Dennis and Kathy said made a lot of sense to me," Goodman says.

All of this will give the museum a bigger story, one that will encompass the history of the mob in America. "That opened up the entire world of organized crime," Barrie says. "You could go deep into the stories, whether it was Chicago or New York, because they all ultimately had a connection to Las Vegas."

The first challenge Barrie and the museum's board face is how to get their hands on the goods—the kinds of artifacts and letters and photographs and memorabilia that will attract visitors to the museum and bring the history of the mob alive. Mobsters aren't exactly known for keeping diaries or scrapbooks, and Barrie already knows the horrors of trying to assemble a museum collection from scratch. When he was launching the Rock and Roll Hall of Fame, he'd been told that sixty thousand pieces of memorabilia had been collected—only to find just "five or six cardboard boxes" of second-rate stuff. Barrie had to scramble to put together a creative team and launch a global search to build a massive collection of rock artifacts.

This being Las Vegas, the mob museum would compete with anything Barrie has done before in both budget and size: forty-two million dollars for seventeen thousand square feet of exhibits, a cultural spectacle in a city of spectacles. But the old courthouse, which has been placed on the National Register of Historic Places, comes with conditions: its walls and architectural features cannot be altered. And the courtroom on the second floor, where Oscar Goodman got his start, is considered sacrosanct. Not because of Goodman, but because in 1950, the courtroom had been a stop in the legendary Kefauver hearings, when a special investigative committee chaired by freshman senator Estes Kefauver of Tennessee toured the country to expose an innocent America to the world of organized crime. The televised hearings, which featured testimony from some 600 witnesses, became a national sensation, viewed by more than thirty million people. But when the hearings reached Las Vegas, they were forced to adjourn after only half a day. The reason? "When they were asked to appear," Barrie explains, "all of the mobsters left town."

The old courtroom will be the centerpiece of the new

museum. And this time, with their former lawyer running the show, the mobsters themselves are prepared to cooperate.

Barrie and the museum's board get some unexpected assistance from the blitz of media coverage that accompanies the project. VEGAS MUSEUM OFFERS A MOB HISTORY YOU CAN'T REFUSE reads a headline on National Public Radio's website. VEGAS TO REMEMBER ITS FOUNDING FATHERS WITH A MOB MUSEUM reads another in the *Seattle Times*. SHRINE TO THE WISE GUY: LAS VEGAS BUILDS MOB MUSEUM WITH FBI SUPPORT trumpets the Associated Press. Suddenly, the phone at Barrie's office begins ringing at all hours. The callers aren't just collectors who possess some rare piece of memorabilia, but people who had been personally acquainted with organized crime—everyone from retired mob associates to former FBI agents.

The agents, Barrie says, put him and his wife Kathy in touch with "some of the mob figures they had worked with who had gone into witness protection." A meeting is set with one of them, the former hit man Frank Cullotta, known as the elder statesman of the mob in Vegas.

How does one prepare for a meeting with a former hitman? wonders Kathy Barrie. When Cullotta meets the museum's team, he is out of witness protection and has already spilled everything to writers and filmmakers, including for the Martin Scorsese movie *Casino*. Cullotta knew the inner workings of the Chicago outfit in Las Vegas, the crimes committed, the individuals involved, and the documentation left behind. "He told us what it was like for him being so deep in the Mafia," says Kathy Barrie. "It was like meeting the mob in one person."

"Frank, what was it like playing yourself, killing the guy in the movie?" she asks Cullotta of a scene in the movie, *Casino,* in which a character based on Cullotta commits a murder.

"Kathy," he replies, "them guys deserved to die."

Susanne Dalitz calls. Her father, Moe, who played a pivotal role in putting the city on the map, came to Vegas in 1950 as the behind-the-scenes owner of the legendary Desert Inn after a career in Ohio as a bootlegger and rum-runner during Prohibition. Dalitz knows her dad will be a central figure of the mob museum, and she wants him treated with respect. Yes, he had been called "America's most secretive and most successful mobster" in a 2009 biography entitled *Mr. Mob.* But he was also a licensed casino owner, a hotelier, and a civic leader who built hospitals and supported local charities. His daughter "opened up her home to us, and her father's papers," hoping that we would "present a fair representation of her father's life and legacy," says Kathy Barrie.

Barrie and his team meet with family members of the late crime boss Sam Giancana, and his Vegas-based girlfriend, the singer Phyllis McGuire. The son of Robert Mayhew, a longtime aide to Howard Hughes, has a wealth of artifacts—including the long memos Hughes wrote by hand when he was living like a hermit on the top two floors of the Desert Inn. Others come forward with guns that they insist were used in notorious crimes. Upon analysis, though, most of the guns don't turn out to be true artifacts. For instance, one gun, reputed to have been owned by Bugsy Siegel, wasn't even manufactured until after his death. "Most of the time the guns aren't legitimate," Dennis Barrie says, "because they threw the guns away after they committed a crime."

But along with the trash comes the gold. A collector offers up the barber chair in which Albert Anastasia, underboss of the Mangano crime family and a cofounder of Murder, Inc., a mob-related group of contract killers, was slain at the Park Sheraton Hotel in New York. Victoria Gotti, widow of New York crime boss John Gotti, donates one of her late husband's suits and enables the museum to acquire Gotti's red 1972 Jaguar XKE.

Then one day, "out of the blue," Dennis Barrie gets a call from the niece of a show-business entrepreneur named George Patey. "I have the wall," she says. On February 14, 1929, in what became known as the St. Valentine's Day Massacre, seven members of a bootlegging gang were lined up against the wall of a Chicago garage and gunned down in a hit believed to have been ordered by Al Capone. Patey's niece says her late uncle purchased the wall when the garage was being demolished and had it reassembled, brick by brick, behind the urinals in the men's room of his Roaring Twenties–themed restaurant in Vancouver, Canada. "When the restaurant shut down, he gave the wall to his sister in Las Vegas," says Dennis Barrie. "She had it stored in her suburban garage, each brick wrapped and identified." The museum buys the wall, all three hundred bricks of it.

"Everyone on the board was making and receiving calls, including Ellen Knowlton, formerly with the FBI, and Robert A. Stoldal, the longtime Las Vegas TV executive," says Kathy Barrie. "All were instrumental in attracting and acquiring donors and artifacts."

As the calls multiply and the collection grows, Dennis and Kathy Barrie and the museum's board realize that they are developing something more than "a cartoony version of organized crime," as Dennis puts it. The museum is shaping up to be a deep look into the history of the mob in America. If they can pull it off, the museum will not only feed what he calls the public's "fascination with the underworld, the dark version of the American Dream," it will revitalize Las Vegas's downtown.

It's a long shot. But in Las Vegas, long shots sometimes pay off.

When the National Museum of Organized Crime and Law Enforcement opens on February 14, 2012—the eighty-third anniversary of the St. Valentine's Day Massacre—the Mob Museum (as it's more commonly known) is mobbed. The street is closed off by the police, and the museum's front hall teems with hundreds of invited guests cheered on by thousands of excited onlookers. THE MOB MUSEUM IS A HIT, MAN reads the headline in *USA Today*.

It's a grand opening like no other, in a city that reinvented the meaning of grand. But this time, instead of movie stars and the monied class, the guests of honor are mobsters. Henry Hill, the snitch who sold out his Lucchese crime bosses to the FBI and inspired the Martin Scorsese movie *Goodfellas,* has flown in, fresh from witness protection, flanked by two bodyguards. Reputed former Boston capo Vinny Ferrara, known as "the Animal," is mingling with local luminaries in the front hall. Meyer Lansky II, grandson of the powerful "mob accountant" whose empire stretched from Miami to Vegas, is in attendance. So is the man known to the museum's creators only as "Tom Machine Gun," a shadowy figure who sold the Mob Museum his tommy gun—always calling from a pay phone, and never using his real name. Even two of crusading, mob-exposing Tennessee senator Estes Kefauver's daughters attend the grand opening.

Oscar Goodman arrives like a star in an old-fashioned patrol car flanked by two Las Vegas showgirls dressed in white. He cuts the ribbon with his trademark giant martini close at hand. He served three back-to-back terms as mayor, but after twelve years, his wife, Carolyn, succeeded him in 2011—the only known instance of one spouse succeeding the other as mayor in the United States.

"Are you the mayor?" someone asks Oscar Goodman at the event.

"No," he responds, "but I'm sleeping with her."

Then the doors are thrown open, and the crowd gets its first look at the museum. It's a veritable Disneyland tour celebrating the city's unique culture. But instead of Walt Disney, the man who welcomes visitors—in the form of a life-size cardboard cutout in the lobby—is the lanky figure of Oscar Goodman, who shares stories of his clients and their alleged crimes as part of the museum's audio guide.

Today, visitors begin the forty-five-minute audio guide tour—with more than forty stops—on the second floor, where the old courtroom has been meticulously re-created down to the historic 1950s paint colors and original benches to look as it did the day the Kefauver hearings came to town. "The hearings are about to begin!" booms a voice. Giant screens unfurl from the ceiling and videos play, transporting visitors back to when the crusading senator attempted to expose the truth about the mob.

On display is Estes Kefauver's battered briefcase and his raccoon-skin cap, which he began wearing after an opponent accused him of being a "raccoon-like communist puppet." Another exhibit showcases Oscar Goodman's old briefcase, which he called his Gelt bag, the audio guide explains, "since he used it to carry his money, or Yiddish *Gelt*, home after defending clients."

As visitors pass a police lineup, mug shots are taken through one-way glass. Notorious gangsters are seen captured in photographs from old government files: Mickey Cohen, Joey "the Clown" Lombardo, Lucky Luciano. A short film featuring Al Capone is projected onto the actual brick wall from the St. Valentine's Day Massacre, telling the story of the bootleg wars that led to the massacre. There's a framed ticket from the 1919 World Series, believed to have been "fixed" by the New York City gambler and racketeer Arnold Rothstein. There's an old awning from the Arizona Club, a saloon that predated the city, and a dazzling display of artifacts from the Flamingo, the casino that started it all: canceled checks, yellowed ledgers, a slot machine, even one of the pink ceramic Flamingo figurines that Bugsy Siegel personally handed out to his two hundred guests at the casino's grand opening on December 26, 1946.

The expansive Skim Room, its walls papered with hundred-dollar bills, shows visitors exactly how much cash the mob skimmed annually from each casino to avoid having to report it as taxable income or share it with investors: a grand total of three hundred million dollars "easy" from the Flamingo, Sands, Thunderbird, and Riviera between 1950 and 1960. The "Getting the Money" exhibit tracks eight bundles of five thousand dollars in cash, for a total of forty thousand dollars—"the amount Maishe Rockman could carry back to his partners in Cleveland"—as it's passed from one mob hand to another on its eastward journey.

True to Goodman's promise when he first enlisted help from the FBI, the legendary law enforcement officers who tried to stop the mob are also represented. One exhibit displays the gun, holster, and hat of Ralph Lamb, the heroic county sheriff "who worked with the FBI to build a file on mobsters that he and others suspected were moving into the desert town," according to the museum's website. The exhibit extols Lamb's toughness: he "slapped the cologne" off Handsome Johnny Rosselli, the Chicago Outfit's man at the Stardust, and "reportedly greeted a rolling herd of

Hell's Angels by first destroying some of their motorcycles, then giving the men haircuts." The Nevada Gaming Control Board's black book of "excluded persons" is on display, as is the execution chair from the Nevada gas chamber, in which thirty-two prisoners were put to death.

"The museum mixes attraction and repulsion, sentimentality and hard-edged realism, relish and disgust," the *New York Times* observes. "Like a gangster movie, it seduces us with these figures on the one hand, and with the other reminds us of the demands of justice." With more than one hundred seventy employees and an annual operating budget of around thirteen million dollars, the museum quickly makes good on Oscar Goodman's dream of a revitalized downtown Vegas. Four hundred thousand visitors flock to the Mob Museum annually, spending double-digit millions a year in the once-blighted downtown. And they don't just visit—in museum parlance, they *linger*. "The average linger time is two and a half hours, which is unheard of," says Kathy Barrie.

For Oscar Goodman, it's a moment to savor. The son of a Wharton-educated lawyer whose grandfather owned a bar in Philadelphia, Goodman earned his University of Pennsylvania law degree and headed west, like so many others before him, to make his fortune. Once scoffed at for his alleged mob connections, he rose to become not only one of the city's most elite and influential players, but part of the city's history.

About halfway through the audio tour, as visitors peruse memorabilia from the movie *Casino,* Goodman shares the story of how Martin Scorsese cast him to play himself in the movie, representing the mob affiliate Frank "Lefty" Rosenthal, on whom the character played by Robert De Niro is based, and Tony "the Ant" Spilotro, who inspired the character played by Joe Pesci.

But there was a "big problem," Goodman tells museum visitors on the audio tour. "I can't memorize. I couldn't remember a darn line. As far as the production was concerned, I blew line after line after line." Scorsese had to have cue cards made for Goodman and shoot multiple takes to make sure he got what he needed. "I finally got through it," Goodman says, "and breathed a sigh of relief."

Goodman was embarrassed to have blown his lines. But one day, he learned that he was in good company. He was on the set of a TV show, once again playing himself, and he remembered something the actor Laurence Fishburne had told him. Goodman told him the story of how he had struggled in *Casino.* "Well, don't be embarrassed," Fishburne told him. "Because Marlon Brando needed cue cards, too."

Brando's famous role in *The Godfather,* arguably the greatest mob movie of all time, is of course also well represented in an exhibit in the Mob Museum, brainchild of Oscar Goodman.

"From being a villain to the naysayers," Goodman says, "I became a visionary."

Chapter 8

THE HEALER AMONG THE HUSTLERS

THE SAPPHIRE LAS VEGAS POOL AND DAYCLUB

WITH THE SUN high in the desert sky and the glittering spires of the Strip stretching out before her, the young woman stares through the windshield at her future home. Her name is Kaitlyn. The twenty-one-year-old nursing student sits behind the wheel of her old Toyota Camry, packed with all her earthly belongings—her books and clothes, her pots and pans, her pictures and posters. She's fleeing her one-school, two-church hometown, where nothing ever happens, for the city where everything does.

"Oh, my God, oh, my God!" she screams, taking in the sights of Las Vegas for the very first time. "I'm actually going to live here!"

Earlier that day, she stood in the driveway of her childhood home in California, bidding farewell to her mom and dad and little brother. Her parents couldn't understand why she was leaving. "The same people I went to elementary school with here are the same people I went to high school with," Kaitlyn explained. "There's no room for growth. Nothing that I will ever become, other than a wife and a mother."

"What's wrong with that?" her mother asked. "Why do you have to leave? And why does it have to be Las Vegas?"

Kaitlyn had already considered other options. New York? Too far and too cold. Los Angeles? Closer, but too big and too sprawling, with too much traffic. Then it hit her. The town whose very name conjures "money, good times, and beautiful people." The town "everyone wants to go to." The two words that, for as long as she can remember, "just kind of called my name." Las Vegas.

I'm going to meet some pretty awesome people in Vegas, she thought. *There's not a single famous person that hasn't been to Vegas.*

Now, after years of planning, she's ready to set off. If her father is apprehensive about how his beloved daughter will fare in Vegas, he tries not to show it. "I love you and I know you're gonna do good," he tells her, his eyes filled with tears.

It's an eight-hour drive to Sin City, but Kaitlyn's not going for the sin. She's going to care for the sick and the injured. She'll be attending nursing school and working as an emergency medical technician with a Las Vegas ambulance service.

Little does Kaitlyn know that she will find her future—and earn her fortune—in a swimming pool.

Kaitlyn's nursing school is in Summerlin, a planned community built by the heirs of Howard Hughes on twenty-five thousand acres he purchased on the edge of Las Vegas. The apartment she rents is a one-bedroom, tiny and scruffy, "but it's all I could afford at the time with my salary"—ten dollars an hour as an EMT.

Her visits to the grand resorts on the Strip are limited to the back of the ambulance—never a limousine—dressed in her drab EMT attire: tactical pants, blue work shirt, steel-toed boots. The calls come nonstop, one after another. A heart attack at Caesars. A stroke at the Sahara. A birth at the Bellagio. Drunks, drugs, delirium. For her first year in Vegas, this is her life: everything an emergency, sirens wailing, crazy hours, saving lives—being on call nights, weekends, every spare hour in between.

But while Kaitlyn keeps her head down at work and school, she's also keeping an eye on the young women of Las Vegas, the movers and shakers, the ones who seem to have conquered the city. They come from all over the world, and in every club and casino, the women all appear to have one thing in common: breast augmentation.

"If you want to make good money in Vegas," Kaitlyn says, "you have to get it done."

Nothing over the top, she thinks—just a boost to get herself noticed, to give herself a crack at a better-paying extra job. But when she calls one of the city's myriad cosmetic surgery specialists, she's staggered by the price they quote.

Fifty-four hundred dollars. Far beyond the reach of a student making ten bucks an hour as an EMT.

Kaitlyn is undeterred. She calls her ex-boyfriend back home and asks him to lend her the money. Once she undergoes the procedure, she assures him, doors will open and she'll pay him back—with interest.

Her ex-boyfriend agrees. The procedure takes a few hours, followed by a few weeks for recovery.

Two days post-op, Kaitlyn looks in the mirror, and begins to cry—with joy. "I felt so happy and overwhelmed," she says. Kaitlyn feels reborn. More confident. More outgoing. It gives her "a new outlook on life," she says. From this point forward, she puts on makeup and styles her hair every single time she steps out her front door.

She is becoming a citizen of Las Vegas.

Gone is the drab attire of a small-town nurse-to-be. Now, when Kaitlyn goes to her closet, she reaches for "something revealing"—silks and satins and body-hugging clothes that reflect her newfound confidence.

It doesn't take long for her investment to pay off. Only a few weeks after her recovery, a job offer wafts in on the hot desert breeze: working as a "promo girl" for a liquor company. "You stand there, hold drinks, smile, look pretty, and try to get people to buy it," she's told.

Promo girls are everywhere in Las Vegas. Resorts and nightclubs spend thousands for young women "just to hang out," says Las Vegas VIP superhost Steve Cyr, who sits beside his friend Kaitlyn one night in Barry's Downtown Prime, a new steakhouse in the Circa Resort and Casino. "When you go to the club, why do you think there are forty girls there? They're just hanging out? No. They're there because they're getting free drinks and they're getting paid. They're there to flirt with the guys and give 'em hope. Prime the pump."

"The technical title for a promo girl is 'atmosphere model,'" adds Rich Baldwin, a connoisseur of all things Vegas and a longtime friend of Kaitlyn's and Steve Cyr's. "They're the ones at the day-pool clubs, the nightclubs, and everywhere else where they want to sell you a fifteen-hundred-dollar bottle of vodka. The guys come to spend money, and it helps a lot if there is a group of hot girls who they think they have a shot with. As I always say, 'Alcohol is the ultimate social lubricant,' and most guys want to look like a big spender. So they'll spend a fortune buying drinks for the atmosphere models and everyone else at the club."

The pay for a promo girl is an hourly wage, plus tips—several times more than what Kaitlyn earns as an EMT. And she'd get to make her own hours.

She thinks about it, but not for long. She's determined

to keep her steel-toed feet on the ground. But she knows that time is short. "There's always going to be younger, prettier girls to take your spot," she says. At twenty-one, she figures she has seven years to cash in on what seems to be her most valuable asset in the club world of Las Vegas—her beauty—before she "ages out," as she calls it.

She promises herself that she won't "get lost in the industry," the glittery world of Vegas entertainment that leaves so many young women broken and broke. So she takes the job, while also continuing to work for the ambulance service and studying for her nursing degree.

Her first client is a beer company. The job is simple: hand out free samples of beer at a place called Sapphire.

The next afternoon, Kaitlyn walks into Sapphire Las Vegas, which bills itself as the world's largest gentlemen's club—a massive complex of stages, VIP skyboxes, private rooms, and bars. She gives her name at the check-in desk and is directed to the swimming pool out back. After walking through the pool's restaurant, where lunch is being served, she passes a kiosk selling everything from sunglasses to bikinis embossed with the dazzling blue Sapphire logo, turns a corner, and...*gasps*.

Sprawling before her is not just a swimming pool. It's an entertainment venue: three pools in a mammoth Las Vegas dayclub totaling forty thousand square feet. And even now, in the early afternoon, a party is raging. Five hundred people swimming and dancing and reclining on lounge chairs and daybeds and in VIP cabanas. DJs in elevated booths, blaring hip hop and party music, the nonstop songs of summer in the eternal summer city. A full staff of topless female bartenders racing to keep the cocktails flowing, a popular drink being an elixir served in a watermelon rind, while a seemingly endless spray of champagne hovers over the pool like mist. Some young women wear pink wristbands, which identifies them as "entertainers" from the adjoining Sapphire gentlemen's club, where as many as three hundred women perform every night in the club (but not at the pool, whose entertainment doesn't include the Sapphire dancers). The club has 13,000 entertainers in its database.

Kaitlyn's eyes grow big as moons. "Everybody's splashing in the pool, everybody's singing, everybody's dancing, everybody's having a good time," she recalls. And everybody's *topless*. All right out in the open, in broad daylight.

Kaitlyn has arrived at the Sapphire Pool and Dayclub. It's the pinnacle of the dayclub revolution in Las Vegas, which began with a Sunday party called Rehab, at the Hard Rock Hotel and Casino in 2004. Back then, the resort was looking for a way to turn its guest-only swimming pool, which was selling an anemic ten thousand dollars in drinks on summer weekends, into a profit center. One day, after returning from a boat party on Lake Mead, the hotel's nightlife director had an epiphany: turn the

Hard Rock's swimming pool into the world's first dayclub pool party.

Rehab was an instant sensation. Partygoers in swimsuits lined up around the block to get in; liquor sales instantly hit ninety thousand dollars a day. The pool party gave birth to the now-raging Las Vegas celebrity DJ revolution, as Paris Hilton, Kim Kardashian, Drake, and Shaquille O'Neal showed up to spin tunes. The Hard Rock had discovered a way to turn day into night—and in Las Vegas, more night means more money. By 2007, Rehab was raking in about six million dollars in the course of its twenty-one scheduled Sundays.

But the party was just getting started. Lindsay Lohan, Justin Bieber, Puff Daddy, Dennis Rodman—they all flocked to Rehab, where daytime partygoers engaged in activities like "making it rain," during which hundred-dollar bills were tossed to the crowds from cabanas above the pool. It wasn't uncommon for regulars to spend one hundred thousand dollars a season on VIP cabanas. The dayclub even inspired a reality TV show, *Rehab: Party at the Hard Rock Hotel*.

The party raged for fourteen years, unstoppable even when undercover cops arrested seven people on narcotics charges and one for solicitation of prostitution in 2009. By the time Rehab closed in 2018, almost every major resort in Las Vegas had its own pool parties: Wet Republic at the MGM Grand, Ditch Fridays Pool Party at the Palms, Drai's Beachclub at the Cromwell Hotel and Casino, Tao Beach Dayclub at the Venetian. By the time Kaitlyn walked into Sapphire, the club was on its way to winning the *Las Vegas*

Review-Journal reader's poll for Best Day Club eight years in a row.

Unlike the entertainers and the bartenders, Kaitlyn keeps her top on. She's working as a promo girl for the beer company, not Sapphire, so she isn't required to follow the club's topless dress code. She walks around in her black shorts and tank top bearing the beer company logo, handing out beer. Then one day, in the middle of the mayhem, a man approaches her and introduces himself as one of the bosses at Sapphire.

"Do you wanna work here?" he asks.

By now, Kaitlyn knows that what she's making as a promo girl is small change compared to what the Sapphire day pool can offer. The man standing before her holds the keys to the big money, a cash advance on her youth.

"He gave me his business card," she says, "and I started the next day."

Now when Kaitlyn drives from her apartment in the suburbs to Sapphire, she enters the entertainers' locker room, punches in, and is handed a pair of blue bikini bottoms with the Sapphire logo on the back. She removes her top and heads to the pool. The pay is actually the same that she made as a fully clothed promo girl. But with her top off, she discovers a world of difference. Drinks that used to sit untouched on her tray suddenly fly off it. Young men order bottles of champagne and whiskey from her at one thousand dollars a pop—or more. Kaitlyn is "bringing bottles out left and right," and the corresponding tips are enormous.

She's earned serious money on the side to have a couple of drinks with a guy, and even more to sit at a table with a group of men at a resort's meganightclub. All talk, no touching. "The thing I appreciate about Sapphire is that it's a very safe environment while also being a very fun environment," she says. "At the end of the day, it's a job."

One day, a real estate investor from Tennessee shows up. As Kaitlyn serves him shots in his nine-hundred-and-fifteen-dollar-a-day cabana, he asks, "What would it take to go to VIP with you?"

Kaitlyn studies the gentleman. He's dressed "head-to-toe Gucci"—not a good sign. "Nine times out of ten, people dressed head to toe in Gucci don't have money, because they spent it all on their clothes," she says. "People who come in with 'dad shoes,' those are the ones who have the money."

"I'm not a dancer, I'm not an entertainer, so I'm not allowed to go to VIP," Kaitlyn tells him. "Unless you buy me off the floor." Which means paying whatever she asks for precisely one hour of her company.

She sets her price, which is sizable. The man happily pays—in cash.

In the VIP room, Kaitlyn, as a nondancer, is required to keep her top on. He drinks and they talk about life. She tells him about her work as an EMT and her classes at nursing school, and he gives her investment advice. He enjoys the conversation and the champagne so much that he pays for a second hour. Kaitlyn is now holding more money than she has ever held in her life.

"It was like a high," she says. Not just the money, but what it could buy her: a better place to live, time to herself, a nursing degree, a future.

By the time the five-month day-pool season comes to a close, a week after Labor Day, Kaitlyn has earned more than she would have ever dreamed possible before landing in Las Vegas.

As promised, she repays her ex-boyfriend the fifty-four hundred dollars he lent her for the breast augmentation—with interest.

Kaitlyn's not just making money, she's also making connections. Two months after she starts working at Sapphire, one of her fellow cocktail servers comes to her with a proposition.

"We should dance at Rhino," her friend says.

Kaitlyn knows the place: the Spearmint Rhino, a legendary gentlemen's club where four hundred exotic dancers serve a Who's Who clientele. The club's owner, John Gray, known as the Lord of the Lap Dance, ran a Las Vegas construction company before figuring out how to turn exotic dancing into big money by adding an element of fantasy to the experience. "We don't want people to feel embarrassed," he once told *The Guardian*. "It's about getting value. It's a one-to-one experience. There's nothing seedy in it."

Kaitlyn had never danced on a pole or table before. But by this point she's fully embraced the animating spirit of Las Vegas: extreme risk brings extreme rewards.

"I have no idea what I'm doing," she tells her friend, "but let's go!"

After heading home to pick up some lingerie, they drive to the Rhino for an audition.

"What's your name and where are you from?" the manager asks the two women.

They give their names and hometowns.

"Okay, walk back to that wall."

They turn and walk back about ten steps.

"Okay, turn around and walk back."

They do as they're told.

"Okay, you're hired," he says.

The audition is over. Along with a punch card for the club's time clock, Kaitlyn is given a stripper name: Cosmic.

Out on the floor, before her first dance, Cosmic is nervous but drinks whatever the bartender gives her, and the mix of alcohol and adrenaline soon has her ready to go. She knows what she needs to do. The goal isn't merely to "shake your butt for dollar bills," she says. The goal is to *perform*—to convince the clientele to take you back to a private booth or the VIP room. That's where the *real* money is. Not in the twenty-dollar lap dances, which wear you out. Not in the tips you get for being up onstage twice a night, for two songs per appearance. "I've made zero dollars up on the stage, and I've made seven hundred dollars in dollar bills up on the stage," Kaitlyn says. But in the VIP rooms, the sky's the limit. "You set your own prices. You can charge whatever you want." Just to dance, talk, and drink with the clientele, who always want more, and which Kaitlyn never supplies.

"Half of them you sit and you drink champagne and just talk, and the other half you give them dances," she says.

Now she's holding down three jobs—serving cocktails at the Sapphire day pool, dancing at the Rhino, and riding to and from emergencies in the ambulance—and attending classes at nursing school. There's not a moment to waste. Four years and counting since Kaitlyn arrived in Las Vegas, she knows time is short before she "ages out" and is replaced at age twenty-eight. "In Vegas, there's a lot of Kaitlyns," says a friend.

What sets her apart, in Kaitlyn's estimation, is that she hasn't let the money go to her head. "A lot of these girls out here, that's all that they care about—money, money, money, money, money." In the quest for cash, and all of the designer clothes and handbags and jewelry it can buy in the boutiques along the Strip—the "stuff that's not going to matter in five years"—they end up working for too many years just to maintain their lifestyle. "You could work in some of these casinos as a cocktail server until you're fifty," Kaitlyn says. "But if you've been working in this industry since you're twenty-one, like I have, you should have plenty of money saved up."

In January 2022, she becomes a cocktail server at the Tao Beach Dayclub at the Venetian, where customers dance and frolic and dip in plunge pools under the noonday sun in a forty-seven-thousand-square-foot "Asian-inspired tropical oasis," according to the Tao Beach website.

"It's a move up," says Kaitlyn. "The clientele is high class, the money tends to be better, and you're selling more of a good time as opposed to a sexual image. And we can keep our tops on."

Over her four years in Las Vegas, Kaitlyn has banked roughly three hundred thousand dollars—which she has been "saving and saving and saving to pay all cash for a house, which is happening in February 2024. I'm building it from the ground up." She still works part-time as an EMT, for roughly the same salary, though she got a small raise. "I got thirty cents more an hour in the last year," she says. With her bachelor's degree, she dreams of one day opening her own "med spa"—a combination medical center and day spa, providing a wide array of cosmetic procedures to the city's clamoring clientele. Her business ambition mirrors the twin paths her life has taken since she arrived in Las Vegas: the small-town girl committed to caring for others, and the big-city entertainer who knows how to take care of herself.

"I'm hanging on to my hometown values," she says. "Never forgetting that relationships and people are always going to be more valuable than money."

Chapter 9

WHAT HAPPENS HERE, STAYS HERE

R&R PARTNERS ADVERTISING AGENCY

TWO MOMS, MIDDLE-AGED, middle class, in middle America. Best friends. They're sitting in a nondescript conference room on folding chairs, sharing their thoughts about Las Vegas with a group of strangers. They're part of a focus group assembled by Billy Vassiliadis, the Las Vegas advertising wizard who oversees the ad campaigns for a city that is built on ad campaigns. Suddenly these two ordinary, all-American women—"with a couple of kids and schools and doctor's appointments," Vassiliadis says—have the room's complete and undivided attention.

They're revealing their deepest secret. And it's a wild one.

Every year, the women confess, they save up their money and tell their families they're going to a spa or low-key resort in the Midwest. "A mom's escape weekend," they call it. Just for three or four days. To sit by a pool with a book, get a massage, maybe have a glass of wine over dinner. A chance to relax and recharge. They pack their bags and kiss their husbands and kids goodbye and head off to catch their flight. But when they get to the airport, they don't board a plane to some boring spa or meager heartland hotel. Instead, they head for the destination they dream and scheme about all year long.

Las Vegas.

They've never told a soul before now about their secret getaways. And they never do anything to betray their husbands or families: their wedding vows are sacred. But the escape that Vegas affords them is sacred, too: the resorts, the restaurants, the pools, the shows, the gambling, and the drinks, lots of drinks, all of which keeps the two women sane for the rest of the year. They may spend their days "on life's treadmill," as Vassiliadis says, but stepping off it for their surreptitious three-day adventure is when they really, truly come alive.

The women strike a chord in Vassiliadis. Like them, he had arrived in Vegas from the heartland and immediately felt liberated by his new hometown. "Doing things here that I would never do anywhere else," he says. "I mean, it's a place where people transform. You see it in what they wear, and the level of energy they have, and the kind of activities that they do. The city literally becomes an escape, a transformation, where people become free. Free from being judged, free from calendars, free from schedules, free from picking up and dropping off, free from mom's house for dinner on Sunday, free from whatever it is they feel obligated to do."

He soon discovers that the two women's story is merely the tip of a mammoth iceberg of longing and need. The researchers that Vassiliadis and his advertising agency, R&R Partners, send out to conduct focus groups across America and interview people on the Las Vegas Strip hear similar themes over and over: A "very mild-mannered, very polite" woman saves her money all year to leave her humdrum life behind and blossom into a strutting peacock of fashion and fun on the Strip. A guy who feels judged by nosy neighbors, even in his own backyard, for the simple act of having a beer, can't wait for his annual stroll down the Strip with a huge, fancy drink in his hand. Because in Vegas he feels free. A creative young man, who never gambles in his normal life, mails his winnings home to preserve his cash and keep the fun going.

"He told us Vegas is where he feels like a king, and he wasn't going to lose his shirt and, in the process, lose that feeling," says strategist Kirsten Gunnerud, who led the research. "By mailing his money home, it actually kept that good feeling going even longer.

"To bring all these stories to life for the team, the image I shared was of a shook-up can of soda exploding," she continues. "People were hungry for a place where they could go and just feel totally free for a minute. Where no one thought or cared about what they said or did and where no one at home would ever have to know. Vegas was the pressure valve. I didn't realize until I started working on this account how deeply ingrained in human nature this need is, to 'let go' of it all from time to time. To let our 'wild' side out. And for many, Vegas is the only place where they felt they could.

"There, they could disappear from who the world wanted them to be, to freely explore who they themselves wanted to be—people their normal lives might not recognize. Which then, ironically, gave them the power to go back to their normal lives again."

There is a world of desperation out there, seekers flocking to Vegas to be unleashed, to lose themselves and in the process sometimes find themselves, in a rite of passage shared by civilizations "since the beginning of time," says Gunnerud. "Almost every pagan culture had some event or ritual where people were allowed to freely let their wild side out and escape from the day-to-day for a short period of time: back to the Mayans and Egyptians and Romans. They recognized this truth and gave people that outlet."

"I can wear a crazy shirt and nobody tells me I look stupid," one person tells the researchers.

"I drink margaritas when I'm there, but at home I don't even drink," says another.

"I feel like a lion in Vegas: powerful, respected, listened to, honored, full of strength and energy," says a third.

Interviewees reveal exploits that run the gamut from

"the surprisingly benign to the most hedonistic extreme," says Gunnerud.

The research leads to an idea, which leads to an advertising campaign they call "Adult Freedom." This will soon become the linchpin of the consumer TV campaign for R&R Partners' biggest client: the Las Vegas Convention and Visitors Authority, which has an annual advertising budget of fifty-eight million dollars a year. R&R are the pros who, according to the *Las Vegas Sun,* have learned "to sell Vegas, the way Nike sold shoes and McDonald's sold burgers—by setting a scene and telling a story." They're the ones, in short, who tell the world why the world should come to Las Vegas.

And the ones who will unleash the bold new image of Las Vegas are Billy Vassiliadis and his team at R&R Partners.

Billy Vassiliadis first landed in Las Vegas at age eighteen, a Greek American boy choosing to attend the University of Nevada, Las Vegas, despite the snickers from his high school classmates back in Chicago. *What are you going to study? Slot machine repair?*

But Vassiliadis soon discovers that he has a knack for selling people on things. In 1982, after graduating from college, Vassiliadis finds himself running the campaign for a long-shot candidate for sheriff of Las Vegas.

And winning.

With the win came the rewards, and soon he was

on the phone with the king of Las Vegas advertising: Sig Rogich.

Vassiliadis knows the Sig Rogich story. Rogich was five years old when his family emigrated from Iceland to America and eventually settled in Las Vegas, where his father got a job as foreman at a factory making the city's most iconic symbols: neon signs for casinos. With a degree in journalism and marketing, Rogich worked briefly as a journalist, then in TV advertising, before entering the political arena, writing speeches and handling other duties to help elect candidates like Paul Laxalt as governor of Nevada. After opening his own agency, R&R Advertising, in 1973, Rogich began to shape the city's image, becoming one of Vegas's most powerful and influential figures. He socialized with the likes of Frank Sinatra and Wayne Newton as his agency became the largest in the state of Nevada, spearheading the massive Las Vegas Convention and Visitors Authority contract and, according to the *New York Times,* representing "Howard Hughes's casino hotels, home builders and car dealerships."

Introduced to Billy Vassiliadis by a mutual friend, the political adviser Kent Oram, Rogich put Vassiliadis on retainer before hiring him as a full-time R&R employee several years before the agency won the Las Vegas Convention and Visitors Authority contract. Soon, Billy became an account manager and, later, "basically an office manager" at R&R, says Rogich.

Vassiliadis oversaw the agency when Rogich went to Washington, DC, in 1984 to work for Ronald Reagan as one of three directors of the Tuesday Team, which created the highly acclaimed "Morning in America" campaign for Reagan's landslide reelection. Later, George H. W. Bush asked Rogich to serve as director of advertising for his 1988 presidential campaign. After Bush was elected, Rogich served in the White House as a senior assistant to the president, and in 1992, he became US ambassador to Iceland. Upon his return from DC and Iceland, Rogich sold R&R to Vassiliadis and his partner, who renamed the agency R&R Partners.

Vassiliadis, in the words of the *New York Times,* is now "the pied piper of Las Vegas." Known as Billy V—"the most powerful unelected person in Nevada"—he oversees the largest ad agency in the state. His wife, Rosemary Vassiliadis, followed him out to Las Vegas in 1983 and has since become the director of the city's Harry Reid International Airport. Billy Vassiliadis not only serves as the advertising point person for the Las Vegas Convention and Visitors Authority but is a major player in every aspect of the city's life. His client list, the *Times* reports, "includes home builders, miners, ranchers, liquor distributors, hospitals, airlines, utilities, telecommunications firms, and the big casino hotels on the Strip." If you have something to sell in Las Vegas, Vassiliadis is the one you want advertising it.

No one knows the power of a good slogan better than Billy V. It was R&R that came up with "Nobody Does It Better," in response to Atlantic City's legalization of gambling. It was R&R that coined "The American Way to Play," celebrating the revival of patriotism in the wake of Ronald Reagan's victory as president. It was R&R that minted "Resort Bargain of the World," the mantra that brought Vegas back from the 1987 recession by promoting cheap shrimp cocktails and bountiful buffets. The agency created "Las Vegas: Open 24 Hours" (a campaign focusing on the new megaresorts and attractions on the Strip) and variations of the freedom theme, including "Freedom to Start Your Own Party" (during the 2000 presidential election), plus "Vegas Calling" (with comic Don Rickles on the phone, asking temptingly, "Don't you want to come to Vegas?").

These later ads were a departure from the 1994 campaign designed to bring families to Vegas, promoting the city's kid-friendly attractions. That, Vassiliadis now decides, was a mistake. The family era of Vegas is over—its death knell sounded by the shuttering of the MGM Grand theme park in 2002. "Las Vegas being a family destination is absolutely terrible in terms of setting ourselves apart from the competition," Vassiliadis tells *Las Vegas Mercury* magazine in 2004. "We needed a campaign that would once again give adults a sense that they can create their own experience here—within the bounds of legality, of course." So Vassiliadis gives his creative team a new directive—one that draws on the spirit of the two heartland housewives from the focus group and their "mom's escape weekend."

Vassiliadis is determined to create an ad campaign that will excite the masses and distill the magic of Vegas in a few words and images. Not just a catchy tagline, but a *story,* one capable of ushering in a new era—something bigger, better, and brasher than anything that has come before.

Every member of the creative team at R&R, around twenty-five of the company's two hundred twenty employees, begins working feverishly, each hoping to be the one to strike on the concept for the new campaign—the story, images, and tagline—that would reinvent the city. What is it that makes Vegas *Vegas*? Out of the all-star talent devoted to the task, no one in their right mind would have placed a bet on two junior-level twenty-somethings to be the ones who would strike advertising gold.

The two young ad men bouncing ideas off each other in their side-by-side cubicles at R&R Partners have been in town less than a year, and both still look like tourists, dressed in flip-flops, shorts, and T-shirts.

Jeff Candido, age twenty-six, moved to Vegas from San Francisco, where his college degree and advertising aspirations had been met with "closing doors and pink slips." When a job offer came in from R&R Partners, he didn't hesitate. "You only live once," he says. But so far, his work hasn't exactly been glamorous—mostly slot machine come-ons and scripts for the in-room videos that hotels on the Strip use to promote their amenities. He's also known for coining the racy tagline for Thunder from Down Under, the all-male, all-Australian strip show,

WATCH A REAL SWORD FIGHT! "I presented it to my supervisors within the agency, but it never went any farther than that," he will say.

In the cubicle next to him sits Jason Hoff, twenty-three years old and fresh from New York City, where he'd been freelancing at ad agencies. But when the economy reeled after 9/11, ad jobs had dried up. "The only work I could find was a temporary job as a secretary on Wall Street," Hoff says. He sent his portfolio everywhere he could think of, and received a response from what he considered the most unlikely place: R&R Partners in Las Vegas. Three weeks into the new job, his work has been even lower rung than Candido's: churning out flyers for various attractions around town. "Telling potential clients that there's a $9.99 buffet at Circus," he says. "Things like that."

Hoff and Candido are determined to do something big and smart and fun and bold—"swinging for the fences," as Hoff puts it. "That was the bond, that was the magic, that was the desire."

Their ticket out of their cubicles crosses their desks one day in the summer of 2002. It is the "biggest, juiciest assignment at R&R," Candido says—a summons to create a new ad campaign for the Las Vegas Convention and Visitors Authority, the agency's biggest client. This time, the bosses at R&R make clear, they want to push the limits. They don't want the "happy smiley kind of work, the things you typically think about tourism advertising," says Hoff. They want to "bring the city's advertising back to a more authentic tone, something of the bad-boy town." Hoff and Candido are struck by one central idea in the brief: "The stories you come up with in Vegas, the stories that become the highlight of people's lives, the stories that keep people coming back, aren't necessarily stories you want to tell everybody."

The two young guns look at each other and smile. This is why they got into advertising—to tell stories in a *different* way. They know that the agency's other teams, with far more experience, are also vying for the big prize. So they work nights and weekends, pausing only long enough to grab lunch at the Suncoast, where they know they can win enough money at the three-dollar blackjack table to pay for the eight-dollar buffet. They keep returning to the idea that "the things in Las Vegas are the things you can't put on TV."

It's a tantalizing thought. But it's also a creative conundrum. How do you make a TV ad that tells the kinds of stories you can't put on TV?

Hoff and Candido hit on a solution. They won't tell the stories in full—they'll only hint at them. "Because when you let people fill in the blanks," explains Candido, "they usually fill it in with something raunchier than you can ever actually tell them to begin with."

From that germ of an idea, they begin kicking around potential taglines, scribbling down their thoughts on yellow-lined legal pads. It's a nonstop brainstorming session. "Hanging out together, talking, throwing ideas back and forth, throwing out lines, go home and think about it and come back the next day and start all over again," says Hoff. As they write, they read their ideas aloud:

"Anything Goes!"

Lame.

"Where You Know How It Goes."

Lamer.

"Keep It Between Us."

Hmm.

"Get In on the Secret."

Getting warmer.

Then, as if by magic, they both read out loud a line they've independently scribbled on their legal pads. It's a line that's been spoken throughout time, a "five-word phrase uttered sotto voce by long-ago traveling salesmen and sailors on shore leave," according to the *Washington Post*, along with anyone else adrift, alone, naughty, and free:

"What Happens Here, Stays Here."

The two young men look at each other. They smile. Then they laugh. They immediately *know*.

It's a line that conveys a big idea in a split second. A line that promises freedom. And secrets. A line that is clearly meant for adults, not kids. A line that makes you want to know *more*.

"It was radical," says Candido. And it was *different*. R&R had long moved past selling Las Vegas by focusing on the things that Vegas offers: the resorts, the casinos, the restaurants, the shows, the showgirls, the shops, the swimming pools. The agency had realized that you don't have to tell people about all that—everybody already knows it. Candido and Hoff's tagline doesn't state what's obvious. It hints at what's *hidden*.

"It has legs," one of them says.

"I can already see it on a T-shirt," says the other.

"It will work!" they exclaim in unison.

They take their idea to R&R's creative director, Randy Snow. They know the agency wants something new, but they also know that the "What Happens Here" concept will be an uphill battle. R&R's ads for Las Vegas once highlighted what Billy Vassiliadis calls the city's "ten billion dollars in infrastructure on the Strip"—the resorts, neon lights, showgirls, casinos, and swimming pools. This new idea, by contrast, will tell you nothing about Vegas. It tells you that it *can't* tell you.

Candido and Hoff launch into their pitch to Snow. They have rough scripts and "a few little images," says Hoff. Each script tells the story of people in Las Vegas, without telling what they actually *did* in Vegas. "We must have written a couple hundred versions in a million different ways," says Candido.

Maybe it's a husband and wife, searching for a Vegas tattoo parlor before heading to the airport, not to get a tattoo—but to have one removed. Then the screen cuts to black. In the center, above the Las Vegas logo, are five little words: WHAT HAPPENS HERE, STAYS HERE.

Maybe it's a bride-to-be and her girlfriends in the back of a limousine early in the morning, clearly exhausted. Then one of them starts laughing, and the laughter is contagious. You can't help but wonder what they're laughing about. Followed by: WHAT HAPPENS HERE, STAYS HERE.

Or maybe it's an older woman in a casino bar or a coffee shop, writing a postcard to the folks back home. But when she looks it over, she quickly reconsiders and smudges out some of what she's written. Followed by: WHAT HAPPENS HERE, STAYS HERE.

"We liked it because it introduces a tiny truth, one that everyone knows but has not been publicized," Hoff later tells the *Washington Post*. "We felt the truth was the way to go."

"It makes you smile," adds Candido. "It makes you remember the last bet you placed, the last girl you talked to, the last thing you did in Las Vegas that you wouldn't do anywhere else."

"We want to be like that little reminder in the back of your head," says Hoff. "We want to scratch that little itch, fan that little flame of: *I'd love to get away with something stupid for a few days.*"

"Interesting," creative director Snow responds. He takes the "What Happens Here" concept upstairs, along with several other ideas, eventually meeting with Billy Vassiliadis in the agency's Creative War Room, its walls painted in camouflage and adorned with an image of a giant hand grenade.

"I think we can move forward to Rossi with these," says Vassiliadis. Meaning Rossi Ralenkotter, then the marketing director of the Las Vegas Convention and Visitors Authority.

As Rossi Ralenkotter listens to the advertising executives deliver their pitch in his office, his initial reaction is positive. But he has concerns. "It did capture the essence of what had become our new advertising brand, which was 'Las Vegas—Adult Freedom,'" he says. "And the campaign would give visitors permission to have fun in Las Vegas. However, many of the commercials would not be filmed here, so our city's many images and attractions would not be shown in the ads. This required an explanation of the strategy behind the new campaign to our hotel stakeholders and the board members of the Las Vegas Convention and Visitors Authority."

Even Billy Vassiliadis has "lingering doubts," says Randy Snow. "So we tested the ad both with and without the tagline. I mean we showed it to people and got their response."

The sample ad concept they showed was "Mistress of Disguise," which depicts a woman in stiletto boots and a skimpy top blatantly flirting with her driver from the back seat of a limousine. When the limo arrives at her destination, the woman steps out transformed, speaking in a proper British accent and dressed conservatively. She brushes against her limo driver and heads off, speaking on her cell phone.

The response comes back positive: the tagline wraps it up. WHAT HAPPENS HERE, STAYS HERE is "the bow on the package," says Snow.

They still aren't ready to begin production. Ralenkotter has approved it, but the Las Vegas Convention and Visitors Authority is a tax-funded public entity headed by a board that was at that time composed of five representatives from the resort industry and six local politicians. "Now we had to sell it to the board," says Snow.

"It was a little rugged at first," Vassiliadis admits. "It's not a very Chamber of Commerce kind of spot."

Calling the new campaign "Vegas Stories," Billy Vassiliadis and his agency's executive vice president Rob Dondero meet with each board member separately, telling the prospective stories of "What Happens Here, Stays Here" over and over again. Some members flatly don't like it; others are hesitant.

"This does not present us in a good light," one board member supposedly complains.

"This is on the naughty side," adds another.

"Somebody coming to the Consumer Electronics Show and getting their tattoos removed before flying home isn't going to help us sell conventions in Las Vegas," says another.

Shortly after that, Candido and Hoff get the word.

"Guys, this is the one," Snow tells them. The convention authority is on board. "They've decided to do 'What Happens Here, Stays Here.'"

Candido and Hoff look at each other in disbelief. A few months ago, they were writing flyers for $9.99 buffets. Now they are riding what Hoff calls a "fast-moving train." The convention authority wants to "go out big"—meaning the first ad will debut nationwide, in the biggest advertising forum of them all: the Super Bowl.

Candido and Hoff are now the creators of one of the biggest ad campaigns in the history of Las Vegas. Other members of the R&R creative team begin working on the campaign, writing scripts, contributing ideas. Even the president of the Las Vegas Convention and Visitors Authority, Manny Cortez, comes up with an idea.

"Why don't we do something about weddings and wedding chapels?" he asks.

A spot is quickly written: an attractive young couple stands outside one of the city's quickie wedding chapels. They've just gotten hitched. He doesn't speak English; she only speaks English. She kisses him on the cheek and says, "I have to get back to my convention." Then they go their separate ways. Cue: WHAT HAPPENS HERE, STAYS HERE.

Once the scripts are finished, a director is hired for the first year's spots, one of the world's greatest commercial directors, Bryan Buckley. Actors are assembled and locations secured. "I was so excited, I was beside myself," says Hoff. "This was the first TV shoot I'd been on in my entire career."

They shoot a dozen variations of the idea, including the bridesmaids laughing in the car, the woman crossing out her secret line on the postcard, and the newlywed couple who don't speak each other's language.

"One had the camera panning around a hotel suite," remembers Candido. "There were empty liquor bottles over there, and chicken feathers in the corner, and a live tiger. Just this whole scene of, *What happened in this Las Vegas suite?* The housekeeper is cleaning up and finding all this random assortment of stuff under the bed and in the closets." But the ad doesn't make the cut. Maybe the hotel didn't want to show one of their rooms being abused. Whatever the reason,

Candido thinks of the rejected idea years later, when he sees the movie *The Hangover*. "I was like, *goddammit!*" he says.

Finally, the actual ads are shown to the board. One board member argues that the ads could be seen as depicting the city as a place for cheaters and thieves, like "Mistress of Disguise," the ad featuring the woman flirting with the limo driver. "Doesn't this feel exploitive to you?" the board member asks Billy Vassiliadis.

He doesn't agree, but the thought shakes him. "I called my research people a week before the spot was supposed to air and said, 'Go to San Francisco and show it to women. I want to make sure this does not look like we are being exploitive.'"

The researchers stop random shoppers in a mall and show them the spot on a portable screen. "Overwhelmingly, the women we showed it to, pretty much across the board, said, 'No, not exploitive, but empowering.'"

They settle on "Mistress in Disguise," the ad featuring the woman flirting with the limo driver, as the first to run on national TV during the Super Bowl.

Days before the spot is scheduled to air, one board member, the CEO of one of the major resorts, calls Vassiliadis.

"Are you willing to risk your account on this campaign?" he asks. Meaning the convention authority's fifty-eight-million-dollar advertising budget.

"Yes," Vassiliadis replies.

"I hope it works," the CEO says. "Because you just did."

But the battle isn't over. Just before Super Bowl weekend, a letter arrives at R&R Partners. "It said, 'We are not accepting your advertising,'" Vassiliadis recalls. As far as the NFL is concerned, whatever happened between the "Mistress in Disguise" and her limo driver in Vegas should stay in Vegas.

The letter is forwarded to the R&R Partners public relations department, and then sent, along with dubs of the ad, to national news outlets. Suddenly, "What Happens Here" is prime-time news—what people in the ad business gleefully refer to as "earned media."

"NFL spokesman Brian McCarthy said Monday that the commercial was rejected last month after league officials reviewed it, though he did not specify why the league turned down the ad," reported CBS News in one of many stories about the commercial. "Most of the news stories actually ran parts of the ad as part of their story," says Randy Snow. "For which, of course, we paid nothing."

The only thing better than running a big expensive ad is having the media tell everybody about it, for free. "It was a huge story," says Vassiliadis. "They were talking about the spot that the NFL wouldn't run before we ran it a single time. 'What Happens Here' was off and running."

The ad finally runs in January 2003, not at the Super Bowl but almost *everywhere* else. In a skit on *Saturday Night Live,* Ben Affleck declares, "What happens in Thailand, stays in Thailand." At the Academy Awards, host Billy Crystal jokes, "Remember, what happens at the Oscars, stays at the Oscars." On *Meet the Press,* William

Bennett, the moralizing former education secretary who had been captured on video playing the slots in Las Vegas, complains, "Apparently, WHAT HAPPENS HERE, STAYS HERE applies to everyone but me."

The phrase quickly enters the pop culture lexicon, a five-word summation of life on the wild side. "A stroke of marketing genius," the *New York Times* raves. On *The Tonight Show*, Jay Leno asks First Lady Laura Bush if she saw the all-male Chippendale's revue when she was in Las Vegas earlier that week. "Jay," she replies, "what happens in Vegas, stays in Vegas." When he asks her about her last argument with the president, she tells him, "What happens in the White House, stays in the White House."

And then there's the revenue—lots and lots of revenue. In 2004, just over a year after the ads first air, Las Vegas has a record-breaking March, with more than three million visitors. Perhaps most telling, the airport in Las Vegas becomes the first in the nation to return to pre-9/11 traffic levels. Vegas is back, and bigger than ever.

As for the two women in the heartland who started it all by telling the focus group about their secret Vegas getaways, no one seems to know what happened to them. "That was over twenty years ago," one of R&R's researchers says. "And they were anonymous, so we wouldn't be able to share their names regardless."

Perhaps they're still slipping away each year to Las Vegas, for weekends that not even their husbands or kids or friends know about. Drinking and gambling and both losing and finding themselves, living it up in ways that might scandalize everyone back home. Sharing a secret in this city where they understood, long before an ad agency dared to say it, that what happens here, stays here.

Chapter 10

THE QUEEN OF LAS VEGAS

THE STRIP

SHE ISN'T SURE what her young husband is going to do with his life.

"But from the first date," she says in an interview years later, "I knew we were going to do it together."

Elaine Pascal Wynn is a young wife and mother headed to Las Vegas in July 1967 with her husband, Steve, and their ten-month-old daughter, Kevyn. They're moving to Vegas so Steve can gamble everything they've earned on a new life in the desert.

Elaine is a self-professed "good girl" who has triumphed at everything she's undertaken. In high school in Miami, she was named Miss Miami Beach—not to mention Best Looking and Most Likely to Succeed. She moved to California to major in film studies at UCLA, was named Spring Queen, and had been on her way to a career in Hollywood as an actor, writer, or director. But now she is Mrs. Steve Wynn, and "in those days you did what your husband said you should do, and I've always been a good sport. So when he said he wanted to move to Vegas, I said, 'Okay, let's try it,' and off we went."

As the young family steps off the plane on that July day, they are instantly enveloped by the blistering heat, the likes of which Elaine has never experienced before, even in her torrid hometown of Miami.

"What *is* this?" she asks.

This is her future.

Their first stop: a grocery store, to buy milk for the baby. Steve has a job working the graveyard shift as the slot machine manager of the new Frontier Hotel and Casino. He has purchased a 3 percent share in the operation for seventy-five thousand dollars, money he made partly by running his father's bingo business back east. Elaine is a stay-at-home mom, raising their daughter and supporting her husband, meeting him for dinner at the hotel restaurant during his nightly break. While he works in the flashier side of the city—the "showgirls, feathers, and sequins," as Elaine calls it—she introduces him to the other side of town, the Las Vegas of family, education, worship, culture, and charity. As they get to know their neighbors and join the local Jewish temple, meeting the city's movers and shakers, her initial fears turn to fondness. She finds herself falling in love with Vegas, with the hotels and the hustle, the gambling and the gamblers. As one of the other Vegas wives told her, not long after she arrived: "Once you get the desert sand in your shoes, it's hard to kick it out."

That sand fills Elaine Wynn's shoes, from mom sandals to stiletto heels, for nearly six decades. As she helps her husband create the new Las Vegas through a succession of lavish resorts, each grander than the last, each defying the limits of imagination, scale, praise, and profits, along the way Elaine rises from devoted young wife to tough matriarch in her own right, a woman *Vogue* will christen "the unofficial Queen of Las Vegas." To do it, she will have to step out of the shadow of her husband, one of the most legendary and influential figures in the city's history.

Steve and Elaine meet, fittingly, over gambling.

Both of their fathers are gamblers. Jules "Sonny" Pascal is a handsome hustler, a salesman who "made enough money to have a good roof over our heads," Elaine says, but who likes to test his luck at the table. One day in 1962, over a hand of pinochle in the card room of the Fontainebleau in Miami Beach, he meets a fellow card player: Mike Wynn, the son of a vaudevillian, who has turned his passion for gambling into a profession, running bingo games up and down the East Coast. "Our fathers liked to play cards and bet on games," Elaine says.

Jules and Mike wager on anything that moves. So one year just before Christmas, as 1960 turns to 1961, they decide to place a bet on their kids. Both are headed home from college for the holidays: Elaine from UCLA, Steve from his English literature studies at the University of Pennsylvania. Their dads roll the dice by setting them up on a blind date.

"Dear Elaine," she remembers Jules writing her in the only letter she ever receives from him while at college, "I have met a fantastic young man, and when you get home from school we are all going out together." It's a quadruple date: Jules and Mike with their wives, Lee and Zelma; Elaine's brother with his girlfriend; and Elaine with Steve. Jules and Mike have arranged for them to all attend a game of jai alai, a competitive sport that was legal for betting in Florida. "That was their idea of a good first date," Elaine will recall.

The odds are ten to nothing that Elaine Pascal will give Steve Wynn anything more than a passing glance. She's accustomed to what she calls "*Miami Vice* boys," suntanned young men who dance the cha-cha and the merengue. Steve, by contrast, is a "very Ivy League guy—hair parted on the side, wore blue-and-red-striped ties," she says. But with a single glance, she sees past his buttoned-down surface to something deeper burning within. They quickly ditch their folks and the jai alai and drive to the Fontainebleau. There, dancing cheek-to-cheek with Steve in the Boom Boom Room, Elaine Pascal, who was going places, is stopped in her tracks.

"He was whip-smart, articulate, very scholarly," she says. "I thought he was brilliant, even at the age of nineteen. He swept me off my feet. He was meteoric."

Almost immediately, they begin to talk of marriage. But Elaine's father, strangely, is adamantly against it.

"That's ironic," Elaine tells her dad, "because you fixed us up."

"This is the wrong thing," he insists. Elaine and Steve are still in college, he points out, and Steve, who was planning to attend law school, doesn't have a job lined up after graduation. "You're going to be a drain and a burden on us and Steve's parents," her father frets.

So Steve Wynn sits down with Elaine's father. There, in the Pascal family's living room, he launches into what will become his trademark, his superpower: a vibrant, charismatic, compelling presentation. He lists all of the reasons he wants to marry Elaine, and all the things he'll do to support them.

Jules Pascal isn't budging. So Steve turns to Elaine.

"Will you marry me?" he asks. Right in front of her father.

"Yes," Elaine says.

Before the wedding comes a shock: Steve's father, Mike Wynn, dies while undergoing open-heart surgery, leaving behind $350,000 in debt. By the time Steve and Elaine are married three months later, Steve's young bride is well aware that there is no one else to run Mike Wynn's bingo games. "Steve felt it was incumbent upon him to settle any debts that his father had," Elaine says. "Steve took his father's place in running the bingo business. He called the numbers; I counted the cash. I became a bingo marm."

Thus begins their partnership.

The bingo games are no mere lark. Mike Wynn had built a sprawling, commercial bingo operation in multiple cities along the East Coast. "If you ran a bingo parlor, some people looked at you like you were a bookie," Steve's mother, Zelma Wynn, would later tell *GQ* magazine. But Mike Wynn didn't just sell bingo; he sold escape. "See these women over here, Steve?" Wynn once recalled his father telling him. "Every one of them knows that they're not going to win tonight. This is all about diversion— forgetting your troubles and woes."

Steve ratchets the games up a notch, turning them into full-blown extravaganzas, complete with costumes and ceremony. Elaine, who has transferred from UCLA to George Washington University, where she will graduate with a BA in political science in 1964, is at his side, booking the buses to shuttle players to and from the games, organizing the food and drinks, selling bingo cards and other supplies at the door. "I made fifteen bucks a day, and that was enough to take care of my food for the week at George Washington University," she says. "What I realized in the years I've been married to him is if you don't share his life, you get left behind," Elaine tells the *New York Times* in 2008.

The bookie to whom Steve's father owes money turns out to have a heart. "Listen, kid," he tells Steve. "Your father's debts died with him. You're off the hook." Steve and Elaine become friends with the bookie and join him on a trip to Las Vegas. Steve had visited Vegas once before, accompanying his dad to open a short-lived bingo parlor above the Silver Slipper Casino. But Elaine has never been, and her first reaction to the town isn't joyous. "Anything that had to do with gambling was tough on me, because of my dad," she says. "I just remember being very nervous about that environment." She and Steve accompany the bookie to the Sands, where they take in a performance of the Rat Pack: Frank Sinatra, Dean Martin, and Sammy Davis Jr. at the height of their swinging 1960s peak. But not long afterward, the bookie ends up having a heart attack—"which is why," Elaine explains, "we got close to his partner, Charlie Meyerson, who became one of our closest friends and most precious business colleagues."

Elaine and Steve have managed to save some money from their bingo operation. So when an opportunity arrives to invest in the Frontier Hotel and Casino, Steve assembles a group of investors—"some people from New York who had manufactured our bingo cards and other supplies," Elaine will recall—and they ante up for a small stake in the operation. Steve's investment, which his wife calls "worker bee points," comes with a sweat-equity discount: the Frontier will shave a fraction off the cost if Steve moves to Las Vegas and works in the casino.

So, like so many before and after them, Steve and Elaine Wynn bet their lives on a piece of the action.

"Because there is nothing more glamorous," Elaine says, "than to say you own a piece of a casino."

As she settles into her new life in Vegas, Elaine discovers that the town is "a paradox." On one hand, it's "quite provincial, with real people working in real jobs and raising real families." On the other hand, there are the resorts and casinos, the shows, the stars, and the criminal underworld that finances and profits from them. Elaine is determined to live in the real world, the nine-to-five Las Vegas of child raising and grocery shopping, while her husband lives in the other world, the "twenty-four-hour town," working the graveyard shift at the Frontier. That is how, in their first year in the city, their future is written not on the Strip, but at a dinner table. They join Temple Beth Sholom and are invited to the home of Jerry Mack, a local banker, for the Jewish holidays. "It was just the most wonderful gesture," Elaine tells the author Jack Sheehan in his oral history, *Quiet Kingmaker of Las Vegas: E. Parry Thomas,* "because Steve and I were brand new and didn't know anybody, really." By then they have met Jerry Mack's partner, a man who can make buildings—and fortunes—rise out of the desert: E. Parry Thomas, the city's most prominent banker.

A friendship is immediately born. Like everyone who meets Steve Wynn, Parry Thomas is captivated by the newcomer's charisma and energy. But he's also struck by Steve's wife. "When you talk about Steve Wynn, you have to mention how wonderful the woman he married is," Thomas would tell Sheehan in his oral history. "She just sparkles and has an exceptional intellect." According to Sheehan, the banker could see that Elaine was a force to be reckoned with—a "remarkable woman who, he felt, was the equal of Steve. He suggested that because she was so classy, she softened Steve's rough edges."

Steve Wynn is nothing short of amazed at the connections. "What are the chances of coming to this growing young city of Las Vegas, a young Jewish kid from Utica, New York, in the bingo business, and being adopted by the most powerful man in town?" he will say.

Steve sells his shares in the Frontier to Howard Hughes, who ultimately buys the entire hotel. The move winds up saving Steve Wynn from ruin when several other partners are found guilty of being fronts for Detroit mobsters, according to a 2008 New York Times article: "Wynn was cleared of any mob connections in the investigation, which resulted in some convictions of partners and led to the sale of the Frontier to Howard Hughes." Wynn emerges unscathed—because a wiretap shows that he was not only not associated with the partners, but "that the guys from Detroit hated me, because I was screwing them all by helping sell the joint to Parry Thomas and Howard Hughes," he later tells Sheehan.

"Thank goodness for that wiretap, or it would have been a short happy career," Elaine says in the oral history. "That would have been the end for us in Las Vegas."

Instead, it's only the beginning. Steve and Elaine make a sizable profit from the sale of the Frontier. But Steve is out of a job. "We didn't have any prospects," says Elaine. They consider leaving Las Vegas and returning to the East Coast, but Thomas encourages the couple to stay. "The town is growing," he tells them. "It needs young professional people who have been highly educated. Don't leave. We'll find stuff for you. You'll own the place."

Thomas is in a position to find them plenty. First, he gets Steve work as a liquor distributor, and from 1968 to 1972, Wynn Distributing Company grows into a major player. Thomas then finds Steve the one thing that can turn a Vegas player into a king: land.

One day in the summer of 1971, Steve takes his wife out to see the little slice of nothing, "a bastard property" draped with power lines, as Thomas described it, at the corner of Caesars Palace and Flamingo Road. "It was a narrow strip," Elaine says. "But you know: location, location, location." Only one hundred sixty feet wide and fifteen hundred feet deep, the land had been owned by a racetrack gambler deep in debt before Thomas convinced him to sell the property to Howard Hughes.

But that's the catch. When Steve offers a Hughes associate $1 million for the land, the offer is rejected. Hughes *never* sells, he is told. "He buys."

So Parry Thomas pulls off a miracle. One Sunday, a note arrives, which Steve paraphrased in Sheehan's oral history as saying: "You may offer this property to Mr. Stephen Wynn, liquor distributor. But you are to stress that we want no publicity whatsoever...considering that this will be the first sale we've ever made, although it's an inconsequential transaction." The note is signed "HRH"— Howard Robard Hughes.

For Steve, it's a seminal moment. "I ran outside and told Elaine and started jumping up and down," he said in the oral history. "I yelled that I'd just bought the corner next to Caesars Palace for a million dollars. Fuck! I couldn't believe it. I didn't immediately know where I was going to get the money, but I knew it would be easy."

As Steve would tell Sheehan, "That purchase from Howard Hughes still ranks as the most thrilling real estate deal of my life. That's number one and it's a long way down to number two."

But Hughes was just the first hurdle. "The question now," Thomas would say, "was how was Steve going to motivate Caesars to buy the property from him."

His wife knows the answer: Steve will bluff. "The property had tremendous value because it was right next to Caesars Palace. So Steve threatened to build a hotel casino right on that corner. Anybody that knows real estate knew that piece was far too valuable for Caesars to let anybody have it."

In 1972, Caesars buys the property from Steve Wynn for $2.25 million. "Wynn's personal share of the profits: $700,000," states a 2005 *Vanity Fair* article entitled STEVE WYNN'S BIGGEST GAMBLE. Now the Wynns have enough capital to become serious players in Las Vegas—as well as a "bank roll" for the future, Elaine says.

What's next? At first, nothing. The couple heads to Sun Valley for a few months, where Steve works as a ski instructor. "We became ski bums for a winter," Elaine says. Then, one gorgeously sunny day in March, on a ski run together, the couple finds themselves all alone in the middle of a slope. "There was nobody above us and nobody below us," Elaine recalls. "And Steve looks at me and says, 'I think it's time to go home now.'"

Back in Las Vegas, they buy their first home. Thomas finds them something new: an investment in a downtown resort. Steve begins buying stock. Then one day, a bar owner he knows from his days as a liquor distributor tells him that a group of employees in the casino at the resort are embezzling money. With help from Thomas, Steve gets a seat on the board of directors. Before long he takes over, cleaning up the place and expanding the hotel and casino. It becomes his first property in Las Vegas:

The Golden Nugget.

By the time they have their second daughter, Gillian, Elaine is more determined than ever to do her part to improve what she sees as the "civic evolution of the town." She throws herself into every aspect of the community: the schools, the hospital, the charities, the arts. Steve, always quick to recognize an asset, puts Elaine in charge of community outreach for the Golden Nugget. "I became an advocate for all things that would be good for our employees," she says.

WHAT REALLY HAPPENS IN VEGAS

Resorts require endless employees—the "talent," Elaine calls it—and she becomes the gateway for a flood of families relocating to Las Vegas. Whether it's the armies of employees on the casino floor or the hand-picked executives in upper management, they all have questions about schools and housing and doctors and churches and just about everything else. Elaine has the answers. Through her office, she creates scholarship programs and art programs and relocation programs and other civic-related activities. "Because the Golden Nugget is a public company, Steve had me become a board member," she says. "I was the person representing the company in the community. I lived and breathed and saw all that was going on."

One day, Steve surprises his wife with a question. "Would you take over the running of the Golden Nugget?" he asks. The move would make Elaine one of the few female CEOs of a major Las Vegas resort. She declines.

"You're going to go off skiing and I'm going to be stuck here on the weekends," she tells her husband. "I didn't want the nine-to-five responsibility of overseeing a property."

She and Steve fall into a working relationship that lasts for half a century. "It takes fifty years to be an overnight sensation," Elaine says. Her office is just down the hall from his, and she becomes a primary sounding board. "We talked about everything that he wanted to do, that he was interested in doing, who he was doing it with, why he was doing it," she says. "I would get involved in personnel conversations and expansion conversations."

And expansion, for Steve Wynn, is seemingly limit-less. He is on his way to becoming what could be called the Wizard of Wows, the man credited with re-creating and revolutionizing Las Vegas via a collection of resorts more akin to Walt Disney, Wynn's spiritual mentor, than to Bugsy Siegel. "We don't build these places for kids," Steve will later say. "They couldn't afford it. We build 'em for the child in each of us."

With Elaine at his side, Steve turns Vegas into a financial rocket ship, launching the corporate takeover of American gambling and ushering in an era of red-hot growth for major hotel chains like Hilton and Marriott. But a rocket ship needs fuel. It arrives one day from an unlikely source: Michael Milken, the financier known as the junk bond king.

"Michael Milken was our savior," says Elaine. "We'll be forever grateful to Michael. He was always a great sup-porter and friend, and he's like a brother to me."

Long before Milken pleaded guilty to securities fraud in the early nineties, his investment firm, Drexel Burnham Lambert, handed Wynn and his company one hundred sixty million dollars in the late 1970s to open a Golden Nugget resort in Atlantic City. A few years later, Milken financed most of the six hundred thirty million dollars for what Elaine calls Wynn's first "lollapalooza": the Mirage, a colossal Polynesian-style resort, which opened with 3,044 rooms, 2,300 slot machines, nearly 6,400 employees, and 1,000 palm trees beneath a soaring sixty-foot atrium with its own waterfall, quarter-mile swimming pool, and dolphin habitat. The cost of building the resort borders on madness, a price tag so high that it will require the casino to rake in a staggering one million dollars a day just to break even.

Steve, always seeking to maximize the value of his land, wants to build the Mirage right up to the sidewalk on the Strip, taking advantage of every square inch of real estate. But Elaine immediately recognizes the move as a mistake. Her husband's strength is his vision. Hers is making sure the vision will work. And what he's envisioning for the Mirage might not.

"You're not going to have any perspective of this magnificent building if you put it right up on the sidewalk," she tells him. "This is not New York City. We're not landbound, where we have to have it right on the curb. If you set it back there will be a perspective as people drive by and walk by, and they will be able to perceive the building at a better angle than if it's right flush in their face on the sidewalk."

Steve listens to her. "It's probably the best advice I ever gave him," she says. Because pushing the building back makes room for what will become the Mirage's crowning feature: an enormous faux volcano, fueled by natural gas, erupting on the hour from sundown to 11 p.m.

Elaine also comes up with an idea for the grand opening of the Mirage on November 22, 1989. The first guests at the resort will be Siegfried and Roy's white tigers. The illusionists, who will be bringing their act to the Mirage, drive up in their vanilla Rolls-Royce with two gigantic white tigers from their show in the back seat. Then they'll lead them on leashes into the first new resort built on the Strip in sixteen years—the one that will become the new standard for all the megaresorts that follow.

Elaine is confident; Steve is nervous. Nervous "that nobody is going to come," she says. "Despite a massive PR campaign." As usual, Elaine is right. More than one hundred thousand show up in the first twenty-four hours. At the appointed hour, after Siegfried and Roy make their grand entrance and put the tigers in their glass-walled habitat, the barricades come down and the crowd rushes through the front doors—only to come to a halt, stunned.

"It was a pristine, exquisite environment, nothing like it ever seen in Las Vegas," Elaine says. "And there was a collective moment when everyone came through, stopped, and broke into applause." For a moment, Elaine, who "had never been to a hotel opening like that before," feels like the world has invaded her home, this perfect, immaculate wonder she and Steve and their team have created together. "I felt like saying, 'Don't anybody drop cigarettes on the carpet!" But she is grateful for the crowds. The casino quickly surpasses one million dollars a day, earning forty million dollars in its first month. Steve and Elaine cofound Mirage Resorts, which eventually expands into eight hotels and thirty-five thousand employees.

"We never looked back," Elaine says. "It was a success from day one."

♣

By the time the Mirage opens, Elaine and Steve have been divorced for three years. But they are still living together. "Steve neglected to move out," Elaine will later explain. In 1991, they remarry, and Elaine continues to provide her husband with guidance and support behind the scenes, careful not to steal the spotlight from the showman.

"Listen, we had a partnership that was working very well," she says. "And I was never confused about who bore the burden of the enterprise. It was always Steve. He was always the visionary. He was always the risk taker, the financial architect, the one who could articulate what he was trying to do better than anyone else. I was there to complement and supplement that vision and that activity."

In 1993, only four years later, Mirage Resorts opens Treasure Island: a four-hundred-thirty-million-dollar hotel and casino right next to the Mirage, with a pirate theme and a fiery sea battle that breaks out every fifteen minutes on the resort's front yard lagoon. The two pirate ships had been delivered to Treasure Island with Michael Jackson and Steve Wynn standing on one of them as it was transported down South Las Vegas Boulevard. "Cannons thunder and pirates plunder!" Steve's voice booms from hidden speakers. "Treasure Island at the Mirage! You can travel the seven seas and never see anything like it again!" And in true Wynn style, Steve ushers in the present by blowing up the past, timing Treasure Island's grand opening to coincide with the demolition of the Dunes hotel and casino.

The implosion is spectacular. Elaine is so nervous that something could go wrong that she has splits of champagne passed out to invited guests watching from the bleachers across the street, and the crowd is soon buzzing from the alcohol and the adrenaline rush. As the multitudes look on, the Dunes collapses into a cloud of dust, and a fireworks display lights up the sky. It is, as Elaine puts it, "another fabulous, harebrained opening."

On the site of the old Dunes, Steve envisions his next resort, centered around a sea of water. "I was advocating for the name Beau Rivage," says Elaine, French for beautiful shoreline. "But we have a dear friend, Ann Anka," singer Paul Anka's wife, "and she said, 'Beau Rivage is not the right thing. You have to go to Italy. You have to see Bellagio.'"

Bellagio. Steve likes the sound of it, the way it would roll off a gambler's tongue. He and Elaine head to Italy, where they check in to the Villa D'Este, the legendary hotel on Lake Como. There, on a boat with Paul and Ann Anka, they see the future. Not the scruffy town of Bellagio a few miles away, but the Vegas *fantasy* of Bellagio—a lushly wooded, Italian-themed resort, set on a beautiful lake.

It would be yet another revolution, another wow from the Wizard of Wows, a high-end wonder that will set a new standard for opulence. It would import the world's best chefs, house one of the world's finest art collections, and offer an indoor shopping mall—in the style of the nineteenth-century Galleria Vittorio Emanuele II in Milan—featuring the world's most luxurious brands. As always, Elaine is involved in practically every aspect, from the dining to the decor to the designer shops. For the hotel's lobby, a soaring atrium, she looks to her personal collection of works by the renowned glass artist Dale Chihuly. She and Wynn interior designers Roger Thomas and Jane Radoff visit Chihuly's boathouse and residence, where Elaine sees the future of the Bellagio's atrium.

A profusion of gigantic glass flowers, called *Sea Forms by Chihuly,* appears underneath the swimming pool, shimmering beneath the water. "So when you were swimming, you were looking at this explosion of color and glass," Elaine recalls.

"I want that on the ceiling of the lobby of the Bellagio," Elaine tells Chihuly.

Chihuly creates a sculpture, *Fiori di Como,* consisting of more than two thousand massive glass flowers. It fills the atrium ceiling of the Bellagio's lobby, one of the biggest and most audacious exhibitions of the artist's career, setting the tone of wonder and awe for all that follows.

The Wynns—Steve, Elaine, and their daughters Kevyn and Gillian—become known as the first family of Las Vegas. And with the glory comes the pain.

In July 1993, the phone rings in Steve Wynn's office. "Mr. Wynn, we have your daughter," is all the caller will say. Twenty-six-year-old Kevyn has been kidnapped, and the caller is demanding more than a million dollars in ransom. Without telling Elaine what's happening, Steve goes to the teller cage in the Mirage and withdraws $1.45

million in cash. Hours later, after the ransom is delivered, Kevyn is found bound but unharmed in a car at the Las Vegas airport.

Only after their daughter's safe return does Steve tell his wife about the ordeal. "I was spared the agony of the hours of anguish that occurred between the time she was taken and the time we got her back," Elaine remembers. "So thank God. That would've been hell for me. And he knew it and that's why he opted to do it."

In early 2000, Steve receives another late-night phone call. This time, it's Kirk Kerkorian, the owner of MGM Studios and the force behind the two megaresorts his studio built in Las Vegas. "We were getting ready for bed," Elaine says. Steve takes the call in the bathroom. When he emerges, his face is grim.

"He's going to put in a tender offer for the company tomorrow," he tells her.

"Oh, no," Elaine replies.

If Kirk Kerkorian wants to buy Mirage Resorts, he will get Mirage Resorts. All the hotels, all the casinos, everything that Steve and Elaine and their organization have created in the desert and beyond.

"You build your empire," she says, "and here comes Genghis Khan."

Steve sells it all to MGM for $4.4 billion.

But he can't quit, can't retire, can't rest on his past conquests. He must top himself, to create one more *wow*, like Harry Houdini had to perform one last death-defying trick—one last impossibility made real. "The next thing that was going to upend Bellagio," Elaine will remember. "That's no small feat."

This one will be named after its creator—the Wynn—and the grandeur of the resort must match the grandeur of the name. In 2002, two years after selling their life's work to MGM, Elaine and Steve cofound Wynn Resorts, an empire that will eventually stretch from Vegas to Macau to Boston. They've learned from their past: the erupting volcano at the Mirage, the fiery pirate show at Treasure Island, and the dazzling fountain at Bellagio had all been freebies, as Elaine puts it. The signature attractions were all front and center—you could see them from the street, without entering the hotel. This time, though, they're building a resort across from a shopping mall. How can they turn the front entrance into something spectacular if it's constantly being bombarded by the lights from the signs across the street? What would be "the hook" in the front lawn that draws the multitudes to the Wynn? "We were really struggling with what to do," Elaine recalls.

Late one night, after a planning session that had dragged on for hours, Elaine is pondering the design challenge on her drive home. "I'm thinking and I'm thinking, and I pick up the phone," she says. Steve Wynn answers. "It must have been around 11:30 p.m. I tell him, I think I have a proposal. Let's shut the whole thing out. Let's create a magic garden, a mountain, a wall. As people drive down the street, they're going to be intrigued by what's behind the wall."

An enormous mountain is built, landscaped with thousands of trees and plants, to separate the Wynn from the Strip. Behind the mountain lies the shimmering Lake of Dreams. This time, though, guests have to *enter* the resort to behold its wonders.

"The new resort is immense," marvels *Vanity Fair* magazine in 2005. "It includes 2,700 rooms, 18 restaurants, two theaters, a man-made mountain, 1,960 slot machines, an 18-hole golf course, an artificial lake, two ballrooms, a 38,000-square-foot spa and fitness center, topiary gardens, a museum with priceless works of art from the Wynn Collection, thirty-one boutiques, five swimming pools, a car dealership (Ferrari and Maserati), and two wedding chapels." But the biggest wonder of all is the resort's price tag: $2.7 billion. "To put that figure in perspective: it is $300 million more than the U.S. government spent last year to fight the global AIDS crisis," the *Vanity Fair* story continues. "Another point of comparison: $2.7 billion is roughly $1 billion more than the cost of the Freedom Tower, the 1,776-foot skyscraper going up at the site of the World Trade Center, in New York."

The opening, on April 28, 2005, is as spectacular as all the others—"like mounting the Normandy invasion," Elaine says. But this time, all of the chips are pushed out on the table. As usual, Elaine helps in overseeing the myriad details, the stress so intense that she and two other executives temporarily end up in the hospital, Elaine with a respiratory infection. The resort was "our last stand," she says. "I was doubling down on my commitment. I was just not going to have it fail."

Steve literally puts his signature on the resort, a blazing lighted logo with the single word WYNN scrawled across the top of the curving golden edifice, punctuated by a defiant period. By then, though, Elaine has begun to emerge from her husband's shadow. "She was like a willow, beautiful and blowing graciously toward her husband," the legendary singer Phyllis McGuire tells Cathy Horyn of the *New York Times* not long after the Wynn opens. "She was totally, 100 percent, behind her husband. That's not as true anymore. She's more her own person."

The Wynn is another staggering success. Another winner. Another *wow*. A resort that matches and, some would say, even exceeds the glories of Bellagio. But this time, at age 63, Steve greets his triumph in a new way. This time he doesn't go looking for another vision, another resort to trump the last one, another lollapalooza.

Steve Wynn could always envision the future of Las Vegas. But by the time the Wynn is completed, he can barely see it. In 1971 he'd been diagnosed with retinitis pigmentosa, which would gradually destroy his vision. By 2010, he is legally blind.

As always, Elaine is there to support him. "Mr. Wynn leans on Elaine figuratively and literally, often throwing an arm around her as she guides him through the property," the *New York Times* reports. *Vanity Fair* writer Dominick Dunne was once sitting at dinner with the Wynns when it became obvious that Steve couldn't see the fork next to his plate. "To the left, dear," Dunne heard Elaine murmur. Steve "immediately picked up the fork and went right on talking and eating," Dunne wrote.

In 2006, while Steve is giving a tour of his personal art collection to a small group of friends, his diminished eyesight causes him to accidentally jab his elbow into Picasso's 1932 portrait of his mistress, Marie-Thérèse Walter, titled *Le Rêve* (The Dream). "There was a terrible noise," wrote director and screenwriter Nora Ephron, who witnessed the disaster. "Smack in the middle...was a black hole the size of a silver dollar."

"Oh, shit," Steve says. "Look what I've done."

Steve, who had arranged to sell the Picasso painting for $139 million, is forced to call off the deal. Elaine is there to console him. "First of all," she tells him, "it's only a thing. And second of all, aren't you glad it was you who did it, and not somebody else? This is a sign. We are not supposed to sell this picture." (In fact, with Steve's knack for timing, he has the painting expertly restored, and in 2013 sells it to the same buyer for $155 million.)

Elaine doesn't discuss what happens next. But it's written across headlines.

Steve buys a new superyacht and begins spending

more time away from Las Vegas. A younger woman, more than twenty years his junior, enters Steve's life while he is still married to Elaine. Steve and Elaine divorce, for the second time, in 2010, and this time it's for keeps. Steve calls it the costliest divorce in American history; Elaine emerges with half of Steve's share in Wynn Resorts. Steve marries the younger woman in 2011.

Then things get ugly.

"In 2018, she found herself an outsider, having been ousted from her office and the Wynn Resorts board after the divorce," according to a 2022 *WSJ Magazine* profile.

Thus began an epic fight, both in court and in the boardroom, whose details have been written across endless court documents and headlines. But all that matters now is this:

Elaine wins.

The fight isn't merely a financial issue for Elaine; it's a woman's rights issue. Maybe she thinks of her mother, Lee Stollman Pascal, who had sailed from the Russian city of Pinsk as a little girl in the 1920s, passing beneath the Statue of Liberty to make a new life in America. She worked as a self-taught pianist in silent movie theaters and, after marrying Jules Pascal, crafted custom clothing and handbags on the side. But her independence and creativity were stifled by the times she lived in. "She had thoughts of her own and a mind of her own," Elaine will say, "but she was definitely subservient to my father." Now this immigrant woman's daughter, who helped build Las Vegas into a modern mecca, would no longer be subservient to anyone.

Elaine is now the largest individual shareholder of Wynn Resorts.

For so many years, Elaine thought of Steve as the hero of her story.

Turns out *she* is.

Elaine Wynn remains in Las Vegas, focusing not only on the resort and casino side of the city, but also on the side of town that she recognized, embraced, and graced with her considerable time and devotion from the start: the Las Vegas of families, education, sports, culture, faith, and charities.

Elaine Wynn may not have sought the spotlight, but she found it nonetheless.

"In one of the most testosterone-driven cities on earth," *WSJ Magazine* noted, "a woman outlasted and out-maneuvered them all."

Chapter 11

UNMASKING THE JACKPOT WINNER OF THE MASK

TREASURE ISLAND

ROBERT TAYLOR'S LIFE is as unremarkable as his name.

An accountant from Phoenix, Arizona, Taylor rises at 6:30 each morning and returns home at 5:00, day after day after day. He's twenty-seven and single—no kids, no big passions, no recreational pursuits. "I hang out with friends, go to the gym," he says. "I don't have any hobbies."

"Very mundane life," he adds.

Twice a year, though, Taylor leaves that life behind and flies off to Las Vegas. He's been going since he turned twenty-one, when his father, James, introduced him to the idea of a Vegas getaway. Since then, it's become something of a family ritual twice a year, packed with bright lights, amazing meals, and nonstop fun.

On Saturday, January 8, 2022, Taylor and his dad bring Robert's younger brother to Vegas for the weekend to celebrate his college graduation. After dropping off their luggage at the Luxor, where they're all staying in the same room, the three men decide to go "casino hopping" before dinner. At 5 p.m. they take an Uber to the Mirage—his dad's favorite—and spend a little time in the casino. Then they board the two-minute tram to Treasure Island.

There, in the casino, Taylor slid some cash into a slot machine called The Mask.

The Mask is a riotous 1994 hit movie starring Jim Carrey as Stanley Ipkiss, an ordinary bank clerk not unlike Robert Taylor, whose own unremarkable life is upended when he finds a green wooden mask floating in the river of his hometown, Edge City. Taking it home, he puts it on and is magically transformed into a manic character called The Mask, a zany, green-faced, fast-talking superhero who fights crime, wins the girl of his dreams, and runs amok over everyone who'd bullied him. At Treasure Island, The Mask slot machine features scenes from the movie and screams the lines that Jim Carrey uttered into infamy:

Smokin'!

Somebody stop me!

It's showtime!

The machine, unoccupied amid the crowded slots surrounding it, seems to beckon Robert Taylor. It's big and modern, with its flashing lights and giant screen. "It looked like one of those newer video games," Taylor says. "It was calling my name."

Taylor orders a vodka cranberry. With his father at his side and the promise of a Saturday night in Las Vegas stretching before him, he puts the first of several bills into the machine. It responds with a swirling symphony of light and sound, sirens and salutations, as Robert Taylor joins Stanley Ipkiss in what the slot machine's marketing materials describe as "his madcap adventures around Edge City."

Before long, Taylor is into the machine's "bonus feature"—a chance to spin the wheel at the top of the slot, the realm where the ever-growing progressive jackpot resides. Right now, according to the bright lights on the machine, it stands at $229,368.52.

For a moment, Taylor's a gladiator. It's man against machine—which can deliver a life-changing jackpot. Not some dry number on an auditing form in his office back in Phoenix. Here in Las Vegas, numbers flash in dazzling lights for all to see, promising riches beyond belief.

The wheel spins. The lights blaze. The slot screams.

It's showtime!

The machine's frenzy rises to a deafening, blinding crescendo, only to...*stop*. Freeze. Flashing now only:

ERROR MESSAGE.

ERROR MESSAGE. ERROR MESSAGE. RESOLVING PROGRES-
SIVE PRIZE.

PLEASE WAIT.

And, at the top corners of the screen: LINK DOWN.

Taylor is soon surrounded by casino attendants, who struggle to resolve the problem. They open up the back of the paralyzed machine and reboot the system. When it finally responds, it offers Taylor another chance to play the bonus feature. But when he tries, no dice. "The same thing happened," he says. "It froze up again."

It was like a cruel trick. The mocking mask. Jim Carrey's leering grin. The frozen machine. The attendants shaking their heads. "Sorry," they tell him. "The machine has malfunctioned."

"I was out of luck," Taylor recalls. "They cashed me out, and I left."

He's reimbursed for the money he's dropped into the machine, plus another fifteen dollars for his trouble. Accompanied by his brother and father, he walks out of Treasure Island, heads south on the Strip, and crosses over to the Venetian, where they have dinner reservations for 6:30 at Smith and Wollensky. Afterward they catch the comedian Sebastian Maniscalco's show at the Wynn and hit the casino at the Luxor. The next day they will join the Las Vegas Raiders tailgate party at Allegiant Stadium. But on that Saturday night, when Taylor finally gets to bed at 3 a.m., his head is still filled with visions of that frozen slot machine.

It looks like he'll be heading back to Phoenix a loser.

"I just thought I was super unlucky," he says.

Three days later, the call comes in to the Nevada Gaming Control Board.

It's from the operator of a bank of slot machines at the Treasure Island casino. One of their machines had malfunctioned on Saturday night. Unable to get it fixed, the casino had paid off the player—no name, no address, just some guy who had tried his luck and then vanished into the night. But forty-eight hours later, when a repair crew finally got the slot machine back online, they made a startling discovery.

The guy's quarter had paid off.

He had won the jackpot—almost two hundred thirty thousand dollars.

The man who takes the call is named James Taylor, who has the same name as Robert Taylor's father. But this James Taylor is chief of the gaming board's enforcement division, the high sheriff of Nevada casinos, overseeing one hundred twenty employees responsible for investigating gambling crimes across the state. He and his team were the ones who busted Dennis Nikrasch, a Chicago hacker who used a handheld computer to steal sixteen million dollars in jackpots from slot machines over the course of twenty-two years—the largest theft in Las Vegas history. They were the ones who vanquished the "bill validators," crooks who figured out how to trick slot machines into mistaking one-dollar bills for hundred-dollar bills. They also unmasked a band of cheats who they suspected (but could never prove) were in cahoots with dealers. The players planted hidden cameras under their sleeves so they could make the right bet at the right time.

In addition to criminal investigations, which James Taylor calls "the most fun," he and the enforcement division are responsible for resolving any disputes between casinos and patrons involving amounts greater than five hundred dollars. "If you have problems with the casino and they work it out with you, fine," he says. "But if they don't, you can call our office and we will have agents come out, look at the video, test the machine, talk to witnesses. And we will make a determination whether or not the casino should pay you that money."

The case of The Mask slot machine falls into the dispute category. But instead of getting the casino's money back from a crook, Taylor and his agents are tasked with giving it away to a winner. After all, the lure of Vegas only works if gamblers are confident they'll be paid their winnings, in full. Nevada casinos, which collected some $13.4 billion in wagers in 2021, are strictly regulated, and it's James Taylor's job to ensure that money won is money paid.

The Mask machine, it turns out, is part of a vast network of slots called wide area progressives. Every machine in the network continues to accumulate the same large jackpot, even when no one is playing them. So long as someone, somewhere, is playing one of the connected machines—even as far away as Atlantic City—the jackpot pool continues to grow. And like a lottery, the money in the pool legally belongs to the people who paid into it. It's not the casino's money to take. Nor does it belong to the state. It belongs to the players. And if a player wins—even if there's a slot machine malfunction—the casino cannot keep the jackpot.

The clock is ticking. Gaming regulations state that if the winner cannot be found in thirty days, the unclaimed jackpot gets rolled back into the machine. That means the money goes to the next winner—and the individual who won the first time around goes unrecognized, and unrewarded.

James Taylor, the sheriff of Vegas gambling, is determined not to let that happen.

He must unmask The Mask's winner and get him his money.

It's been four days since the mystery player hit the jackpot at Treasure Island. The delay in determining what happened with the machine's malfunction—compounded by how long it took the gaming control board's technology division to pass along the information to enforcement—has made it even tougher for James Taylor and his team to track down the winner. If they're going to solve the case, they'll need to act quickly.

Taylor summons Dan Nuqui, one of his most seasoned field agents, and runs down the basics. There's little evidence to go on: the winner received his forty bucks in cash, so there's no paper trail to follow. "He didn't leave behind any bread crumbs," Taylor says. "There's nothing—no name, we don't know where he was staying in the city. Treasure Island didn't have any information on him when he left. They offered him forty dollars, and he said, 'Okay, thanks, have a good day,' and took the money and walked out of the casino."

The chief gives Nuqui his marching orders: find the winner and deliver the money, to ensure "that the public trust in the gaming industry remains strong." He also tells Nuqui where to start. "He's going to use a credit card to buy a cup of coffee," Taylor says. "He's going to do something to leave a trace at that casino. Go pull the tape."

Meaning the CCTV footage.

Every casino in Las Vegas is equipped with countless security cameras, and every machine with a jackpot of two hundred fifty thousand dollars or more has its own dedicated CCTV camera. "If you look around, there's video everywhere," Taylor says. "All those black balls in every corner and ceiling—those are video cameras." To maintain a gaming license in the state of Nevada, casinos agree to give the gaming control board unlimited access to their CCTV video.

But this is January 2022, in the midst of the coronavirus pandemic. Mask regulations mean that people's faces are obscured—all the cameras catch are hair and eyes, rendering standard facial recognition programs useless. Add to this the quickly diminishing time element: most casinos record over their old security footage after seven days. "So we had two days left to watch the tape," says Taylor. Nuqui orders the CCTV footage from the evening in question from Treasure Island, other resorts, and the entire Strip. "Outside, inside, everything," Nuqui says. "So we could follow them from camera to camera."

Nuqui starts with the video from the malfunctioning slot machine. He sees the winner hit the jackpot. He sees the confusion that follows. He sees the winner and his two companions milling around the frozen machine for nearly forty-five minutes while several casino attendants try to assess the problem. He sees no clear faces around The Mask machine. Only masks.

Finally, he watches the technicians tell the winner it will take another day or two to figure it out. They hand him the forty dollars for his trouble. Then, around 5 p.m., the winner and his companions depart, exiting the frame of the slot machine's dedicated camera.

From CCTV camera to CCTV camera, Nuqui watches hours upon hours of video, following the masked winner, guided only by the man's clothes and his companions. They never use a credit card, never check in anywhere that required identification, never do anything that Nuqui can follow up on. "I watched them walk out of Treasure Island and then turn southbound on the Las Vegas Strip," he says.

There they merge into the multitudes strolling the Strip—and the trail goes cold.

But the time from the machine's malfunction to the winner's departure from the casino is only half the story. CCTV cameras are present in practically every inch of Las Vegas. So if Nuqui can follow the winner forward in time from the point of the jackpot, he can also trace where the winner came from *before* he hit the jackpot.

Nuqui obtains earlier videos and starts to rewind. He watches the trio emerging from the tram to Treasure Island—which only comes from one resort: the Mirage. He watches the footage again and again in reverse, following the winner backward in time from camera to camera. Nuqui would have been lost, along with the jackpot winner, if not for one thing: outside the Mirage, a camera captured the winner arriving at the casino, exiting an SUV.

The image is blurry. It's captured from a distance, so it's pixelated and grainy. And the sun has just gone down between the towering walls of the Mirage, so the lighting is hazy at best. "Really crappy video," Nuqui says.

Nuqui calls a friend, an investigator who's a supervisor at the Nevada Transportation Authority. The cop, who comes over to watch the video footage with him, notes that the SUV appears to be in a line for vehicles from rideshare programs. But without a logo on the SUV, it's difficult to tell if it's an Uber or a Lyft or one of their competitors.

Another stroke of bad luck: the SUV doesn't have a front license plate. What it does have, though, is a small emblem on the grill, blurry and partially hidden in shadows.

A clue.

Nuqui plays the tape over and over, trying to make out the emblem. It's oblong, which leads him to believe the vehicle is a Ford. He searches through online images of Ford SUVs, narrowing down the possible models one by one. After settling on two or three, he begins calling the rideshare companies.

Another roadblock. Rideshare companies walk a fine line between assisting police investigations and protecting the privacy of their customers. Sometimes it takes a warrant to get their full cooperation in criminal matters. But this isn't a criminal case, so a warrant isn't an option, and the rideshares are reluctant to share information. To even correspond with Lyft, Nuqui has to create a law enforcement "rider account" and submit an inquiry online.

After confirming that Nuqui is a bona fide agent with the gaming control board, a Lyft supervisor asks, "How much was the jackpot?"

"All I can tell you is it is a life-changing amount," Nuqui tells him.

The supervisor makes an exception. If Nuqui can supply the time of the ride in the supposed Ford, he'll cross-reference Lyft's records and let him know if there's a match.

The results come back fast: no match.

Next, Nuqui tries Uber, forwarding the presumed make and model of the Ford and the time the ride ended, according to the time stamp on the security footage.

It doesn't take long before someone at Uber calls back.

They have an exact match—but the identity of the rider can't be released, due to privacy policies. Thinking fast, Nuqui comes up with a solution: he'll write an email and Uber will forward it on to the mystery rider. Uber agrees.

> We confirmed that one of your registered riders/vehicle occupants may be entitled to a large sum of money after gambling in a Las Vegas casino. The patron left the casino before they could be paid out. The recorded video shows they used a ride share loading/unloading lane of the casino's (Mirage) driveway at approximately 17:01 hours on 01/08/2022.
> If possible, we would like the driver/vehicle information (to confirm it's the correct vehicle on the video) and the rider information (name/DOB and contact information) to confirm if they are the correct person to receive the payment from the casino. Any assistance you can provide would be greatly appreciated.

Uber sends the email to Robert Taylor's brother, since it was his Uber account that had been used to book the car. Two days go by: no response. Uber follows up with a phone call: no answer. Finally, Uber sends a second, more urgently worded email—and the brother finally responds.

In an age rife with email scams, the brother is

understandably skeptical. A big jackpot? Out of the blue? It seems like the oldest trick in the book. Still, the brother forwards the email to their father, James, who agrees to call the agent.

"I'm a state police officer with the Nevada Gaming Control Board," Nuqui tells him, "and I believe your son won a sizable jackpot at Treasure Island on January 8, 2022. I just want to make sure the money goes to the right person."

James Taylor is still skeptical.

"Would you feel more comfortable if I send you an email through my government email account?" Nuqui suggests.

Robert's father agrees, and Nuqui sends him the case number and some images from the video cameras, plus his contact information and state ID.

"Okay," Taylor tells Nuqui. "I'll forward your contact info to my son and we'll go from there."

"A life-changing amount of money," Nuqui repeats, this time directly to the winner, Robert Taylor.

The accountant is back in Phoenix, sitting in his office, awash in audits. It's January 28, nearly three weeks after the investigation began, and Nuqui has at long last gotten the call he's been waiting for: "Hello, this is Robert Taylor, and Uber told me to contact you in regards to a slot machine error."

Nuqui starts by confirming Taylor's identity. He asks him to supply his driver's license, so he can check it against his stay at the Luxor. He also asks him to describe what happened with the frozen slot machine that night at Treasure Island. Convinced that he's found his man, he then asks Taylor the most important question:

"Do you know how much you won?"

"No," Taylor says. "I just remember it went to the bonus game and it just froze. So I didn't know what was going on."

"Bro, you won just short of a quarter million dollars," Nuqui tells him. "$229,368.52 to be exact. That's why we've been trying to find you. And if you hadn't taken an Uber that day, we probably wouldn't have."

Stone-cold silence.

"I can't believe you guys found me!" Taylor finally exclaims.

Back in Las Vegas, Nuqui's boss is on the line with Treasure Island.

"We found the kid," he tells them.

Treasure Island doesn't just wire Taylor his winnings. The resort flies him and his family back to Vegas, all expenses paid, making a media event out of the big jackpot. They want the message sent far and wide: what happens in Vegas *pays* in Vegas.

Taylor finds himself back at The Mask slot machine. This time, Jim Carrey as The Mask isn't frozen, but tipping his yellow hat, his green face swirling amid flashing lights and blaring sirens. Taylor poses with his giant cardboard check for $229,368.52 beside the gaming board chief, both of them wearing coronavirus masks as the story goes viral worldwide.

"Such a good kid," chief James Taylor says of the winner. "Very shy and reserved. He did one interview that night with the *Las Vegas Sun,* and by Monday morning we had *Good Morning America, Inside Edition, Fox News,* and the *Washington Post* all lined up for interviews. He turned them all down. He just didn't want any press."

Back home in Phoenix, ever the accountant, Robert Taylor banks the entire amount. "I'm gonna use it to pay off some student loans," he says. "And I'm trying to plan a vacation with my family, to do something kinda fun." Maybe he'll return to Vegas and once again stand before that riotous Mask machine. For a quarter he'll let the wheel spin and wait for his life to transform, like the character in the movie, from lowly clerk to lucky crusader, from mundane to magical.

It's the quintessential Vegas story: a fortune won, and lost, and won again. As Jim Carrey's masked hero continues to shout from the slot machine, for all to hear: *It's showtime!*

Chapter 12

RISK CITY

THE STRAT

MORE THAN ONE thousand feet above Las Vegas, a young man stares down into the mouth of his fear. Harnessed and connected to a cable and two thin guidewires, he is preparing to leap from the STRAT, the tallest freestanding observation tower in America. At 1,149 feet, the spire is a dazzling feat of imagination and engineering, the ultimate dare in the city of daring. But the young man who is about to leap is not filled with exhilaration, but with excruciating, heart-palpitating *fear*.

His name is Badri, and his eyes are welling with tears.

A skinny grad student pursuing a master's degree in computer science in the Midwest, Badri has paid $129.99 to take the SkyJump, a death-defying leap that has become something of a daredevil ritual in Vegas. He stands on a tiny platform, the city sprawling in every direction beneath him. Far below—829 feet below, to be hair-raisingly exact—at the base of the tower, his family crane their necks skyward to see if the terrified twenty-two-year-old will actually take the leap. A cousin and a friend have accompanied him to the top, ready to make the jump. But now, standing next to them, Badri isn't so sure this was the right move. He wishes he had stopped off on the way up in one of the shops outside the STRAT's casino. Maybe the Magic Shop, where he could have found a trick or totem to help him conquer his fear. To quell his panic, he mentally chants a mantra:

I can do it. I can do it.

It doesn't work. The doubts are louder:

I can't do it! I can't do it!

He thinks about all of the enormous technicolor Sky-Jump signs and slogans covering walls and gigantic video screens that he had passed at the SkyJump's entrance: OVERCOME FEAR...I FACED FEAR...ICONIC AND HOLY S*&T! One sign covers an entire wall. "How Do You Measure Up?" it asks. A needle hovers over a range that rates a jumper's level of courage, from Coward to Chicken to Normal Person to Adrenaline Junkie to Daredevil.

Badri thinks of himself as a Normal Person. A good student, a nice guy, everything pretty regular—except when it comes to heights. Ever since childhood, before his family moved to America from India, he's had the same frightening dream, over and over. *I'm in a forest. Running. There are people behind me. Chasing me. Hunting me. All of a sudden, there's a cliff ahead. I'm falling off the cliff. And at that moment, I wake up.*

Now he's fully awake, and the dream is *real*, the cliff looming before him, so dizzyingly high in the sky above Las Vegas. If he jumps, he'll plummet past the revolving Top of the World restaurant, which he passed in the elevator on the way up. The restaurant is one floor below 108 Drinks, the cocktail lounge that offers jumpers a complimentary Liquid Courage alcohol shot from 3 to 5 p.m. Many leapers would have fortified themselves with a drink. But Badri is doing the jump stone-cold sober.

The SkyJump attendants are strapping him in and double-checking the cables. "Who wants to go first?" one asks Badri and his two companions.

Badri and his cousin don't hesitate. "Sravani!" they scream in unison, yelling out the name of their friend.

The minute Sravani hears her name, she begins yelling, too.

"Are you sure I can do this?" she shrieks. "Are you sure I can? *Oh, my God, oh, my God, oh, my God!*"

She stands on the edge of the platform. Then, taking a deep breath, she steps off the platform and out into the void. Arms outflung, mouth open, eyes shut tight, she's falling, falling, falling, a tiny speck in the desert sky, screaming all the way down.

Seven hundred and eighty hundred feet into her descent, a "descender" machine at the top of the tower begins to slow her freefall, finally bringing her to a graceful rest on a circular landing pad. She's still shrieking at the top of her lungs. An attendant attempts to calm her.

"You okay?" he asks. "You good?"

Sravani stops screaming. She flashes a thumbs-up.

"It's *awesome!*" she declares.

Badri is up next. Sravani and the rest of his family shout encouragement, as if he could hear them from almost two-tenths of a mile up in the sky.

"You gotta man up, Badri!" calls another cousin, a businessman from Texas who's previously made the bloodcurdling jump himself. He turns to the rest of the group. "Once you jump, you feel like you're the king of the world," he says, as if he's speaking directly to Badri. "Partying. Dancing. A man!"

From its lawless days in the Wild West to its roots in organized crime, a daredevil spirit has always run through Las Vegas. But the actual moment the city becomes synonymous with risk taking can be traced to November 1967. More than a half century before Badri stands atop Las Vegas on the SkyJump platform, another young man decides to stage a death-defying spectacle in the very heart of the city. He has come to Caesars Palace for a boxing match. But the moment he spots the resort's fountain—the fabulous, endlessly long fountain erupting in cascades of water in front of the hotel's neo-Roman facade—he *knows*.

He has to jump the fountain on his motorcycle.

His name is Robert Craig Knievel, but he calls himself Evel Knievel. A stuntman and relentless self-promoter, he is determined to make his vision a reality. So he begins sweet-talking Jay Sarno, the founder, developer, and front man of Caesars. Jumping the fountain—all one hundred forty-one feet of it—will be a feat no one has ever attempted. It will be more than a mere stunt. It will be history.

Sarno, a visionary himself, understands better than anyone the magic that helped turn Las Vegas from a dusty frontier outpost into one of the world's most popular tourist destinations. It's not gambling, or drinking, or swimming pools, or sex. It's *publicity*. His grand new palace has been making its mark in its first ten years, but if some crazy fool wants to jump a motorcycle over the fountain, only another fool would say no.

The date is set for New Year's Eve. The nation is roiled by the turmoil of the 1960s, and Evel Knievel aspires to be its hero, "a cross between Elvis Presley and Liberace," as he later says. Now, on the morning of December 31, 1967, he is greeted with a hero's welcome. As many as one hundred thousand fans swarm the Strip, standing atop cars and walls and even signs, eager to watch an action junkie defy death—or perhaps meet it. Knievel has hired actor and director John Derek to film his jump (along with Derek's camerawoman, aspiring actress Linda Evans). Whether Knievel succeeds—or spectacularly fails—footage of the jump will be a sensation on national TV.

"The louder that Evel beat the drum, the more they listened, wondering just what kind of individual was this who would risk death for the enjoyment of others," *Cycle News* will report in 2004. "Some said he was crazy. Knievel's extravagant flamboyance only fueled the fire further."

Making his way to the fountain in the flamboyant jumpsuit that will become his trademark, Knievel stops by the Caesars casino, where he places a hundred-dollar bet on a single hand of blackjack—and loses. A shot of Wild Turkey at the bar and he's ready to go.

The fountain has been fitted with two ramps to propel Knievel and his four-hundred-pound Triumph Bonneville 650 TT across the water: one for takeoff and another for landing, with the cascading waters in between. As Knievel starts his bike and the crowd roars, a new epoch in Las Vegas is about to begin: the era of extreme sporting events.

Knievel guns his bike, and goes airborne.

He knows immediately that something is terribly wrong. The bike suffered a sudden loss of power on the takeoff ramp, and the abrupt deceleration didn't provide enough of a lift. Soaring across the fountain, he quickly loses his battle with gravity. He hits the landing ramp with a horrendous thud, and the handlebars are ripped from his hands. Tumbling off the ramp, his body careens across the street and into the adjacent parking lot of the Dunes.

Knievel is now on his way not to glory, but to the hospital. According to press reports, he spends the next twenty-nine days in a coma and awakens with a broken pelvis and femur, broken hip, wrist, and fractured ankles. But later accounts cast doubt on the long coma, the hero hovering between life and death. "It was all a fabrication, all horseshit," Jay Sarno Jr. is quoted as saying in the biography *Evel* by Leigh Monteville. "My father and Knievel were like two giggling, sneaky teenagers. They were putting something over on everybody. They were a couple of promoters." In Vegas, all it takes is the right publicity to turn a spectacular failure into a lucrative success.

Whatever the extent of Knievel's injuries, the crash helps anoint Las Vegas as the capital of extreme sports. Not only does ABC's *Wide World of Sports* decide to televise the jump and its bloody aftermath—"the most devastating crash ever filmed," according to one account—the network winds up paying a higher price for the footage than if it had done a deal with Knievel from the start.

The doomed jump becomes a part of Vegas legend. In 1989, two decades after Knievel's failed attempt, his son Robbie, then twenty-six, successfully makes the jump his father missed. After soaring over the fountain on his Honda CR500, *Sports Illustrated* reports, Robbie "avenged the blot on the family escutcheon…roaring into an underground garage where five paramedics and a brain surgeon waited to, if need be, splice him back together again." In 2016, to celebrate the "daredevil legacy" of both Evel Knievel and Las Vegas, the Red Bull Air Force—an extreme sports team sponsored by the extreme sports drink—parachutes from a plane at night in jumpsuits festooned with red, white, and blue LED lights, landing in front of Caesars.

Now, petrified SkyJumper Badri stands waiting to join

Knievel and all the thrill seekers who followed in the late great stunt artist's wake. Except that those who brave the SkyJump don't fly horizontally across a fountain or canyon or river. They go vertical—the length of almost three football fields. Straight down.

Like Knievel's jump, building the STRAT tower was an act that could be viewed as either courageous or just plain crazy. It was the brainchild of the swashbuckler known as the Polish Maverick, Bob Stupak, who dreamed of Vegas marvels no one had ever imagined. Stupak was a gambler who defied the odds: he even cheated death in 1995, after crashing his Harley at sixty miles per hour and breaking every bone in his face, looking "worse than anything you could see in a horror movie," as his friend the legendary Las Vegas–based singer Phyllis McGuire told John L. Smith of the *Las Vegas Review-Journal*.

Soon after arriving in 1971 from Pittsburgh, Stupak purchased a casino called the Vault in downtown Vegas and renamed it Glitter Gulch. He was "perhaps the greatest huckster in Las Vegas history," wrote the *Review-Journal*. In 1974, he opened a small "slot joint" he immodestly christened Bob Stupak's World Famous Historic Gambling Museum and Casino. After that place burned down, he took "the worst piece of real estate on Las Vegas Boulevard, a site fit only for a car lot," and transformed it into a space-themed hotel and casino he named Bob Stupak's

Vegas World—a gaudy operation that, thanks to Stupak's gift for publicity stunts and sloganeering, nevertheless pulled in one hundred million dollars a year in gambling revenues during its peak in the mid-1980s.

In 1990, Stupak experienced his grandest vision of all. Flying over the city in a private jet at two thousand feet and reveling in a magnificent Las Vegas sunset, he had an epiphany: a resort and casino built not in the desert, but in the sky. Complete with a restaurant and amusement park, the aerial resort would bestow upon everyone in his adopted city the same glorious view he was enjoying from the jet. He would build not merely a tower, but the Stratosphere Las Vegas, the biggest, tallest, and brashest in the world.

"All he had to do is risk everything he owned," reported the *Las Vegas Review-Journal*.

Originally designed at more than 1,800 feet high, Stupak's tower was soundly rejected after concerns were raised about it being a hazard to passing airplanes. So the gambler cut a deal. He lowered the height to 1,149 feet but added a roller coaster and freefall ride at the very top of a concrete stem, a spire of nothingness in a city where every square inch of real estate is precious. "You couldn't build it today," says Stephen Thayer, the VP and general manager of the STRAT hotel and casino. "The financials just don't work. Think about how much of it is unusable elevator space. It's only the small part at the top you can do something with, so most people wouldn't go and build something like this."

The tower opened in April 1996, at a cost of five hundred fifty million dollars, and it quickly bankrupted its creator. Like so many in Vegas, Bob Stupak gambled everything, and lost. He died in 2009 at the age of sixty-seven, but his tower, a monument to both his lunacy and his legacy, lived on. SkyJump opened the following year, and Oscar Goodman, then the mayor of Las Vegas, marked the occasion by proclaiming April 20, 2010, SkyJump Day. Guinness World Records certified it as the highest leap of its kind in the world. In 2013, a mere three years after opening, SkyJump welcomed its one hundred thousandth jumper; its two hundred thousandth came only two years later.

The Stratosphere changed hands several times, passing to new owners who couldn't figure out exactly how to renovate it, until March 2018, when Golden Entertainment announced plans for a makeover costing one hundred forty million dollars. The resort was later renamed the STRAT Hotel, Casino & Tower.

The jumpers line up to take the leap: tourists and gamblers and action junkies and celebrities of all stripes, their names commemorated on a CELEBRITY SKYJUMPERS plaque at the entrance. They come from all over the world to jump off of the tower, tethered only by trust, a cable, and two thin guidewires. They come to soar over the city of moxie and money, in the ultimate Las Vegas baptism: risk. Some risk everything at the tables, or the wedding chapels, or a host of high-flying activities, from parachuting to paragliding. But others prefer the most extreme thing Vegas has to offer. One man is so enamored with the SkyJump, it's said that he has taken the plunge one hundred thirty-two times.

Badri, the computer science student, has signed the legal releases and suited up in the green SkyJump custom jumpsuit. He's completed his safety checks and has been guided into the SkyPod, where the doors open to reveal a large vertiginous platform, like a condominium balcony in the sky. As he waits his turn, someone takes his picture, as if he were an astronaut on a historic mission, documenting the bravery to come.

But he's *not* feeling brave. He's still terrified. Now that he's harnessed and connected to the cable and guidewires, though, there's no turning back.

"Badri," comes the command, "you're up next."

The hot desert air grows thin. His heart beats in his throat. His mouth is dry and his eyes are filled with tears. He is guided to the lip of the platform. From up here he can see *everything*: the city shimmering in the midst of a vast desert, with its endless cycle of winning and losing, of fortunes won and fortunes lost, of garish ideas and grand innovations all coming blazingly true. Suddenly, against all expectations, Badri finds himself flooded with an overwhelming sense of awe. The view of Las Vegas opens something deep inside him.

The countdown begins. "Ten, nine, eight…"

I can do it, I can do it, Badri thinks, repeating the words over and over in his mind.

"…seven, six, five…"

And not only will I do it, but I will do it with my eyes open, so I can see everything and feel everything.

"...four, three, two..."

Badri grasps the handles anchored to the platform on either side of him, steadying himself.

Now, at last, he is ready to face his fear. He has conquered the nightmare he's had since he was a kid back in India. Nobody's chasing him now. The cliff has vanished. This is Las Vegas, and it's real.

"Can I jump?" Badri screams into the wild desert wind.

"Yes!" comes the reply.

Then...he leaps. The guide wires keep him centered and the cable keeps him secure but in no way restrain him. He flies through the air, a man on a string, plummeting to Earth at forty miles an hour.

He's in freefall, and he is free. The fear is gone, replaced by a feeling of euphoria and empowerment. "Like I can do anything in the world," he later says. His eyes are open, he is transformed: from petrified grad student to valiant SkyJumper.

"King of the world, man!" his cousin shouts as Badri plummets, then slows.

Now he is landing, the machinery slowing and controlling his fall. His feet touch down in the landing circle, and attendants rush to release his harness. He's not merely a survivor of the most extreme sport in a city of extremes, but a champion, ready to embrace all that Vegas has to offer. To dine and gamble and dance. To move past his deepest fears and embrace his deepest desires. To risk everything. To become one with Las Vegas.

"He can do anything now!" shouts his cousin. "He's *invincible.*"

Chapter 13

THE INVASION OF THE SUPERCHEFS!

SPAGO LAS VEGAS

SHELDON GORDON DREAMED in shopping malls.

"Entertainment retail" is how the visionary real estate developer described his concept. Before he died in 2017, his dreams had become lucrative megamall realities, smashing the status quo with what Gordon described as "never-before-seen features" in each successive property: the first shopping center monorail system running through the Pearlridge Mall, located just outside Honolulu; a "merchandise bridge" at the Valco Fashion Park mall ferrying shoppers over an eight-lane highway in Cupertino, California; the "first and only spiral escalator in the Western hemisphere" in the

Westfield San Francisco Center. When an underground oil field on the prime corner of La Cienega and Beverly Boulevards in Los Angeles is seen by many as a barrier to development, Gordon devises a solution: stacking his mall above five levels of parking for the auto-obsessed city and designing a structure that bends around the drilling site.

Thus is born the monolithic mall called the Beverly Center.

Then comes the ultimate canvas: Las Vegas. In 1990, Gordon, who could be called the Michelangelo of malls, is preparing to create a mall he is convinced will revolution-ize Las Vegas, betting that he can attract enormous new crowds to the city if it had more to offer than gambling.

He calls his magnet for the masses the Forum Shops at Caesars Palace. No mere shopping center, it will be a vast Roman-themed megamall connecting Caesars Palace with the new Mirage resort next door via moving walk-ways that only go one way—the way the gods of Caesars want it. Once shoppers are in the mall, "the only way out is through the casino," the *Los Angeles Times* reports not long after the mall's 1992 opening.

But not before passing through what, in the early 1990s, is perhaps the wildest, most creative, and soon to be among the most lucrative shopping experiences in the world.

It begins as it usually does for Gordon: with a stretch of barren land—in this case, the old Formula One racetrack beside the mushrooming Caesars resort. In 1987, Cae-sars leases the land to Melvin Simon and Associates, the builders of the Mall of America, the world's largest mall in Bloomington, Minnesota, and to the Gordon Company, helmed by Sheldon Gordon. Designed to evoke the Roman Forum, the Forum Shops at Caesars Palace will be created complete with Roman architecture, "ruins," and fountains, plus animatronic statues that come to life and a sky that cycles every hour from day to night.

"To create the Forum Shops, Mr. Gordon once again did the inconceivable," his marketing materials say. "While everyone told him it would not work, he bet everything he had to finance the project."

It will be over the top, even for Sheldon Gordon.

"The new shopping complex adjoins the Caesars casinos, cost an estimated one hundred million dollars and promises to add new depth to our understanding of the term excessive," the *Los Angeles Times* reports. "The statues talk. The false sky evolves from sunrise to sunset... Animatronics-driven, laser-laden and high-end down to its subterranean valet parking lot, the place is a model of mallsmanship and a marvel of manipulated egress," the article continues, noting that "the proprietors have arranged their exits to keep you in until you render unto Caesar a visit to the gaming rooms."

"The shopping wonder of the world," it's called, this Roman-themed realm that will offer twenty-seven apparel shops, specialty stores, three art galleries, and one high-end jeweler. The maestro of malls naturally needs to feed the masses, to fuel their shopping and keep them in his gilded Roman domain for as long as humanly possible.

Gordon needs *restaurants*.

His Forum Shops will eventually have fifteen. But Gordon didn't become a mall magnate by thinking small. He decides that his Forum's "anchor" restaurant will be one of the most innovative and most successful restaurants in America, a temple of contemporary Californian cuisine, beloved by Hollywood studio bosses and movie stars alike: Spago.

If Gordon can get Spago, other successful chefs and their restaurants will surely follow.

It seems like another stroke of Sheldon Gordon genius. All he has to do is convince Spago's Austrian celebrity chef, Wolfgang Puck, to leave his booming LA-based empire and gamble on a developer's wild dream in the desert.

"Sheldon, you are crazy," Puck tells him.

Noon at Spago, in West Hollywood. The restaurant is closed, but Gordon is, as always, fully open for business. He'd rushed into the culinary hot spot in a whirlwind, his suit jacket askew, a sheaf of architectural plans under his arm, talking a mile a minute about how Puck can earn fresh fortune and fame by importing Spago to the Forum Shops at Caesars Palace.

Puck takes one look at the plans—the fountain-filled Roman architecture, the moving animatronic Roman statues, the fake Roman sky turning from day to night—and dismisses them: "This looks like a circus, not a shopping mall."

At this moment in the early 1990s, Las Vegas is a

culinary backwater of America, a laughingstock landscape of all-you-can-eat buffets, national chains, and retro
delicatessens.

The *New York Times* will later observe that "the odds of
finding sophisticated food in Las Vegas were slightly less
than the chances of financing a child's college education
on the roulette wheel. In the old days high rollers were
wined and dined extensively on institutional hotel fare
and further lubricated with champagne, limousines, and
tickets to see Liberace or Ann-Margret. The masses ate at
the $5-and-under restaurants and took taxis."

Most of the respectable restaurants—"the gourmet
rooms," as they're called—were in the major resorts. But
even the high-end restaurants there catered "primarily to
the comp crowd," once observed Tom Kaplan, now executive vice president of development and design at the Wolfgang Puck Fine Dining Group. The food was "ridiculously
overpriced, such poor quality, the wine had no diversity,"
he tells the *Las Vegas Review-Journal*, later adding, "There
were some good locally owned restaurants, but the rest
were dominated by the hotel restaurants."

At this point in his stellar career, Puck, then forty-one,
does not need to gamble, especially not on Las Vegas.
His groundbreaking restaurant Spago is famous for its
casual, open-kitchen concept with dishes focusing on
fresh ingredients, including high-end pizza, which helped
launch the revolution known as California cuisine. With
it, Puck became "the cop at the intersection of fine food
and celebrity," according to the *New York Times,* "whose

tastes mirrored that of an entire generation. Or, by simple chronology, led it."

By the time Gordon brings his plans to Spago, Puck is at the helm of a budding empire, including four restaurants—Spago in West Hollywood, Granita in Malibu, Chinois on Main in Santa Monica, and Postrio in San Francisco—collectively earning $25 million a year, according to the *Times*. "His packaged foods bring in $10 million more," the article continues, noting also Puck's three cookbooks and his monthly appearances on *Good Morning America*.

Riding high in Los Angeles, Puck is a star among stars. Spago is the epicenter of the entertainment industry and the setting for superagent Irving "Swifty" Lazar's ultra-exclusive annual Oscar party.

Puck might have brushed off Gordon's cockamamie Forum Shops at Caesars Palace plans, and his even more audacious prediction that Las Vegas—*Las Vegas!*—would one day become the new culinary capital of the world. But because Gordon is a regular customer at Granita, Puck's Malibu restaurant (and because, for Wolfgang Puck, the customer is king), Puck feels compelled to at least listen to the pitch—on this day and many more to come. "I could not get rid of him," Puck later recalls.

"Open Spago in Las Vegas and you will see, it will be amazing," promises the developer.

"Sheldon, go away," repeats the chef.

Unbeknownst to Gordon at the time, Puck does have a Vegas Achilles' heel: boxing.

Born in Austria, his mother was a pastry chef who later married Josef Puck, a coal miner and boxer who adopted young Wolfgang and gave him his surname. Puck was drawn to boxing but eventually followed his mother into the kitchen. He was fired from his first job—peeling potatoes in an Austrian hotel—but didn't give up. Rising through the ranks, he was soon cooking in some of the most prestigious restaurants in Europe before landing in America and making his mark in Los Angeles.

Through it all, Puck retained his love of boxing, regularly visiting Las Vegas, the capital of the sport, for boxing matches at Caesars Palace. He'd flown on the Caesars jet with Henry Gluck, the chairman and CEO of Caesars World from 1983 to 1994, and sat behind Frank Sinatra to watch the fights from the third row. "At Caesars Palace, they probably thought I was a gambler," Puck says.

Sitting beside the chef at many of the boxing matches was one of Las Vegas's visionaries: Joseph Terrence "Terry" Lanni. In his eighteen years at Caesars, eventually as president and COO of Caesars World, Lanni oversaw the company's expansion, both as a resort and as an international corporation.

"Everything happened at Caesars Palace," Puck later says. "Caesars Palace was really the number one hotel at that time."

"Terry Lanni made sure Wolf was treated special," says David Robins, now Puck's executive vice president of domestic operations and culinary director, Las Vegas.

But one thing was missing. After the boxing matches, Puck was, naturally...hungry.

"Where are we going to go eat?" he would ask Terry Lanni.

Lanni would take Puck to the Caesars gourmet room and the local standbys. "Las Vegas was the land of the buffets and cheap-priced food," says Robins.

"When you come out of the fight or the casino for the night, there is nowhere to go for late-night noshing," Puck realizes.

Maybe, just maybe, Sheldon Gordon is not completely crazy.

Maybe Spago can fill a void in the desert, just as Spago filled a void in Hollywood.

Over these dinners, Lanni would tell the famous chef that Las Vegas *needed* him. Lanni is so confident in this shared vision of the future that he convinces Caesars to spend an estimated one hundred million dollars to build Gordon's Forum Shops, instead of using its prime vacant land for additional casino space.

Puck is not afraid to gamble, either. "I always take risks," he says. "A lot of people are risk averse. They're scared. 'Ugh, if I open a second restaurant or third restaurant, I'm going to lose control of the first one.' I never was like that. I always said, 'We have to grow. We have to do more.' So for me it was always exciting to find something new and to do something different."

Finally, he surrenders to the developer's relentless onslaught.

"Sheldon, if you can get the money, and we can control it—if we get 51 percent—I will do it," Puck tells Gordon.

He adds that he'll also require ringside seats for every Las Vegas boxing match.

Out stretches the developer's palm for a hearty handshake.

"No problem, I'll get the money," Gordon promises, along with the ringside seats.

Neither man could have fully known the implications of this historic handshake, or that at this moment, the future of Las Vegas celebrity chef dining has begun.

Gordon gets the money, as promised, and Puck heads to Las Vegas.

One midnight in San Francisco, Puck meets with David Robins, then the twenty-five-year-old executive sous chef at San Francisco's popular Stars restaurant. "He invited me to LA to work at Spago to try out for the chef job in Vegas," says Robins. A week later, the Spago Las Vegas job was his. "You're making the biggest mistake of your life," Robins says the legendary Stars chef Jeremiah Tower tells him when he says he's leaving for Las Vegas. "You're going to the armpit of America."

But here he is, Wolfgang Puck, heading directly into that armpit: walking the vacant site where Gordon plans to put a mall in what is at that time nothing more than a vast parking lot beside Caesars Palace. But the developer is accustomed to overcoming the impossible. And it's here, Sheldon Gordon assures Wolfgang Puck, that a brave new brand of "entertainment retail" will rise up from this hot asphalt to enchant the world.

We'll see, Puck thinks as he listens to the unceasing pitch.

The Forum Shops will soon begin "selling more per square foot than any other mall in America," according to Gordon. Puck hires interior designer Adam Tihany—renowned worldwide for creating bold new interiors in restaurants, hotels, and residences—to design Spago Las Vegas. The restaurant's cool, colorful style, contrasting with the theatrics of the Forum Shops at Caesars Palace, catches the eye of the *Las Vegas Sun*'s restaurant critic, Muriel Stevens.

"Month after month I waited for the temporary walls and the sign saying 'Spago' to come down," she writes. "Finally, it happened. I was in the Forum Shops that night when I realized Spago was alive. I walked over the debris and into the kitchen. Standing there trying to put everything in order were Wolfgang Puck, senior managing partner Tom Kaplan, and corporate executive chef David Robins."

All their chips are literally on the table. Spago Vegas is more than three times the size of the original 4,000-square-foot Los Angeles Spago: 18,000 square feet on two levels, with a swirling grand staircase connecting the restaurant to a 2,000-square-foot banquet space and an outdoor patio jutting out into the mall, allowing diners to revel in the Roman Forum as the lighting constantly turns from day to night.

"I thought it was the most over-the-top mall I had ever seen," says David Robins. "But beneath it all, I could see that it could succeed. What drew my attention was the entrepreneurial mentality and grandness of the developers of that mall," he adds.

Spago's kitchen is as cutting edge as its design. Puck and his team import their own organic produce—a rarity in this early Vegas culinary epoch. They make their own bread and pizza dough, fly in fish from the best seafood purveyors and meat from the best Midwest suppliers, and have wines shipped in from boutique wineries, using many suppliers who had not done business in Vegas before.

"Some people think Las Vegas is just a funny town," Puck tells the *Las Vegas Review-Journal* on July 26, 1992, in an announcement for his new Spago. He insists that Las Vegas is a "real city" being "neglected in fine dining," which Spago will bring to the hungry town.

It all seems perfect. Muriel Stevens's review is a rave. When Puck reads it, he feels sure Spago has hit pay dirt, that golden artery directly into the heart of the action, the never-ending Las Vegas money train.

"When I read the review, I thought we would be sold out for six months," he tells the *Las Vegas Review-Journal*. "You're going to have to beat people away from the door," Gordon assures him.

Then comes opening night, December 1992. The famed chef proudly stands at the gates of his enormous new Spago, in his chef's whites, with the faux sky around him constantly turning from day to night. But on this supposedly starry evening, Puck experiences a nightmare. A measly 60 customers trickle in—which, for a restaurant with seating for 200 in the main dining room, 100 in the banquet room, and another 100 in the patio café, and for a chef whose other restaurants are serving up to 300 or 350 diners a night, is next to nothing.

Later, he learns that December is the worst time to open a restaurant in Vegas. "Vegas was empty," he says.

With the Christmas holidays looming, even the most die-hard gamblers have gone home to their families. And America's hottest chef is stuck in Las Vegas. Even the tiger-taming magicians Siegfried and Roy, are out of town. "The shows were closed and there were no customers around."

"We built a large restaurant in Vegas, café in front, banquet rooms upstairs, and some catering in the community," says Robins. What they were expecting were convention attendees. "Conventions were the main driver of sales in Las Vegas at the time. Today, Vegas has sports teams and music entertainment as a big part of the equation. Before, it was only gambling and conventions."

But there is one big convention in early December.

The National Finals Rodeo, the annual ten-day event that brings the stars of the rodeo world and the multitudes that follow them to the Thomas and Mack convention center. It's a stampede of boots, hats, spurs, and hungry cowboys.

Soon, the stampede finds Spago and bellies up to the restaurant's trademark open kitchen, the cutting-edge concept that is captivating Hollywood, where stars and studio moguls gaze upon Puck and his team as they dish up wonder.

But these customers think the open kitchen is what Vegas is so famous for—a *buffet line.*

They turn their noses up at the menu: the sunny California cuisine, the designer pizzas, the organic this and farm-to-table that.

Where's the beef? they demand. *The ribs...the burgers?*

Puck turns as white as his chef's jacket.

What the fuck? he thinks.

At least it is a crowd. With Christmas looming, the crowds continue to be thin. Many midnights find Puck and his then senior managing partner, Tom Kaplan, sitting on Spago's empty patio, "watching the faux Roman sky cycle through day, night, and into the morning," Kaplan remembers. "Sometimes it felt like we were actually in Rome."

And Rome is falling.

No crowds.

No stars.

Only gloom.

And wine. Lots of red wine. Not to celebrate. But to obliterate. On these lonely nights, the chef and his business partner frequently return to the two-bedroom corporate apartment they share near the Strip with an unsold bottle or two of red wine. "We drank wine in the restaurant in those early morning hours and brought a bottle or two back to the apartment, turned on the TV, and drank some more!" Kaplan says.

The famous chef lies awake in front of the TV until the

wine forces him into an uneasy sleep, from which he bolts awake the next dawn to a singular realization:

"Coming to Las Vegas was a stupid mistake."

Then, from the smoldering embers of what Puck envisions as his first real restaurant failure, Spago Las Vegas starts to catch fire.

The first spark arrives with an emissary from the world of rock and roll.

Every day at 4:30 p.m., maître d' Gerard Izard and head chef David Robins review a list of reservations and VIP guests for the evening.

"Who we needed to take care of," explains Robins. "I learned from Wolf from day one, you always go and touch the table. To make a connection."

One night in early 1993, he looks down at the night's guest list, and one name leaps off the page:

"Sting," he says.

Robins is "super excited. I was a big Police fan growing up," he says. Come dinnertime, "he was at table four in the VIP section. I walked over, nervous but confident, and introduced myself as the chef, and all I can get out of my mouth is 'I'm such a big fan!'

"He said he was a vegan—no meat, no butter—and I cooked a special vegan pasta with seasonal Chino Farms vegetables."

It's the start of a celebrity onslaught. Tony Danza, Jack

Nicholson, Sylvester Stallone, and fellow Austrian Arnold Schwarzenegger arrive for the food and the fellowship. Reputed mobsters mingle with actors pretending to be mobsters when Robert De Niro and Joe Pesci come by while in town to film the 1995 Vegas mob movie, *Casino*.

"The dancers, the Crazy Horse girls, they'd come into the café and we would give them champagne," says maître d' Izard.

"Once a week, and they would come in and slide down the banister on the grand staircase," adds Robins.

Everybody comes to Vegas and, soon, everybody goes to Spago. "And then there were the Las Vegas celebrities like Wayne Newton, Siegfried and Roy," Puck tells a local newspaper. "They got so excited because they could come to us."

The word is out, and the crowds find Spago. "It started to go crazy," says Puck. "We had a line out the door." Diners hoping to gain entry into Spago form a line that snakes through the Roman-themed shopping mall, while developer Gordon hands out slices of fresh pizza to their waiting clientele.

"This is my restaurant," Gordon says proudly as he serves the slices, turning to Puck and adding with glee, "Look at what we have here!"

By the end of 1993, Spago Las Vegas has earned twelve million dollars. By 1997, the *New York Times* reports that the restaurant has "done more than twice the business of the Los Angeles original." By 2008, it had done three times the business of the original.

Las Vegas visionary Steve Wynn comes to dine at

Spago with his wife, Elaine, surely yearning to have something like it at one of *his* resorts.

Eventually, he does.

Following Puck's lead and encouragement, a wave of celebrity chefs follows him to Vegas. At the opening of the new MGM Grand in December 1993, culinary stars include Mark Miller, the Santa Fe–based Southwestern cuisine impresario; Emeril Lagasse, of New Orleans fame; and Charlie Trotter, the perfectionist chef from Chicago.

The *New York Times* takes notice: "Las Vegas has never been accused of excessive good taste, so why have more than a dozen celebrated restaurants from around the nation—including three high-price steakhouse chains, Morton's, Palm and Ruth's Chris—suddenly sent roots into this arid Nevada soil? 'This is a boom town, and the opportunities for business are endless,' said Tom Kaplan, a partner with Wolfgang Puck in the Spago, opened here in December 1992."

In 1998, the "gastronomic ground shook under the High Mojave Desert and the whole world felt the shudder," John Curtas of the *Las Vegas Sun* observes in 2011, referring to the opening of the Bellagio, Wynn's mammoth Italian lakes–style temple to gambling and gastronomy. A mere six years after Puck brings Spago to the city, the Bellagio has sixteen restaurants, many importing brand-name superchefs and restaurateurs: outposts of Sirio Maccioni's oh-so-social Manhattan citadel Le Cirque and Todd English's Boston hot spot Olives; Jean-Georges Vongerichten's Prime steakhouse and Spanish chef Julian

Serrano's homage to Picasso, a prominent artist in Wynn's art collection. "No one hotel on Earth had ever seen such a collection of chefs, designs, wine and food like it," notes Curtas, "brought forth under one (huge) roof."

Then, in 2011, the invasion reaches an early apex.

"You name it, we've got it: More master sommeliers than New York, more great steakhouses anywhere but the Big Apple and more extraordinary French chefs anywhere but Paris," the article continues. "Does anywhere but here have a concentration of 50—50!—world-class eateries along a two-mile stretch of road? Not even close....But outside of food professionals, writers and intrepid foodies, precious few seem to know the depth and scope of what's going on along Las Vegas Boulevard. Even the hotels, both individually and collectively, seem behind the croissant curve when it comes to crowing about the phenomenon that has taken the food world by storm."

Now the secret is out, and practically every major chef, restaurant and restaurant group in the world has a Vegas operation or is planning one. In a statement that would have been inconceivable a decade earlier, the article declares that "Vegas does food better than any place on Earth."

In 2012, mayor Carolyn Goodman awards the key to the city to the chef who launched it all, Wolfgang Puck.

"Wolf was the first and opened the door for celebrity chefs to expand their operations and have some lucrative business opportunities," says David Robins, who came to work at Spago Las Vegas in 1992 and has remained for more than thirty years, overseeing Puck's operations, which in 2023 include five Vegas restaurants and counting. "Today, we have Joël Robuchon, Guy Savoy, Alain Ducasse, Gordon Ramsay, Hubert Keller, Nobu Matsuhisa, Jean-Georges Vongerichten, and a talented roster of many more. And all of that was opened up by Wolfgang having the vision to come to Vegas."

What developers do with cold, hard steel and what Lady Luck does with an otherwise ordinary pair of dice and a deck of cards, chefs from the world over are doing with food: branding it, pushing it to its limits, making it epic and worthy of inclusion in the over-the-top world of Las Vegas.

A new offering in Vegas entertainment begins—"food tourism," it's called, and it works like this:

Sundown in Las Vegas. Three couples from three cities follow a tour guide through the spires of the new Las Vegas, for what will be a bacchanal—the name once used for Caesars Palace's late 1960s eating extravaganza, which took place in a restaurant designed to replicate an ornate Roman temple and featured "wine goddesses" feeding diners tableside grapes.

This, however, is light years away from those gilded, theme-driven days.

"Follow me," says the culinary tour guide, thirty-two-year-old Thomas Svoboda, as he leads his small group through the Aria Resort and Casino and the nearby Park MGM Las Vegas, which together form a billion-dollar beast of a metropolis, with an array of restaurants and bars to satisfy guests from any nation.

The three couples dutifully follow the tour guide's lead. They have each paid one hundred ninety-nine dollars to enjoy four of the best course in four of the city's best restaurants over the course of three hours, all curated—to use the Vegas word of the moment—by the city's premier culinary tour company, Lip Smacking Foodie Tours.

The tour is named Savors of the Strip, and it's a walking tour, which, for an additional sixty dollars, includes a signature cocktail upon arriving at each restaurant, and, for an additional one hundred twenty-five dollars per person, a helicopter ride over the Strip for dessert.

"All right, guys," Thomas continues, "we're gonna get started. *Follow me.* We are visiting four of the best restaurants in the city today and you will all be enjoying the signature dishes those restaurants are known for."

He names the four restaurants: the NoMad Library at Park MGM (whose soaring walls are lined with twenty-five thousand books, some from the David and Peggy Rockefeller collection), Javier's at Aria, Julian Serrano Tapas at Aria, and Maestro's Ocean Club in the Shops at Crystals.

"Please get your appetites ready!" he says. Along the way, the group passes signs—gigantic billboards, really—

advertising the restaurants that have brought cuisine from the world over:

DINE IN 1920s FRANCE IN 2020 VEGAS

WHEN IN VEGAS DINE IN ROME—EATALY

NOODLES FROM ALL OVER ASIA IN ONE PLACE IN VEGAS

A NEW WAY TO TAPAS. YOUR MOMENT HAS COME.

From here, the culinary tourists embark upon a tour of four Las Vegas restaurants, each one fully prepped in advance to deliver the food at practically the moment the group sits down. Thirty to forty-five pampered minutes later, they're out of one restaurant and on to the next.

All of this inspires Damon Raque, the Vegas adventurer from chapter 3, who is looking for a way to top his previous exploits. One evening, Raque and four of his buddies walk from their accommodations at the Wynn Tower Suites to the Palazzo hotel at the Venetian next door.

After incessantly reading and studying the newest and best things to do in Vegas, Raque has planned an extravagant food-themed adventure.

Steak.

Not merely one steak, but a multitude of the best of steaks. One legendary Vegas steakhouse after another, in quick succession. Each steakhouse in close enough proximity so that the entire tour can be done in three and a half breathless hours in a chauffeur-driven Tesla SUV.

Raque calls Donald Contursi—a veteran Las Vegas restaurant aficionado and former waiter who founded Lip Smacking Foodie Tours in 2014 "to showcase the best dishes at the best Vegas restaurants"—with an idea to create a new, custom-made culinary tour for him and four of his lifelong friends.

"Everybody wants to know what the best steakhouse is in Vegas, and I think I've eaten at them all," Raque tells Contursi. "What would it cost to customize a foodie-tour experience with a steakhouse tour?"

Contursi immediately loves the idea.

"What price point do you have in mind so I can curate the best experience at that price for you?" he asks.

"I'm more about the experience than the price," Raque replies. "How about if you work with a budget of five hundred dollars a person?"

"Okay," says Contursi. "And just to explain: I won't have a menu or itinerary to present, but be assured it will be the best of everything. We order for everybody at every restaurant. We pick out the dishes and choose the wine and the drinks. And you come without knowing what you're going to get, even which restaurants you're going to visit. You won't know anything until you arrive. All you have to worry about is to come hungry."

"I love the element of surprise," Raque says.

Raque invites his four friends, telling them to expect

the ultimate in the unexpected. "I can't tell you what it is, but if you trust me enough, commit the money and allow me to put together an experience that none of us will ever forget," he adds.

Without hesitation, they all say, "Done."

That evening, at 5:45 p.m., the five hungry men's first stop is the CarneVino Italian Steakhouse at the Palazzo, "known for their dry-aged beef," says Raque.

The manager is at the door to greet them. A prime table is waiting near the bigger-than-life bull sculpture in the dining room. The beef onslaught begins the moment their rumps hit the seat cushions. Beef cheeks ravioli with twenty-five-year-old balsamic vinegar. An off-the-menu eight- to eleven-month-dry-aged steak fittingly called the Reserva. And, of course, wine, Tignanello Super–Tuscan wine. After precisely forty-five minutes, the boys fold their napkins and are off once again, in a gull-wing Tesla SUV waiting outside.

Ten minutes later, they're pulling up to the SLS (now the Sahara), where they are escorted to its signature steak extravaganza, the Spanish superchef restaurant Bazaar Meat by José Andrés. Again, the manager is at the door and the table is ready. First they pay a visit to the meat locker, where the many varieties of beef are on grand display, followed by a tour of the kitchen. Then, the men are seated and yet another meat onslaught begins: cotton candy foie gras, with a rare Iberian ham sliced tableside; Japanese A5 Wagyu beef seared on a hot rock; and a side of buttery Joël Robuchon–style mashed potatoes and Spanish mushrooms. All accompanied by Rioja wine.

Back in the SUV, the men are driven fifteen minutes down the Strip to the Aria Resort and Casino. First stop: Sage, "a New American restaurant that had the best whiskey selection in all of Las Vegas," says Raque. Six different whiskeys are poured, each with a tutorial from the expert pourer. Thirty minutes later, they are riding the escalator upstairs to Jean Georges Steakhouse for an appetizer of confit egg yolk atop caviar toast, followed by an off-the-menu Japanese Wagyu brisket carved tableside and Silver Oak California cabernet.

Finally, it's time for dessert, not one but six of them, right next door at Bardot Brasserie, the twenties-themed French bistro operated by the acclaimed chef Michael Mina.

With the additional wine and drinks, the total cost comes to twenty-five hundred dollars, or Raque's budget of five hundred dollars per person—which seems like a bargain. "The experience was so fantastic that we each shook Donald Contursi's hand with a hundred-dollar tip apiece," says Raque.

Once they are done, the men head to the Foundation Room, the cocktail lounge on the sixty-third floor of Mandalay Bay, gazing on the lights of the Vegas Strip, almost unable to speak.

"Blown away and in shock," Raque remembers. "We were in a food coma."

Some of the restaurants are now gone, replaced by others, but for Raque and his buddies the memories remain. "Vegas enables you to make memories with people who are important to you, and they stay with you forever," he says.

Chapter 14

MAGIC

THE MIRAGE

"I THINK IT'S my job to rake through the cool stuff of Las Vegas and explain what makes this city distinctive," says John Katsilometes, who is known as Kats. Even his *Las Vegas Review-Journal* newspaper column is titled simply KATS. Kats writes day in and day out, and is published seven days a week, three hundred sixty-five days a year, not including his hundreds of separate columns posted online each year. He's pretty sure he's the only columnist in America who can say that these days. "Nobody does what I do anywhere, at least at this velocity," he says of his column's frequency and reach.

Maybe because nobody else covers a city like Las Vegas, a city with enough never-ending action to fill Kats's daily columns.

He doesn't even cover everything—"I don't dive much into scandal," he says—keeping his stories focused on the winners: the you-gotta-see-thises and don't-miss-thats, and all the exciting backstage and onstage stories about the neon-lit city and its even flashier inhabitants.

Tips on the town's news and happenings come roaring into his laptop and phone incessantly, sending him running off to follow his editor's command: *Get out there!* "They want me in the scene, active in the community," he says of his bosses. "I have to physically be at as many things as I can be."

Every day, he blasts out of his downtown condo and into his 2021 Infiniti QX50 Sport SUV or his rebuilt 1967 Mercury Cougar, blazing through the desert streets, his laptop in his replica Pan Am flight bag, in search of somewhere to start writing. Today it's at a corner table in the Roasted Bean coffee shop in the Mirage Resort and Casino, but he could be anywhere. "I'll be at the Circa Sportsbook or the South Point Showroom or the SuperBook at Westgate, writing from there," he says. At some point, all of the morning's texts and emails will result in a story, a post, or, often, a scoop.

Kats was the first to tell the world when Carlos Santana, a resident performer at the House of Blues at Mandalay Bay, collapsed onstage in Detroit in 2022 (Kats wrote and filed a column from his phone while having dinner at One Steakhouse bar, sitting before the legendary barman and "bon vivant" Johnny O'Donnell), and he had the scoop about the August 13, 2018, death of celebrity TV host, longtime Las Vegas resident, and fellow *Las Vegas Review-Journal* columnist Robin Leach.

Though he usually receives news during the day, Kats comes out with the rest of Vegas at night. He might start with dinner at the Bootlegger Bistro, an old-school Italian restaurant owned by former Nevada lieutenant governor Lorraine Hunt-Bono and her husband, entertainer Dennis Bono. Afterward, he'll usually progress on to a show—or three.

Kats is often front and center before the greats—such as the time in 2011 when he stood just to the right of Yoko Ono and Sean Lennon as Paul McCartney serenaded them with "Give Peace a Chance"—and it sometimes makes him think, *Through what magical portal did I enter to be lucky enough to arrive here?*

"Saturday, Bruno Mars comes back," Kats says. The recording superstar's Vegas shows are revered and always completely booked. "He's sold out his dates," Kats says. "The first four weeks, then the second four, and the next two. *Boom!*"

But nothing is ever sold out for Kats, whose column grants him entry everywhere.

Later in the evening, he might stop by the Laugh Factory at the Tropicana Hotel and Casino, or Jimmy Kimmel's Comedy Club in the LINQ Promenade entertainment district. One of Kats's May 2019 columns noted the talk-show host's Vegas roots: "Kimmel, who actually attended Kenny Guinn junior high and Clark High, isn't a stand-up, but he is funny. 'I am from Las Vegas. I love it here. I have many memories here. I lost my virginity about a mile away from here, in the front seat of an Isuzu I-Mark in the parking lot of the Continental hotel...'"

Kats is currently in a relationship with singer Steph Payne, whom he met when she was called up to sing at an off-Strip music club—yet another night covering everything both high and low that Vegas has to offer.

Covering the nonstop city is a believe-it-or-not feat similar to what has always filled stages and defied belief in Vegas, what the city has always lived on.

Magic.

Kats has seen most of the magicians in Las Vegas, starting with Siegfried and Roy not long after his arrival. But even in what Kats calls a hypercompetitive environment like Las Vegas, where there are more than twenty-five headlining magicians, none of the stars quite compare to a young magician named Shin Lim...

To find Shin Lim, drive down the Las Vegas Strip and take a left on Siegfried and Roy Drive, named for the late tiger-taming magicians who defined magic in the city of magic for three decades. Then, it's into the Mirage, the vast Polynesian-themed resort with its 3,000-plus rooms and its vast casino and its 1,265-seat theater, where Shin Lim stands onstage before sold-out audiences, defying reality.

Some say he is a wizard.

But Shin Lim insists he's just an ordinary man.

He is thirty-one years old. Hair long and flyaway. Slight of build but larger than life. The superstar of Las Vegas magic, ranked the world's greatest "sleight of hand" artist, a genius of illusion, and, some say, a bona fide wizard.

All of which Shin Lim denies.

"I'm not claiming to be any sort of Jesus or God or wizard," he says. "All I'm doing is sleight of hand. I'm just manipulating the deck of cards so well to the point where it *looks* like magic."

It's hours until his first showtime, at 7:30 p.m. But he's performing this afternoon for a spot on national NBC TV, commanding the stage and making the decks of cards in his hand dance. They swirl, twirl, flutter, fly, even burst into flames. Lim calls it card juggling, but watching him do it is nothing short of magic.

In Las Vegas, Shin Lim stares down from twenty billboards in and around the city, a deck of cards flying acrobatically from his nimble fingers. His handsome face flashes from a giant video screen outside the Mirage, a screen so large that it took two weeks to install and a team of structural engineers to certify that the massive load wouldn't bring down the entire hotel. Five nights a week, Lim sells out the Mirage Theatre, in the same resort where Siegfried and Roy and their white tigers dazzled audiences for thirteen years.

It was a feat of magic that brought Shin Lim to Las Vegas, a sleight of hand befitting a city in the sand built on illusion. Born in Vancouver, Canada, the middle of three boys, he spent his childhood on the move, including eight years in Singapore, before the family finally landed in Acton, a town on the outskirts of Boston. He was twenty-one when he decided to devote his life to magic, a college dropout "living in his parents' basement, directionless and depressed," as Dan Morrell writes in the *Boston Globe Magazine*. "He was selling a few tricks, but he had never performed for a paying audience, and his prospects looked dim."

From that basement, Lim could see the future, but not the path to get there. It would be a nearly impossible leap to join the likes of Siegfried and Roy, David Copperfield, Penn and Teller, and the other master magicians who lived and worked in Las Vegas. Lance Burton, famous for making a dove appear seemingly out of thin air, had made it to Vegas after growing up in Kentucky. After a thirty-one-year run of fifteen thousand shows, Burton published a farewell note to the city in the *Las Vegas Review-Journal*, recalling his childhood dream of reaching "this mythical place called Las Vegas. I didn't know where Las Vegas was located. I didn't know anything about gambling or resorts. All I knew was Las Vegas was where the professional magicians lived and worked and I wanted to join them one day."

Lim felt exactly the same way. But what did he have that would catapult him from his parents' basement outside of Boston to the mammoth stage at the Mirage?

The answer came, fittingly, in a deck of cards.

It begins with a violin smashed on the floor.

Shin Lim is six, and his father teaches him to play the violin, demanding daily practice. The strings don't sing; they screech and scream. He hates this violin with such a passion that he finally smashes it to pieces.

The piano is his instrument. By the time Lim is fifteen years old, he is so proficient a pianist that he reduces his teachers to tears of joy. It's an undeniable talent, but it's no ticket to Las Vegas.

Then, at age sixteen, his older brother, Yi, opens the path to his future.

Shin is rapt with attention as Yi shows him a YouTube video of a magician using his thumb and first three fingers to perform a card trick known as a slip force—sliding a card, undetected, from the top of the deck into the middle, where it can then be identified and retrieved, as if by magic. To the young Shin Lim, it's nothing short of a revelation.

"I was like, 'This is so amazing. Like, I can learn sorcery,'" Lim tells Morrell, who notes, "Before that, he had thought magic was some unknowable, mystic trade." But now, he discovers that it's something he can teach himself. "I went on YouTube and I am figuring out all these tricks," Lim says. The door to the world of magic opens wide. He becomes "obsessed" with cards and card tricks. Watching magicians perform on YouTube, "practicing eight hours a day." Finally, two years later, he flies from Boston to Las Vegas for the very first time, sitting in the audiences before the masters, the resident magicians who live and work in the city—including his idol, Lance Burton.

At age eighteen, though, cards don't strike Lim as a ticket to stardom. Music is still where he believes his future lies, and magic is just a "passionate hobby." So after graduating high school, he enrolls in the School of Music at Lee University in Tennessee, concentrating on the piano and trying to forget about performing magic in Las Vegas… until his body rebels.

It had begun during his senior year in high school, when he'd suffered "periodic stabbing" in his wrists. Now, in his freshman year in college, between the endless hours of piano practice and his sleight-of-hand card "obsession," it's turned even worse: his hands have become numb.

The diagnosis: carpal tunnel syndrome, which delivers a swift finale to his future as a concert pianist.

Magic, which had been waiting in the wings, now moves to center stage.

Lim will eventually set himself apart in Las Vegas via his chosen tool of the trade: a seemingly ordinary deck of playing cards. In Vegas, cards are of course everywhere, the very thing that transforms people into winners and losers. "There's some sort of mystery with luck, with playing cards, gambling, and poker," Lim says. "Cards in themselves are mysterious. There's an aura around them that people find very fascinating, and maybe magic has something to do with that. Magic has this mysterious aura around it, too, and there's a kind of luck as well, in winning big. Maybe that's why so many magicians are in Las Vegas."

"The doctor told me I was overusing my hands, and I had to choose between music or magic," he says. "I had to make a choice."

Okay, either you're David Copperfield or you're not, Lim told himself, the *Boston Globe Magazine* reports. *You're either David Blaine or you're not David Blaine.* "I decided to take a gamble on magic," he says.

Lim is determined to deserve mention alongside superstar magicians like David Copperfield and David Blaine. He sells magic tricks online. He competes at small magic events. He builds self-confidence. And finally, in 2012, he throws down the gauntlet: if he can win the Fédération Internationale des Sociétés Magiques World Championship, considered the Olympics of magic and held every three years in cities around the globe, he will follow his passion to Las Vegas.

He enters the tournament—held that year in Blackpool, England—with what he knows best: close-up card tricks.

He comes in sixth. It's a strong showing, but not enough to make magic his career. The boy who aspired to perform wonders has fallen firmly to earth: a college dropout living in his parents' basement.

Then, the phone rings.

It's a tour organizer who watched Shin Lim perform at the world championship and was amazed. He is organizing a twenty-three-city tour of China for audiences of two thousand apiece. *Would Shin Lim be interested in joining?* And, if so, could he do a twenty-minute magic act?

Lim's act is only seven minutes long. He can add thirteen minutes, but he will also be required to speak to the audience in Chinese, which he does not speak. The solution is simple: he won't talk. He will perform his magic silently, set to musical accompaniment.

"I had been following a traditional path," Lim says to Dan Morrell of the *Globe*, who notes, "This was a departure."

Speaking only through his cards, Lim dazzles the Chinese crowds. He's the youngest of the four magicians on the bill, but he emerges as its star.

In 2015, having perfected his routine, he returns to the world championship with a new routine he calls the Dream Act. It begins with a card table on an otherwise empty stage. Lim asks two members of the audience to sit next to him and watch him up close, while he makes the cards dance and change and disappear, pop up in a plastic bag or emerge from his mouth in a puff of smoke. When the tournament ends, Lim is crowned the World Champion of Magic.

Now he's ready for his next big step toward Las Vegas: a spot on a national TV show, *Penn & Teller: Fool Us*. Lim performs the Dream Act, his sleight of hand now set to dramatic music. No words leave his mouth—only smoke. At the end of his six-minute performance, Penn Jillette delivers the verdict.

Card tricks, he says, speaking directly to Lim, "are

silly at their very core." But what he has just witnessed is dead serious, and "wonderful. And I believe that is the only use of smoke I've seen in a magic trick that was sincerely beautiful."

Lim's sleight of hand has fooled the masters.

"I felt it was perfect," says Jillette.

Lim has now risen to the top of competitive magic and impressed two of its biggest stars on national TV. But if he wants to make it to Las Vegas, he needs dramatic new material. He begins dreaming up new illusions, including one involving a crossbow. Then one day, while trying to make changes to his extremely dangerous crossbow illusion, the crossbow, while locked, accidentally and prematurely fires, the blade severing two tendons in his thumb.

There was "just a little bit of blood, but it wasn't gushing, so I didn't think much of it," he later says.

A friend drives him to the emergency room.

"Hey, give me a thumbs-up," commands the ER doctor.

Lim struggles to raise his thumb. "But nothing was happening." The tendons will flex, but his thumb won't move.

"Okay, this is really serious," says the doctor.

Sleight of hand requires all ten fingers, and the ability to bend each of them like a contortionist, at lightning speed. A card magician who can't manage a simple thumbs-up is destined to early retirement. Lim's entire career—and his dream of Las Vegas—seems headed to an abrupt end, just like his concert piano career. After surgery, doctors tell him it will be at least *two years* before he'll be able to begin manipulating a deck of cards again. And even then, he'll only be able to bend his thumb halfway.

He is twenty-four. Now, instead of practicing sleight of hand, Lim spends endless hours in rehab. Day by day, minute by minute, slowly working to increase the range of motion in his hand. Six months stretches to a year and a half. As he sinks into depression—and recreational drugs—Las Vegas seems further and further out of reach.

Finally, through hard work, patience, and extreme will, Lim recovers. But he never regains full mobility in his left thumb. "I can do a thumbs-up now," he says, "which allows me to accomplish about 70 percent or 80 percent of my card tricks. But I still can't do 25 to 30 percent, because my left thumb is not as quick or strong as my right."

As so often happens with artists, the limitation spurs Lim to greater heights of creativity. Because of his injured hand, he must devise alternative ways to accomplish the same effects. In 2017, he puts his new techniques to the test, appearing on Penn and Teller's TV show for a second time. Given all he has endured, there is no guarantee he'll be able to fool the seasoned duo again. But after the performance, Penn Jillette's praise is no less effusive than it was during their first encounter. Lim has done it again.

"Lim is part of a third wave of magic," Jillette says to the *Boston Globe Magazine* in 2017. First, he says, there were the "big spectacle types"—the Siegfried and Roys and David Copperfields and Doug Hennings. Then there was a second wave ushered in by David Blaine "and bad copies of him." Now, Jillette says, there's a new generation of magicians—"and Shin is one of the best"—who perform tricks that require an enormous amount of skill, without a trace of irony.

Jillette tells the *Globe* that there is no wink in Lim's act, no giggle or apology. "I love that there's this era of magic that is pure and honest and direct and sweet and beautiful."

His comeback complete, Lim goes in search of an even bigger audience. While performing in Macau, he meets his Australian girlfriend, Casey Thomas, a dancer then working as another magician's assistant. It's her idea for Lim to go on *America's Got Talent*—she "pushed me to go for it," Lim says.

On September 19, 2018, he appears on the popular TV show and performs a sleight-of-hand trick called 52 Shades of Red, in which the cards in a deck change color as his hand passes over them. Lim wins the competition and goes home with one million dollars.

The next year, he wins again, in a competition reserved for fifty of the best performers from previous seasons: *America's Got Talent: The Champions.*

The show calls him Best in the World.

And this time, it proves to be his ticket to Las Vegas.

The night after Lim's first *America's Got Talent* victory, Bill Blumenreich makes the rounds of the theaters he owns, the Wilbur and Chevalier in Boston.

Blumenreich is a show business legend. He's also

a fixture in Las Vegas, where he has promoted and produced shows with everyone from the Eagles to Fleetwood
Mac to the comedians Kevin Hart and John Mulaney. On
this evening, after the *America's Got Talent* finale, everyone
in his theaters is buzzing with two words: *Shin Lim*.

"Hey, are you going to get Shin Lim?" one staff member
asks Blumenreich. Then another. And another. Until Blumenreich, exasperated, responds, "Who is Shin Lim?"

At home later that night, spurred by his employees, Blumenreich turns to YouTube. He watches and is
instantly "mesmerized." He has worked with many magicians, "going back to the great Harry Blackstone Jr.," he
says, referring to the famed late magician and son of the
legendary 1900s illusionist Harry Blackstone Sr. But this
is different, radical, *new:* a sleight-of-hand artist who can
make ordinary playing cards dance. "I watched all the
video I could find on Shin Lim," he recalls.

The veteran promoter is astounded—and not just by
the card tricks. Reading everything he can find on this
young master of card magic, Blumenreich immediately
senses that Lim has the kind of magic that can transform a
mere act into a global sensation: a compelling story.

"He not only is the best magician I've ever seen," Blumenreich later says, "but he's got a Horatio Alger story. He
grew up in a small town. Magic was the break he needed
to get him out of there. People can relate to that. Because
unless you're from a rich family, most people never really
escape where they grew up. They never have a chance to

make it big, even if they've got talent. But Shin Lim has *it*. He's got *everything*."

Blumenreich knows immediately what to do with Lim. Not tour him around the world, which is a grind and a waste, as Blumenreich realized after promoting the late comic legend Robin Williams's final show in Las Vegas, wrapping up his national tour. Williams had performed in eighty-six cities, and the Vegas show was a money loser—Williams had already done too many locations, had too much exposure. With Lim, Blumenreich envisions a single-city exclusive. "If you want to see Shin Lim," Blumenreich says, "you have to go to the Mirage in Las Vegas."

This is why Las Vegas has become the entertainment mecca of the world. Entertainers are no longer mere magnets for the gaming tables, because the Vegas resorts no longer make all their money on gambling. "There are too many casinos across the country," Blumenreich says. "Gambling's not just in Vegas anymore. When I was a kid, if you wanted to gamble legally in the United States, the only place you could do it was in Vegas. Now there must be a thousand choices. Today, everything in Vegas is a profit center: the hotel rooms, the restaurants, the gift shops, and the entertainment."

As the sun rises in his Boston-area home, Blumenreich is still watching Shin Lim perform on YouTube.

His first call that morning is to his assistant.

"Get this guy on the phone and set up a meeting," Blumenreich says.

The assistant makes the call and comes back with a swift reply: "*They* would love to meet you."

The promoter assumes that "they" means Shin Lim and his management team.

Instead, a few days later, the magician and his entire family—Shin Lim; his two brothers; his mother and father; and his fiancée, Casey—walk into Bill Blumenreich's home.

"He had no representation," says Blumenreich.

They go to dinner at a nearby Italian restaurant. Once they're done, Shin's mother, Mabel, asks the promoter, "So what do you want to do with my son?"

Blumenreich focuses his attention directly on Lim, who has remained silent all evening. "Let me ask you this, Shin," he says. "What is your dream?"

Shin Lim doesn't hesitate.

"Bill," he says softly, "my dream is to have a Las Vegas residency."

"This is your lucky day," replies Blumenreich. "I partner with MGM, which owns the Mirage, which has a beautiful 1,265-seat showroom there."

The big stage at the Mirage was at that moment home to a ventriloquist who had also won *America's Got Talent*. But he won twelve years ago. Shin Lim is hot *now*.

"I think I might be able to convince them to give you the room," Blumenreich tells Lim.

"Oh, my God," Lim says.

It's no mere "room." It's the Mirage Theatre.

"He was thinking of a smaller room," Blumenreich later notes.

"What kind of contract do you want?" Lim's mother asks.

"I don't want a contract," the promoter replies. "As long as you are happy, you stay with me without a contract. And I think you'll be very happy."

With Mabel satisfied, the real work begins. As impressive as Lim's show is, he only has about fifteen minutes of material—nowhere near the hour he'll need to take up residency at a major theater in Las Vegas. So Blumenreich briefly takes Lim on the road to develop a bigger and better routine. Lim puts in grueling hours of practice, incorporating new tricks into his repertoire, relying on both cards and instinct. "I can't think about doing a move, because if I do I'll mess it up," says Lim. "I have to go by my instinct, purely muscle memory."

Because of his carpal tunnel and tendon injury—the "handicap" of his hands, as he calls it—Lim still faces limitations. If he practices for more than an hour at a time, his wrists start to hurt and numbness creeps into his fingertips. Without frequent breaks the pain becomes excruciating. Before every practice session and performance, he puts himself in a Zen-like state, to make sure there isn't too much blood flowing to his hands and to prevent any surge of adrenaline. If his adrenaline is pumping, it causes his hands to shake, rendering him powerless to juggle the cards or perform sleight of hand.

Gradually, painfully, Shin Lim develops an act that Blumenreich deems ready for the Mirage. But before the resort will hand over its giant theater to him, their representatives have to be persuaded that Lim can draw a sell-out crowd, night after night after night. Blumenreich convinces the Mirage to let Lim replace the ventriloquist who is presently on the main stage whenever he has a night off or goes on vacation. Through this piecemeal approach, Lim headlines close to one hundred fifty shows, "doing a lot of business," says Blumenreich.

The Mirage is sold on Lim. The resort offers him a four-year deal, with two five-year options to renew. In March 2020, Lim and his fiancée, Casey, move into a house in the Vegas suburb of Henderson. Here, Lim has at long last realized his dream: a full-time residency on one of the biggest stages in town.

"If Shin wants to," Blumenreich says, "he can probably stay there for the rest of his career."

For five nights a week at the Mirage, after the opening act billed as the Real Life Sherlock Holmes, fog crawls across the stage, and Lim emerges to the roar of the 1,265 people in a sell-out show that "along with Cirque du Soleil's 'O' is the best-selling show in Vegas," says Blumenreich.

Now the previously silent Lim has a lot to say. And what he talks about onstage is almost as amazing as what he does with his cards. As Blumenreich foresaw, what sells the show is the magic of Lim's story.

As the cards dance and fly and disappear—magnified

to epic proportions via IMAG cameras, so the people in the back row can witness the illusions as clearly as those in the front—Lim shares the physical and mental tribulations he overcame on his journey to Las Vegas. Hence the show's title, "Shin Lim: LIMITLESS."

"I want people to feel that anything is possible," Lim says in his dressing room after filming the NBC TV spot, surrounded by what he estimates to be more than a thousand decks of cards. "Even with any sort of limitations you may have. My show in terms of a storyline is about this hand injury right here. You can actually still see the scar. When you feel like something bad has happened to you and you can't accomplish your goal, there's always another route to it. You can always go around. Life is never just a straight line."

What the audiences witness is something beyond magic. It's deeply emotional, almost spiritual—closer to art than artifice. "A lot of magic feels like you're trying to fool someone," Lim tells Lauren Daley of the *Boston Globe* in 2018. His goal is to change all of that through his cards. "To make it more artistic, more visual. My magic is very much like playing a piano. It's sequential. Most magicians talk, make jokes, there's a lot of patter. Mine is always music driven."

He wants his audiences to leave feeling not that they have watched magic, but that they have experienced a magical moment.

"If you watch like a really, really good movie, the music in it is what makes the movie," Lim explains to the *Boston Globe Magazine*. "And a good composer is able to compose the score in such a way that they can make it flow with whatever is happening in the movie. It's the same exact route in my magic."

That's his greatest trick—to make what he does with a deck of cards feel like something far greater.

"Strength," he says onstage each night, "isn't about what you can do. Rather, it's about overcoming what you thought you couldn't do."

The crowd cheers, as much for the man as the magic, a triumph in a city accustomed to achieving the impossible: an oasis in the sand, built on the hope that the cards will be kind.

Chapter 15

THE GREATEST SHOW
ON EARTH

THE *"O"* THEATER

THE CIRCUS TENT glows.

It stands on the beach near the Santa Monica Pier in Southern California, looking ordinary from the outside but holding wonders within.

The man walking inside the tent on this warm fall evening in 1990 isn't easy to impress, much less astound. Steve Wynn has seen it all and seemingly done it all. But like all high-stakes gamblers, he's determined to do it again.

He's already got the hottest show in Las Vegas— Siegfried and Roy and their white tigers—at his newly built Mirage, but he's eternally asking himself, *What's next?*

This, Wynn has been promised by a friend, just might be the answer.

Although, in the beginning, Wynn isn't sure.

"It's breathtaking, it's spectacular, and it should be in Las Vegas!" Larry Ruvo tells Wynn, his longtime friend and former partner, of the blazingly original circus extravaganza he's just seen called *Nouvelle Expérience*. Presented by a group of highly professional and skilled French Canadian performers, the circus is true to its name, a truly new experience: an acrobats-only circus—no animals, only humans doing the seemingly impossible set to music and lights.

Ruvo ran the largest liquor, wine, and beer distributor in Nevada. He had been visiting Los Angeles with his wife, one of their daughters, and one of the daughter's friends when a ticket broker suggested they see the new-fangled circus in the tent on the beach in Santa Monica. He knew nothing about it except that it was a circus, which he thought his daughter and her friend would enjoy. So Ruvo and his family entered the circus tent, from which his imagination and sense of wonder would never really leave.

"It was so extraordinary that I couldn't stop talking about it," he says.

It was not only extraordinary; he felt it was *perfect* for early 1990s Las Vegas, which was then in its cycle of a return to "family oriented" resorts and attractions. *What could be better, more international, more universal, than a show produced with very few words?* Which any audience, from Toronto to Tokyo, could see, hear, feel, and under-stand in exactly the same way?

Upon his return to Las Vegas, Ruvo immediately went to see Wynn, who was in the midst of building his family-oriented resort, Treasure Island.

"Steve, I just saw the greatest circus—" began Ruvo.

"What kind of animals?" Wynn interrupted, according to Ruvo.

"Steve, there are no animals, but—" Ruvo continued.

"I have no interest in seeing a circus without animals," said Wynn.

"You will on this one," Ruvo remembers. "And he said, 'I have no interest.'"

Ruvo wasn't going to give up.

He called Johnny Joseph, who ran the showroom of the *Beyond Belief* Siegfried and Roy show, and the two of them flew back to Los Angeles to see the circus. Joseph was just as astounded as Ruvo.

"So we both went back to Steve," says Ruvo, and they both told Wynn, "This is as good as I've ever seen."

"And Steve looks at me and Johnny and says, 'What do you two not understand? I have no interest in seeing a circus without animals.'"

Next, Ruvo contacted Wynn's trusted associate and executive Bobby Baldwin and brought him to see *Nouvelle Expérience*. Once back in Las Vegas, Baldwin and Ruvo again expressed their absolute, unbridled elation to Wynn.

"Bobby said, 'Larry is 100 percent right, the show is unbelievable. You have to see it.'"

Which is how Wynn finally came to walk inside the tent that held the future of Las Vegas entertainment, a circus with no animals, but abounding in spectacle and wonder.

It's called Cirque du Soleil.

Steve Wynn knows Las Vegas's long history with circuses, knows the story of Circus Circus, the hotel and casino, which opened in the late sixties with trapeze and high-wire acts swirling in the casino over the gamblers' heads. But he also knows that Las Vegas is ready to move beyond entertainment like showgirls, lounge acts, and the old-time stage performers.

Wynn's been creating new experiences in Las Vegas with his over-the-top, spare-no-expenses resorts, but once this show begins, he knows immediately that *Nouvelle Expérience* is absolutely original and brand new.

"It strips away adult cynicism and restores one's sense of childlike wonder," the *Los Angeles Times* raves about the troupe's reinvention of the traditional circus. "Their acrobatics and aerial exploits are a testament to human potential, demonstrating that anything is possible...The acts seem all the more exquisite because of [the] ways in which music, costumes, movement and other elements are integrated."

Cirque du Soleil is "not the kind of circus you'd dream of running away with," explains the *Chicago Sun-Times*. "It's the kind of circus that sweeps you up in a swirl of stardust."

Long after the circus ends, that stardust is surely still swirling through Wynn's mind. He phones the troupe's cofounder, Guy Laliberté, who recalls Wynn telling him, "I want to do some projects with you."

Laliberté, a former fire-eater and street performer, is a shrewd businessman and doesn't show his hand. Instead, he suggests that Wynn see their 2,500-seat Grand Chapiteau (big top) just off one of Toronto's major highways, where Laliberté and his circus troupe will perform for the summer of 1991.

Once again, Wynn steps inside the tent, this time with his ally, Bobby Baldwin. He's soon enveloped by the mysterious, piercing strings of an orchestra. Not the traditionally cheery tunes of a traveling circus, but something deeper, darker, more mysterious. Then, the lights suddenly switch off. Footlights illuminate the stage. What appears to be a tunnel materializes, through which a masked figure dressed like a court jester leaps, before giving way to another jester emerging out of the dark, carrying a briefcase-toting clown wearing a bowler hat and waistcoat. Cymbals clash as strange new clowns emerge, in striped hose, wildly colored breeches, three-pointed hats. A ringmaster and ring mistress arrive, soon to be replaced by four contortionists, who twist their bodies in unison into shapes that seem impossible, somehow stacking themselves in a human tower.

What the hell is this? some audience members surely wonder.

Wynn already knows the answer.

This is a WOW.

The second act is as wild and inventive as the first. Figures in blue, seesawing each other into the air. A blond woman in a pink unitard, turning gracefully in her trapeze high above. A man in doublet and tights, riding his unicycle across a tightrope. A muscleman performing an aerial ballet, suspended by leather straps, to the sound of cello strings. And so much more.

It's all so crazy.

But also intensely compelling.

Wynn is determined to reinvent Las Vegas entertainment in the same way his father reinvented bingo—with spectacle, amazement, fun, and, to use one of his favorite expressions, wows.

"Bobby," Guy Laliberté says Wynn tells Baldwin, seated next to him, "make sure we have a deal with these guys."

The core of the Canadian-born circus troupe that would conquer the world begins in 1980 as a troupe of stilt walkers called Les Échassiers de Baie-Saint-Paul. The name is a portent of the wonders to come: *échassier* means stilt walker, but it also refers to someone who wades in water.

Founded by a stilt walker named Gilles Ste-Croix, the troupe organizes publicity-grabbing stunts, like stilt walking the nearly sixty miles between Baie-Saint-Paul and Quebec City—a feat that earns coverage in a local newspaper called, fatefully, *Le Soleil*. They come up with a show and take it on the road, performing at hockey game intermissions and organizing a weeklong festival that turns the streets of Baie-Saint-Paul into a carnival of street performers. "Little did these early fans and performers know that these embryonic beginnings would lead to something magical, exciting, and revolutionary on a global scale," according to the history on the Cirque's website.

In 1979, Guy Laliberté returns to Quebec from France, where he had traveled "with only 50 dollars in his pocket...doing stilt walking and fire breathing on the streets of European cities," according to the *Associated Press*. Upon his return home, at 20, he joins *Les Échassiers de Baie-Saint-Paul* as a fire-breathing, stilt-walking performer.

In April 1981, Laliberté and several others, including Gilles Ste-Croix, cofound a nonprofit corporation named Le Club des Talons Hauts (The High Heels Club), and begin to reinvent the circus. They "organized a street fair... and put out the call to performers across the continent," according to the *Globe and Mail,* producing "large scale shows...(with) death-defying acrobatic stunts, the clowns who were much more intriguing than those they'd come to know through traditional circuses, the aerial dancers who exuded sex appeal." By 1984, the government of Quebec has awarded Le Club de Talons Hauts a $1.6 million contract to create a circus to tour the provinces in celebration of the four hundred fiftieth anniversary of French explorer Jacques Cartier's voyage to Canada, and Laliberté and his fellow performers take the circus on the road.

"This traveling show offers a unique take on the circus arts: Animal-free, striking, dramatic, beautiful and reflective," according to the Cirque history. Laliberté soon renames the troupe Cirque du Soleil—Circus of the Sun—because he wants "a name that would last forever, a name that would suggest energy and youth and power. So I thought: why not the sun?"

Cirque is soon performing in a big top before audiences of hundreds, but it's only the beginning. Laliberté knows that to thrive, they'll need to expand beyond Canada, especially during the freezing winter months, and the troupe grows to include performers from Europe and Asia. In 1987, Cirque du Soleil embarks on a tour of the United States and turns a profit for the first time. By 1990, they've toured London, Paris, and Japan and then landed on the beach near the Santa Monica Pier, where they first captivate Wynn, the Las Vegas Wizard of Wows.

Wynn is by no means the first to approach Cirque du Soleil. Laliberté has waved off previous offers from Disney and Hollywood, and negotiations recently fell apart with one of Wynn's competitors: Caesars Palace. Caesars's financially conservative leader, Henry Gluck, is known for both his brilliance and his unwillingness to spend—perhaps even for a spectacle like Cirque du Soleil. "After nine months of meetings and conversations, they—Henry Gluck and [Caesars president and COO] Terry Lanni—changed their minds and thought it was too esoteric for the Vegas market," says Laliberté.

Which is exactly what Wynn must like about it.

He approaches Laliberté during intermission at the troupe's show in Toronto. "I want you guys," Laliberté remembers Wynn saying. "We'll put you up at the Mirage." And there's more on the horizon, he tells Laliberté. "I have a new project called Treasure Island."

Within hours, they have a handshake deal to stage *Nouvelle Expérience* in a tent that seats 1,250 behind the Mirage, twice a night, six days a week, for a residency beginning November 10, 1992.

Opening night, however, is a nightmare.

First of all, a rarity in Vegas: it's cold outside. Inside the tent, a calamity: one of the performers, accustomed to sliding with ease on a rope over the audience, falls from the rope and onto the shoulder of one of the guests.

Dead silence.

Luckily, both the tightrope performer and the guest, a friend of Wynn's, are unharmed.

The show goes on, ending with a standing ovation, and from that point on the circus in the Mirage's white-and-yellow-striped tent is a smashing, sold-out success. The *Las Vegas Review-Journal* deems it "the best thing to happen to Las Vegas entertainment in years."

The circus in the Mirage parking lot is merely a trial

run. Wynn's real goal is securing an exclusive Cirque du Soleil extravaganza for his newest resort, Treasure Island Hotel and Casino.

Wynn asks Laliberté and Cirque du Soleil for a show budget—which, according to Laliberté, Wynn accepted—to come up with something earth shattering, something so original and breathtakingly new that it might actually move the center of the entertainment world from New York and London to Las Vegas.

Laliberté knows both entertainment and business. "I grew up in this type of very balanced world of business and creativity. My mom was very, very creative, eccentric. And my father was a PR guy, a wheeler-dealer," he tells *Forbes*. "I really believe that one gift my life has given me is this fifty-fifty creative-business brain."

He goes to every show in every theatrical capital, from Broadway to London's West End and beyond. Always checking out the competition. "That was my job, to know what entertainment was about," he says. In Vegas, he's mostly disappointed. Siegfried and Roy are, of course, the hot ticket during this era—but, to Laliberté, only the first twenty minutes dazzle. The remaining seventy minutes "is a traditional magician show."

Laliberté and his crew of dreamers get to work. Forget pirates. That's for Treasure Island's front lawn, which features a fiery battle with a full-size pirate ship four times a night. Inside the new theater, Cirque du Soleil's first-ever permanent space, they present their newest creation: *Mystère*.

The curtain rises on Christmas Day, 1993. Wynn sits

in the audience in his new resort's custom-built 1,541-seat theater and watches the reactions of the audience as they take in a spectacle on a revolving stage lit by 1,100 spotlights and featuring a cast of characters drawn from mythology. For a theme, *Mystère* tackles nothing less than the birth of the universe.

"You're about to see a show that will dazzle you, and bring you to different stratospheres of entertainment," Wynn told the opening-night audience, according to Larry Ruvo, who talked Wynn into seeing Cirque du Soleil perform in Santa Monica. "If this works and you love this show, it's my idea. And if you don't like the show, it's my friend Larry Ruvo's idea."

When the curtain falls ninety minutes later, the applause is thundering.

"You guys have made a German opera here," Wynn is quoted as telling the show's director, Franco Dragone, surely wowed and maybe even a little overwhelmed by its spectacle and depth.

"You just gave me the best compliment I've ever heard," Dragone replies.

The reviews are equally ecstatic. "*Mystère* is the circus taken to another dimension," raves one reviewer. "Think of the big top combined with a razzle-dazzle Broadway musical and special effects from sci-fi movies. Stir these ingredients, and you get an elegant concoction—a phantasmagoria that made me feel like I had slipped into a sorcerer's dream world."

The *Las Vegas Sun* sees the show as a dramatic cultural

shift, establishing "a new standard for Las Vegas—and anywhere—for an all-enveloping theatrical experience. A quantum leap for circus artistry and production."

Within ten days, *Mystère* is a sell-out. After six months, it makes good on the initial investment. In its first year, with 480 shows at 92 percent occupancy, 683,294 people will see *Mystère*.

"We hit the bullseye," remembers Laliberté. "For years, it was the hot ticket in town."

But Wynn is already thinking of something new.

He's thinking about...*water*.

Specifically, a resort whose theme is water.

The idea is born on a boat in Lake Como, alongside the Italian town with the rippling name: Bellagio.

While Lake Como, a vast body of emerald-green water, is encircled by historic villas, Wynn's Bellagio will become a thirty-six-story resort with restaurants and shops facing an eight-and-a-half-acre constructed lake with a dancing water fountain synchronized to music. "With its seasonal gardens, extensive pool courtyards and its famed water show, Bellagio is showing that what's outside the casino is just as important as what's inside," a magazine notes.

Before the fountain idea is sealed, however, Wynn has a different brainstorm: the lake will feature water skiers, possibly with a new Cirque du Soleil extravaganza. "He wanted us to be part of the waters," Laliberté recalls. "He said 'I want to do the biggest water show outdoors.' For me, I wanted to do the next big Cirque du Soleil theatrical show."

But the idea of working with water is intriguing. Laliberté, writer and director Franco Dragone, and creative director Gilles Ste-Croix start brainstorming concepts. Soon, a vision appears before them of 1950s superstar Esther Williams, known as the Million-Dollar Mermaid for her high-grossing, high-diving "aqua musicals." A former professional swimmer whose Olympic dreams were interrupted by World War II, Williams starred in MGM feature films that brought synchronized swimming and diving to the big screen.

"A theatrical acrobatic performance using water and the spirit of Esther Williams, a water fantasy," is how Laliberté describes it, adding that Cirque du Soleil would be "the first to do a masterpiece in a theatrical water show."

"He got it," Laliberté says of Wynn's initial reaction. Wynn will still have the Bellagio's lake and its show-stopping fountain outside—and then inside the Bellagio's new custom-made theater, designed to resemble a European opera house, he will present Cirque du Soleil's aquatic masterpiece.

Even the name of the show will be centered around water, taken from the French word for water—*eau,* pronounced "oh."

"*O,*" as the show will simply be called, will of course be extremely expensive, Laliberté warns Wynn.

"How much?" asks Wynn.

"Between ninety and a hundred million," says Laliberté.

"Let's start with ninety and see how it goes," Wynn replies, according to Laliberté.

"We ended up at like one hundred five million including the theater," says Laliberté, which he considers "pretty damn good" for a masterpiece. The rest of the Bellagio grows around the "O" Theater, which itself costs an estimated fifty million dollars and must be built first in order to allow the Cirque du Soleil cast and crew time to fine-tune their production.

After years of rehearsal, "O" is ready to make its world debut on October 15, 1998—the world's most expensive production, in the world's most expensive resort, in the world's most expensive and most technologically advanced theater.

For the first time, Cirque du Soleil performs in a theater with a proscenium, a section of stage in front of the traditional red curtain. The production requires an enormous backstage area, where the wizards and performers of "O" create the magic. "What's unique here, and something that you will probably never see again, because no one [else] is going to spend fifty million dollars on a theater, is that the backstage area is bigger than the house," veteran supervisor Steven Dietrich points out later, standing in the darkness of the immense backstage while the show erupts a few feet in front of him. "It would cost twice fifty million dollars to build this theater today."

Backstage in the cavernous space, the show's eighty performers are cuing up—getting into costume, stretching, rehearsing, getting wet—along with the one hundred twenty-five technicians who run the show.

Out front, the first audience of eighteen hundred eagerly awaits the impossible.

As "O" begins, the curtain doesn't merely go up; it unfurls, rising slowly from the floor and disappearing with a gigantic yank as if pulled from the gods above. The red curtain is, of course, iconic, a remnant of performances throughout time. "Hundreds of years ago they had a red curtain," one of the show's veteran clowns, Marcus Weiss, comments. "When this one blows up to the ceiling, it sort of rips your heart open—in a good way—taking you back to the world of transcendence, of magic, a leap into another world."

The world of "O" almost defies description.

Those in the audience on that first starry night beneath the theater's blue glass ceiling will find it difficult to put the experience into words.

Every seat in the brand-new "O" Theater is filled. Celebrities, business leaders, Wall Street titans, Vegas luminaries. They gasp as the curtain disappears to reveal an enormous stage that seems to be composed almost entirely of water. Dominating the 3,650-square-foot stage is a 150-by-100-foot pool filled with 1.5 million gallons of water, illuminated from every direction by an endless array of lights that can make rain seem to fall, or fog to rise from its glistening surface.

It's more than a wow.

It's a theatrical revolution.

"The concept was having this pool of water from which things would emerge and then return to it," Elaine Wynn says, trying to describe the wonders of "O." Synchronized swimmers point their toes in line and leap into the onstage lake; eight acrobats perform on a floating barge; flyers and catchers dive and leap from a hovering steel-frame ship; acrobats launch themselves in the air from an aerial cradle; divers on Russian swings seem to go weightless and then plunge into the blue pool with Olympian ease; cast members costumed as zebras battle a rainstorm while suspended on an aerial frame; four Mongolian contortionists perform handstands in the water. There are aerial hoops and a water-resistant piano and painted carousel horses—while the onstage lake becomes alternately shallow and then deep, thanks to Cirque du Soleil's master engineers.

Dietrich attributes the magic of the show to the universal fascination with water shared by children and adults alike. "In this show, you never know when they step on the surface of that water, if they're going to fall right in or going to walk on water," he says. Below the twenty-five-foot-deep pool's surface is a submerged floor that can be raised or lowered via an array of giant hydraulic pistons, each capable of lifting more than one hundred thousand pounds, enabling the performers to either dive into the water or seem to glide upon it.

"It was an existential exercise," Elaine Wynn says of

seeing "O" for the first time. "All of Cirque's shows are existential. But this one hit it out of the park."

Elaine Wynn has witnessed performances by many of the greats, from Elvis Presley to Barbra Streisand to the Rat Pack and beyond. She's watched the stars perform in Radio City, Carnegie Hall, and the Super Bowl. But the moment that red curtain rises on "O," she's transfixed.

"From the second it started until the minute it was over, my heart was in my throat," Elaine Wynn says.

When the red curtain falls after ninety minutes, the opening night audience is momentarily stunned. No applause, not yet anyway, just silence. "Because you are in such sensory overload that to clap is the wrong gesture," says Elaine Wynn. "There was such a long pause before everybody burst into this enthusiastic response that was transformative for me. It was the single best performance I've ever seen in my life."

"Liquid magic," the *Los Angeles Times* raves. The *Seattle Times* compares it to a "vivid world of Fellini Fantasia and Esther Williams water ballet" where "a fearless corps of acrobatic swimmers create images of rippling, enigmatic beauty." "Spectacular and emotionally thrilling," says the *San Francisco Examiner.* "The whole brew is risky, noisy, sexy and downright stunning," proclaims *Variety.*

The cash register rings as loud as the applause: since its opening, "O" has reached $2.4 billion in revenue. The theater is packed five nights a week, two shows a night, with an occupancy rate "never below ninety percent," according to Cirque du Soleil's executive vice chairman of the board, Daniel Lamarre. Because of the artistry, of course, but also because of the *water*.

The water just draws them in, as Dietrich says.

Cirque du Soleil's enormous success has never surprised Laliberté. Long before he ever came to Vegas, he had a vision in mind. "Growth was one of my targets," he told a *Toronto Saturday Night* reporter in 1987. "Everything is possible—as long as you work for it. People are so much in need of happiness, and at Le Cirque, we define ourselves as the merchants of happiness."

And they've sold a *lot* of happiness. An estimated one hundred eighty million people have now seen at least one of the two dozen shows that Cirque du Soleil has mounted across the globe, and the company has about four thousand employees, including thirteen hundred "artists" from more than fifty different countries. It has expanded into IMAX films and other projects—all based on what Cirque du Soleil shares with the myriad fantasies of Las Vegas: making people "forget what's happening in their day-to-day life," says Daniel Lamarre.

Cirque du Soleil's influence is so profound that Lamarre once met a man bearing a Cirque du Soleil corporate logo tattoo on his arm. "You saved my life," the fan told him. "I was depressed. I didn't know what to do in life. I went to see one of your shows and it clicked that I could do more. I'm indebted to you for the rest of my life."

"We became, as they call it here, Cirque de Vegas," says Lamarre. "That's the expression the locals are using to show that we are intertwined."

As for former fire-eater Guy Laliberté, he's become a billionaire, and, true to his Las Vegas triumphs, a high-stakes poker player. In 2009, he realized a longtime dream: blasting off into space, accompanying two astronauts on a twelve-day visit to the International Space Station. Of course, he was photographed wearing a clown nose beneath his astronaut helmet.

Over time, Cirque du Soleil has added more Vegas extravaganzas to its roster. In addition to *Mystère* (which celebrates its thirtieth anniversary in 2023, the longest-running of all Cirque du Soleil shows) and *"O"* (Cirque du Soleil's most successful show, and the highest-grossing single show in live entertainment worldwide), there's *KÀ* at the MGM Grand ("the most expensive theatrical production in history," with a budget exceeding one hundred sixty-five million dollars, according to *Vanity Fair*) and *Mad Apple,* which debuted in May 2022 at the New York–New York Hotel and Casino, plus shows highlighting musical superstars—*The Beatles LOVE* at the Mirage and *Michael Jackson ONE* at Mandalay Bay. Some visitors say that seeing a Cirque du Soleil show is their main reason for coming to Las Vegas.

The era of Las Vegas entertainment competing with, and maybe even sometimes surpassing, the money-minting casinos has begun.

Chapter 16

THE TRIUMPH OF THE OPERATIC TENOR

THE MGM GRAND GARDEN ARENA

THE TEN-YEAR-OLD GIRL who stares through the car window at the Big Apple Coaster at the New York–New York Hotel and Casino is like a hundred other kids all dreaming of riding one of the greatest roller coasters on earth. Blasting through the desert air at sixty-seven miles per hour, the Big Apple Coaster is a showstopper, climbing two hundred feet, plunging one hundred forty-four feet back down, and careening into a one-hundred-eighty-degree "heartline" twist-and-dive maneuver, which, as the hotel's marketing materials proclaim, has entranced "more than 1.4 million riders with heart-stopping action and excitement each year." VIP riders include singer Usher, magician

Criss Angel, and actor Channing Tatum, all of whom have taken in the Las Vegas skyline while whizzing around—and through—the New York–New York resort's faux skyscraper skyline.

Even though she sees it only at a distance, the girl falls in love with the roller coaster at first sight during the drive from the airport to the Mansion—the MGM Grand's exclusive resort-within-a-resort for VIPs where she and her family will be staying.

"I saw the massive roller coaster and immediately knew I wanted to go and ride it," she later says, "and I was so excited when the day came."

Now, she walks through the ride's jangling entrance, which, this being Vegas, is no mere hallway but "a massive arcade with any kind of game you could imagine," she says. "They also have loud dance music playing throughout the arcade so you really begin to get excited for the ride."

And, oh, is she excited. She stands in a line that can stretch around the block, everyone waiting for those magical, manic three minutes, to leave their everyday lives behind and board the train to rip-roaring wonder.

The ten-year-old is a roller coaster aficionado, having ridden coasters in both America and Europe. "My favorites are the ones that are big and go upside down," she says. "There is an amusement park in my hometown that is open during the summer, and it has so many crazy rides."

The hometown she is referring to is the Tuscan seaside

village of Alpemare, a small town in Italy that neverthe-less hosts a summertime amusement park complete with a roller coaster called Danger Zone, which she hasn't yet been allowed to try. "I want to ride but I have to wait until I'm twelve years old," says the girl. "Because there is an age limit." Thankfully, there is no age limit for the Big Apple Coaster, only a height limit—fifty-four inches—which the girl, tall for her age, easily clears.

A single ride costs nineteen dollars, and a full-day pass is forty-nine dollars. The girl takes her seat in one of the four yellow four-seater coaster cars, designed to resemble New York City taxicabs. As the ride begins, her anticipa-tion ratchets apace with the climbing car.

Click, click, click, higher and higher and higher...and then they're off. For a little over three exhilarating min-utes, she is flying. Up and down 4,777 feet, one of the lon-gest roller coasters in North America.

"It begins with a slow uphill climb, and you are prepar-ing yourself for the huge first drop," she explains. "Then as it creeps to the top, you fly so fast down the steepest hill and you feel your stomach flip as well. The ride is also filled with many fast turns and one huge circle where you go upside down. Everyone is screaming so loud but at the same time, laughing uncontrollably."

When the ride is over, the thrill remains. "So much better than I could have ever imagined," says the girl, determined to ride it again.

And again.

"It never gets old for me!" she exclaims.

But first comes work, at the MGM Grand Garden Arena.

When she steps into the arena later that night, she is no longer just another kid with a love of roller coasters.

She is Virginia Bocelli, and even at only ten years old, she is already a musical superstar.

Before an audience of seventeen thousand, she brings down the house in a duet with her father, Andrea Bocelli, the famed Italian operatic tenor who has captivated the city of crooners, comedians, and rock stars. A recording sensation whose musical releases are an international event, he has sold more than seventy-five million records, has performed for three popes and four US presidents, and has been nominated for five Grammys.

For Bocelli, the city of Las Vegas has been a thrill ride like the roller coaster that has so captivated his daughter, although for him, it's been a steady climb to the top without a single heart-stopping drop.

It begins on August 8, 1998, when Alan Feldman, then vice president of public relations at Mirage Resorts, spots a concert review on the front page of the *New York Times* Arts and Ideas section. Headlined A POP SIDE TO OPERA, FROM ITALY, it describes the rise of Bocelli, "who sold out Madison Square Garden on Thursday night."

The photo accompanying the review shows a long-haired Bocelli, then forty, in a tuxedo, performing with his eyes closed. He'd been diagnosed with congenital glaucoma as a young child, and became fully blind at the age of twelve following a blow to the head from a soccer ball. "He has a voice to bask in: a tenor with warmth and depth that he simply pours out without affectations," writes the reviewer, Jon Pareles, adding, "in the last six years he has made his way from piano bars to arenas."

Bocelli had been discovered by the Italian singer and songwriter Zucchero, "Italy's answer to Joe Cocker," the review said, "and has a multimillion-selling hit that he has recorded in two languages, 'Con te Partirò,' and 'Time to Say Goodbye.'

"As he sang to dying sweethearts and to endless, all-conquering love, Mr. Bocelli was reaching out not just to a particular romance but to Romance itself."

Knowing that Steve Wynn's soon-to-open Italian lakes–themed Bellagio megaresort requires entertainment "and that a meeting about entertainment was coming up," Feldman quickly buys the 1995 CD, *Bocelli,* and is stunned upon first listen. Bocelli's voice, he feels, perfectly captures the romantic spirit of the Bellagio.

Feldman takes the *Times* article and the *Bocelli* CD to the meeting, where, in a room filled with executives, he sits directly next to Wynn. After briefly describing Bocelli, his sold-out Madison Square Garden concert, and his review in the *New York Times,* Feldman slides the CD over to Wynn.

"He slid it back to me," says Feldman.

Wynn—"a Sinatra, Dean Martin, and Broadway show

guy," says Feldman—isn't convinced that an operatic tenor is the best entertainment option to open his new resort. But as the meeting ends, Elaine Wynn gestures toward the CD and tells Feldman, "Just give it to me."

"I played the Bocelli video on our plane to preview this unknown virtuoso for us both," says Elaine. "I immediately flipped and played it over and over again. I said, 'He must be the voice of Bellagio.' As usual, Steve made the rest happen."

A month passes. At the next meeting, Steve Wynn announces what he calls "this great idea." Not only has he licensed Bocelli's "Con te Partirò" for the Bellagio's opening, he has struck a deal for Bocelli to do two opening concerts, on the night of the grand opening and the following night. Even before the big event, TV ads for the Bellagio, set to "Con te Partirò," help send Bocelli's album rocketing up the *Billboard* charts—and fuel fevered expectations for the resort's grand opening.

Bocelli indeed becomes the voice of the Bellagio, most dramatically at the Fountains of Bellagio; his "Con te Partirò" doesn't merely complement the fountains but is an integral part of it—deep, soaring, majestic, almost miraculous, and, befitting the Bellagio's theme, very Italian.

At the opening, Steve and Elaine Wynn and a host of VIP guests stand before the fountain, with as many as twenty thousand spectators watching from the Strip. And while high winds cause the fountain to drench some of the crowd in a cascade of mist, Bocelli's recorded voice majestically rises up from the speakers toward the resort's Italianesque turrets and towers.

For an encore: the two opening-night concerts. "Oh, my goodness, he had the room from the first song," Feldman later recalls. "Steve loved him, and that song, 'Con te Partirò,' which so perfectly accompanies the swaying beauty of the fountains as well as the power of them, particularly at the climax."

"Steve believed in me," Bocelli says, and he felt an immediate kinship with Las Vegas. "My initial impression is the same, confirmed later in the quarter-century of frequentation that followed."

Thus begins Bocelli's conquest of Las Vegas. From his first visit, he says, "I would say that I have known it forever, because that is precisely my perception of Las Vegas: a place that is now so much a part of my life that I could not pinpoint its first approach." He feels the bright lights and high energy the moment he lands, riding into town beneath the shadow of the mammoth billboards along Wayne Newton Boulevard.

And even though Bocelli can't see the city due to his blindness, he feels it so strongly that he can describe it to his kids. "Before leaving on a trip you have to prepare your children for what they will be seeing, so they would be involved and interested," he tells the *Las Vegas Review-Journal* in 2009.

"They experienced Las Vegas through my stories."

Bocelli remembers first coming to the city with his sons, Amos and Matteo, when the boys—now in their twenties—were young. "Twenty years ago when we landed in Las Vegas with the little children," he says, "and after a walk downtown, we reached the lake at the moment when, coincidentally, the fountains were dancing on the water to 'Con te Partirò,' and Matteo, excited, said 'Babbo, but then they know it here, too. *Your song!*'"

With Bocelli's Las Vegas rise comes a revolution: an operatic tenor conquering the city of Frank and Dean, Elvis Presley, Wayne Newton, Cher and Adele. The contradictions of his triumph in Las Vegas aren't lost on him.

"I learned that the 'Neon City' is the capital of joie de vivre and fun, but it is also much more than that," he says. "And it is definitely less superficial and 'venal' than how it sometimes risks being described (by those who talk about it as hearsay)."

Bocelli calls himself "a quiet man." "By nature, I favor tranquility and silence over crowded places," he says. Still, Bocelli can find peace and solitude in a city known for crowds and noise. "Las Vegas does not take away energy from the visitor. On the contrary, it gives it back. Paradoxically, it is not far from what happens among the taciturn, beloved Tuscan hills, where I was born and raised."

In 2005, on a floating stage at the Lake Las Vegas Resort, Bocelli records his 2006 hit album and DVD *Under the Desert Sky*.

In 2007, with the release of his greatest-hits album, *The Best of Andrea Bocelli: Vivere*—and after taking part in the Concert for Diana at Wembley Stadium in London, memorializing the tenth anniversary of the princess's death—Bocelli performs a sold-out show on December 1 at the MGM Grand Garden Arena, where he feels "a great serenity because of the familiarity I feel with the place and the audiences."

He calls the Mansion, where he stays in one of the twenty-nine sprawling Mediterranean villas, his "portion of home, magically landed in Las Vegas." It's a world unto itself, with every conceivable amenity, but when Bocelli ventures out he loves to stop at Eataly, the Italian food and wine emporium founded by his friend, the Italian entrepreneur Oscar Farinetti. Back at the Mansion, he has a tradition of playing the MGM's marble grand piano, acquired by the hotel in a charity auction called Celebrity Fight Night, which Bocelli attended alongside Queen Rania of Jordan, maestro Zubin Mehta, and actor Nicolas Cage. "That piano is a symbol of a strong closeness, made for friendship and shared values with the entire city," he says.

While his days are filled with activities and friends, the nights are why he comes to Las Vegas, and he comes for one reason:

To perform.

"He's coming!" a dozen voices urgently exclaim, across hallways, over iPhones and walkie-talkies, on the loading dock behind the MGM Grand Garden Arena. Suddenly, a flurry of black Escalades arrive, and from one, Andrea

Bocelli steps out wearing a black hoodie, his tuxedo slung over his shoulder in a Dolce and Gabbana garment bag, heading to his Valentine's concert in February 2022.

Somewhere in Las Vegas, somebody is having the greatest night of their life tonight, goes a common expression here.

Tonight, that somebody is multiplied by seventeen thousand—the number of seats that will be filled in the arena to witness what critics call "excellence personified," "a magnificent gift," and "beyond belief."

"If God would have a singing voice, He would sound a lot like Andrea Bocelli," Vegas megastar Céline Dion once famously said of Bocelli, with whom she sang on the 1999 hit "The Prayer."

"To be present and hear this amazing entertainer and all the accompanying entertainers perform was a once in a lifetime experience," writes a fan.

Tonight, Bocelli will be accompanied by a symphony orchestra. An army of musicians in tuxedos and ball gowns takes the stage at 8 p.m. Giant video screens alight. Red rose petals begin falling down on them. Fog fills the stage. And Andrea Bocelli steps into the spotlight.

"Ladies and gentlemen, welcome to Andrea Bocelli's MGM Grand Garden Arena concert," roars the announcer. The crowd roars back and Bocelli begins to sing his romantic standards, from *West Side Story*'s "Maria," to Elvis Presley's "Can't Help Falling in Love," to the song that introduced the world to the Italian tenor: "Con te Partirò."

But the showstopping moment comes early in the second half of the show, when Bocelli sits down on a stool with an acoustic guitar and tells the audience that he will be joined "by a beautiful girl, my daughter, Virginia." Microphone in hand, the young girl confidently walks onstage and stands beside her dad. And the famed tenor and his ten-year-old daughter launch into a stirring duet of Leonard Cohen's "Hallelujah," which, after a live version was posted on YouTube, racked up twenty-seven million views.

The duet brings down the house.

It's 10:30 a.m. the next morning. Ray Torres, the chauffeur, is on location at the Mansion, waiting to transport Bocelli and his family to a private airport for their noon flight.

Instead of Bocelli, his daughter, Virginia, comes running out, followed by a female assistant in her twenties. Virginia has done almost everything there is for kids in Vegas, from indoor skydiving—being suspended in a wind tunnel in a specially designed facility to simulate skydiving—to riding small planes and helicopters over the town and the desert.

But for her, nothing compares to the Big Apple Coaster.

"She wants to ride the roller coaster at New York–New York," the assistant tells Torres. "Do you know how to get there?"

"Absolutely," the chauffeur replies.

Once they are in the Escalade, Torres asks, "Would you like to hear some music?" The answer is a resounding yes.

"How about Adele?" Torres suggests.

"I love Adele!" Virginia replies.

"She's one of my favorite singers," Torres agrees. "And I'm going to play one of my favorite songs." He presses Play, and Adele's 2021 hit "Easy on Me" envelops the car. From the back seat, Bocelli's daughter begins to sing along, not singing to herself, but just as she had the night before: a consummate professional pouring her entire heart and soul into the song.

"It was one of the most memorable, heartfelt, precious moments of my entire career as a chauffeur," Torres later recalls. "I could hear all of the love and devotion that Andrea and his wife, Veronica, poured into their daughter through her voice as she sang."

When Virginia finishes the song, Torres tells her, "That was the most amazing thing I've ever heard."

By the time they arrive at New York–New York and Torres opens the door for Virginia, she has reverted to being a kid and races off in excitement to ride the roller coaster, leaving the seasoned Las Vegas chauffeur with tears of gratitude and joy streaming down his face.

<p style="text-align:center">

Chapter 17

EARNING A NAME AT THE PALMS

N9NE STEAKHOUSE

"WHO IS MALOOF?" asks Barry Dakake.

It's 2000, and Dakake is the executive sous chef at Charlie Palmer Steak at the Four Seasons, the luxury hotel inside the Mandalay Bay Resort and Casino. He has been at the steakhouse for six months, after opening the Las Vegas location of superchef Charlie Palmer's showpiece, Aureole, where the food and wine are part of the show: "wine angels"—young acrobats in skintight apparel, flying through the air on invisible wires, inspired by Tom Cruise's levitational theatrics in *Mission: Impossible*—fetch bottles lined up inside the Wine Tower, a 42-foot, $1.2 million monolith of laminated high-density, super-transparent acrylic.

Chef Dakake is staring at a name on tonight's reservation list: *Maloof*. The name has him stumped.

"Intriguing name," he says, asking the reservationist to enlighten him.

The name, he is told, actually belongs to a family of Maloofs: George and Gavin, brothers from Albuquerque, New Mexico, plus their other brothers, Joe and Phil, sister Adrienne, mother Colleen, and late father, George Maloof, Sr. Owners of the Sacramento Kings basketball team. Distributors of Coors beer. One of the largest single shareholders in Wells Fargo bank, via their Maloof Companies. And developers of the Fiesta Rancho hotel and casino, a friendly, inexpensive mainstay for locals in Las Vegas. ("High-roller treatment for ordinary people," noted the *New York Times*.) After opening the Fiesta in 1994, at a reported cost of twenty-five million dollars to build, the family sold it in 2001 for one hundred eighty-five million dollars.

That, the chef is told, is the Maloof family.

Now, armed with cash from the sale, the Maloofs are thinking even bigger. And younger. They're building a forty-two-story hotel and casino on a deserted lot a mile west of the Strip. They're calling it the Palms Casino Resort. It is designed to appeal to a variety of visitors, from the Las Vegas resident, always searching for a deal, to the hip Las Vegas tourist or worldly celebrity, always ready to rock and roll. The resort will include a massive casino, a fourteen-screen movie cinema with an IMAX theater, two nightclubs, and a three-level spa.

At Charlie Palmer Steak, Dakake keeps seeing *Maloof* on the reservation list. Then one day, he's approached by head chef Brian Massie, who asks: "Do you wanna come work with me at the Palms, for the Maloofs?"

Dakake isn't sure. He's loyal to superstar chef Charlie Palmer, his mentor—the Godfather, Dakake calls him. But money is money. "How much does it pay?" he asks Massie.

"Don't worry about money," Massie says, quoting a sum that blows Dakake's mind. It's twice his present salary.

Dakake goes to Palmer. "Charlie, I have an opportunity," he tells him. "This is what they wanna pay me, but I would love to stay with you. Can you match this number? Please?"

Palmer gives the chef his blessing. "Look, it's a lot of money," he tells Dakake. "It's okay. You can go."

The restaurants at the Palms Casino Resort will include Alize, serving high-end French cuisine; Little Buddha, an Asian eatery inspired by the Buddha Bar in Paris; and the showstopper, N9NE, a steakhouse founded by longtime best friends and Chicago entrepreneurs Michael Morton and Scott DeGraff, who named the restaurant (using a digit in place of *i*) after the age at which they first met.

On the surface, N9NE at the Palms is just another kitchen. Another job for Dakake, who launched his career at his uncle Dennis Clyde Dakake's ice cream and sandwich shop in Johnston, Rhode Island, "washing dishes and scrubbing booth baseboards, but I always wanted to cook," he says. As his uncle Clyde built his family restaurant into a chain, he let his nephew join the cooks behind the stove. "I was fourteen years old, I was nobody, I was a peanut," Dakake recalls. Soon, he is rising up the ranks from short-order cook to prep cook. After earning a degree from the Rhode Island School of Design in 1990, Dakake moves to New York City and becomes a line cook at the original location of Aureole, Charlie Palmer's famous Upper East Side brownstone restaurant. Making a living, but never a name. "Nobody really knew who I was," he says.

Returning to work in his native Rhode Island, his career is sidelined when he's diagnosed with non-Hodgkin's lymphoma. After chemotherapy and radiation, he is in remission when the call comes: *Do you want to help open Charlie Palmer's Aureole at the Mandalay Bay in Vegas?*

"What do we have to lose?" he and his wife at the time, Denise, ask each other.

Dakake arrives in Las Vegas physically weak but determined to make a new life for himself. He helps open two restaurants, Aureole and Charlie Palmer Steak, just months apart in 1999.

But he's never seen anything like *this*: standing here, in his whites, on the opening night of a major new Las Vegas resort.

At 11 p.m. on November 15, 2001, George Maloof Jr. takes the stage in the Palms casino to address the opening night crowd, his image projected on a giant screen. "Tonight, we celebrate a place that reflects the true spirit of Las Vegas, where you can gamble, win, party, and have fun," he declares. "Welcome to the new paradise for locals!"

There's no Eiffel Tower or Venetian canal. No eye-popping décor. No exploding volcano or fiery pirate battle every half hour on the Strip. This place is pure party. This is the Palms.

Bruce Springsteen's *Born in the USA* roars through the casino, accompanied by a stampeding crowd of thousands. "Within fifteen minutes, it was nearly impossible to move," reports the *Las Vegas Sun,* "as bystanders clogged every aisle, filled up virtually every slot machine, and took every seat at the Palms's tables. Hundreds more waited outside well after the casino's opening, unable to get in because the property was at capacity." Among the celebrants: Pamela Anderson, Samuel L. Jackson, Cuba Gooding Jr., Joe Pesci, Charlize Theron...and Paris Hilton, wearing a dress festooned with one million dollars in brand-new Palms casino chips.

Even the celebrities, no strangers to razzle-dazzle, are awestruck by the Palms's hard-partying energy. "This place goes where the Hard Rock didn't go," Vince Neil of Mötley Crüe tells the *Las Vegas Sun.* "It's like the next step. It's rock and roll with an edge. This is the edge, man."

Dennis Rodman, the NBA star known for his tattoos, neon hair, and flamboyant sense of fashion, is more blunt. "I'll be a real good customer of this SOB," he declares.

By now, the era of the celebrity chef is well underway in Vegas, and the city is on its way to becoming "the culinary center of the world," says Dakake. Wolfgang Puck's Spago is dazzling crowds in the Forum Shops at Caesars Palace. Emeril Lagasse is screaming his trademark slogan *"Bam!"* at Emeril's New Orleans Fish House in the MGM Grand. The biggest names in restaurants the world over are opening over-the-top Las Vegas outposts: Joël Robuchon, Thomas Keller, Bobby Flay, Charlie Trotter, Jean-Georges Vongerichten, Sirio Maccioni, Julian Serrano, Nobu Matsuhisa…*Who the hell is Barry Dakake?* He's still a "nobody."

"When Gavin Maloof would come into the restaurant, he would tell his guests, 'If anyone can pronounce Barry's last name, I'll give you five hundred dollars,'" says Dakake. "No one ever came close." (It's pronounced day-CAKE.)

He doesn't know it, but Dakake's about to get an unrivaled view of the relationship between celebrity and Las Vegas, a backstage VIP pass to a never-ending show—with the unlikeliest individual in the center of it all.

The Palms becomes a speeding train, stoked by the power of celebrity. MTV brings its massive audience inside when they send a film crew there to shoot episodes of the hit series *The Real World*. The resort becomes the kind of entertainment establishment that defines a moment in time, what Dakake calls "the Studio 54 of Las Vegas."

Stars and tourists alike come to play out their fantasies, to party nonstop. It's not just the five-star food, or the fine wine, or the clubs, or the crowds. "It's the chemistry," Dakake says. "There was nothing bigger than the Palms at the time. Not bigger as in scale or size. I'm talking about electrifying—casino, restaurants, nightlife, hotel, pool life. It was the complete package. You know when they say sex, drugs, and rock 'n' roll? I never saw drugs, but there was a lot of sex and rock 'n' roll going on at the Palms. It was unbelievable. It was endless."

Only five months after arriving at N9NE, Dakake becomes the restaurant's executive chef. He's becoming the virtuoso of steak in a city rapidly becoming the world capital of steak, renowned for his signature rib-cap steak. But at the Palms, being stuck in the kitchen doesn't mean missing out on the action. Because there's only one way to get to the stage at Rain in the Desert, the resort's mammoth concert venue, without being seen by the crowds: through the kitchen at N9NE. From the day he starts, Dakake is treated to a parade of stars making their way to the stage: Ozzy Osbourne, Third Eye Blind, Britney Spears, Santana, Kiss in full regalia, Gwen Stefani. "Every person who performed live at Rain walked by me in that kitchen," says Dakake.

One night, the kitchen is buzzing. A woman from another era of Las Vegas, the golden age of Elvis, is coming: Lisa Marie Presley, daughter of the King himself, will be performing at Rain. Before the show, her "people" come down to check out the kitchen security and chart the star's path.

"No one can look her in the eyes," one of Presley's advance men warns Dakake.

Dakake isn't impressed by celebrity. "At the end of the day, they're people, just like you and me," he says. "They have to eat. They breathe the air we breathe. They're human beings. I treat everybody the same."

The chef explodes at the advance man. "Who the hell do you think you are?" he says. "You're walking through *my* kitchen, and you're going to tell me not to look in somebody's eyes? Now I'm gonna do it ten times more, just to aggravate you."

Apparently, word gets back to Presley. Because that night, Dakake will remember, when she comes through the kitchen, "she had a smile on her face from here to Chicago."

"I'll be back," she tells the chef. "We'll talk later."

After the show, Presley comes back to the kitchen, sits on the stainless steel counter, and looks Dakake straight in the eye. "C'mon," she says. "Sit down and let's talk."

Dakake does as he's told. Presley peppers him with questions: *How did you get to Vegas? What's your favorite thing to cook? What do you cook at home?* On and on, until a bodyguard interrupts. "We gotta go," he tells Presley.

"No," she replies. "I don't get to do this often. Please wait for me over there."

Presley and Dakake chat for another ten minutes. "A long time to sit down and talk," he says. "Especially when you don't know somebody, and everyone's got eyes on you."

As she leaves, Presley tells him that her half-brother is about to turn twenty-one, and her mother wants to bring him to N9NE for dinner. "Could I have your number?" she asks.

Two weeks later, Dakake's phone rings. "Hello, is this Barry? This is Priscilla Presley. My daughter told me she met you in the kitchen—you're wonderful, a class act." Soon Priscilla Presley and her twenty-one-year-old son are sitting in N9NE. Dakake can almost feel the leather-clad ghost of Elvis in his 1968 prime, floating above them.

Dakake is working in the kitchen when he hears a commotion in the dining room. People are yelling, screaming. He races out to see what the commotion is all about—only to find everyone in the restaurant on their feet, cheering and applauding. Muhammad Ali is walking through N9NE, shaking hands and throwing punches.

The champ sits down at a table and looks at Dakake. "Chef," he says, "you got any bread pudding?"

Bread pudding isn't on the menu. But by chance, Dakake had prepared some the night before, with apricots and raisins and cranberries and Tahitian vanilla ice cream.

"Bring me two," says Muhammad Ali.

The chef personally serves the pudding. When Ali leaves, he hands a busboy one of his famous sketches on a cloth napkin. "The busboy was supposed to give it to me,"

Dakake says. "But it was a big miscommunication, and the busboy kept it." When Ali's memorabilia agent learns of the mix-up, a gift soon arrives for Dakake: a framed photo of Ali knocking out Sonny Liston, signed, "To Barry, Muhammad Ali."

Then the phone rings: It's the champ's wife, Veronica, calling from Beverly Hills to ask a favor. She's trying to get into Spago Beverly Hills, superstar chef Wolfgang Puck's flagship restaurant, but she can't get a table.

"What do you mean you can't get in?" Dakake says. "You're Muhammad Ali's wife!"

"Well, there's twenty of us."

Dakake makes a call, and a table for twenty appears at Spago.

Several years later, Ali returns to N9NE to celebrate a friend's birthday. "Thank you very much for getting us into Spago," he tells Dakake the moment he arrives, clasping the chef's hands.

"He was a beautiful man, a genuine and humble man," Dakake says. "I could see how he could bring peace to the world."

The steakhouse is popular with athletes. Other boxers follow. Joe Frazier, Ali's onetime nemesis, now in a wheelchair. Tommy Hearns, the Motor City Cobra, the first boxer in history to win titles in five separate divisions. Sugar Ray Leonard, one of the greatest of all time.

There are the legends of baseball: Duke Snider, Stan Musial, Derek Jeter, Reggie Jackson, Ernie Banks. The all-time hockey great Gordie Howe. NFL quarterbacks

Tom Brady, Joe Montana, Dan Marino, and John Elway. Swimming legend Michael Phelps, who comes to stay at the Palms for a week after winning six gold and eight bronze medals at the 2004 Olympics. Dakake cooks for him every night. "Steak, lobster—he was hungry!"

Some of the athletes don't even bother with the dining room. They walk straight into Dakake's kitchen for dinner. "I would set a table with a tablecloth, and the guys would eat," the chef says.

There are more basketball greats than Dakake can count: Bill Walton, LeBron James, and more. Dakake greets them all, serves them their favorites. To the rest of the world they might be stars, but in Dakake's kitchen they're "just normal guys," hanging out with a friend.

One night, Charles Oakley, the retired NBA veteran who played for the Chicago Bulls and the New York Knicks, tells the chef he wants to repay him for all the fabulous food and service. "You take care of me all the time when I come in here," Oakley says. "What can I do for you?"

Dakake, who by now has seen and done almost everything a Vegas chef can see and do, has one unfulfilled wish: to meet Oakley's good friend and former Chicago Bulls teammate, Michael Jordan.

"If MJ's in town, bring him to my restaurant for dinner," Dakake says, half joking.

"C'mon, man, that's all you want?" says Oakley. "That's easy. Book the private dining room Sunday night, fifty people."

Sunday night comes. A party of fifty, with an assortment of NBA players—past, present, and future—floods into the private dining room. All the best food and wine, amassing a giant bill. But no Michael Jordan.

"Man, I don't think he's gonna show up," Dakake says.

"Barry, it's *Michael Jordan*," says Oakley. "He doesn't show up until everybody's in the room. That's how he rolls."

The entrance, when it finally comes, is beyond anything Dakake was expecting. "There's this aura, this presence," he says. "The door opens and then *boom!* It's Michael Jordan. In a blue fedora hat. Blue shirt. Blue pants. Blue belt buckle. Blue shoes. Blue socks. His college colors, right? He's got a bag in his hand."

"Chef Barry?" Jordan says.

"Yeah?" Dakake stammers, as if he's never seen a star before.

"I heard a lot about you," says Jordan. "I'm here tonight because of Charles, and for you. If I like my dinner, what's in this bag is gonna be for you."

Jordan orders one of Dakake's favorites: lobster risotto. When the chef returns to check on him, Jordan flashes a wide smile.

"C'mon, let's go back in the kitchen," he says. "I've got something for you."

There, amid the rush of dinner service, Jordan opens his bag and hands the chef an NBA jersey emblazoned with his name and number. Dakake looks up at the kitchen's large plate-glass window, which allows the restaurant's diners to watch the chefs in action. "Remember the scene from *The Twilight Zone,* where William Shatner's on the plane and this gremlin is looking through the window?" he says. "Well, there had to be thirty or forty people looking through the kitchen window with their camera flashes going off. Michael Jordan's got the jersey spread out. And he's signing it to me."

One morning, Dakake takes the elevator at the Palms. He's headed for the restroom, and he's praying the car doesn't stop. But it does, and an older gentleman steps in. At first, Dakake stares at the floor, hoping to avoid conversation. Then he sees the man's shoes—soft-soled sneakers.

Who the hell is this? Dakake wonders, his gaze rising from shoes to corduroy pants, and, finally, the belt with a buckle in the shape of…Spider-Man.

It's Stan Lee! The creator of Spider-Man, X-Men, Doctor Strange, Thor—all the legends of Marvel Comics.

"What do you do?" Lee asks Dakake, who's now forgotten about needing to go to the bathroom.

"I'm a chef here at the restaurant."

"Boy, am I hungry," says Lee.

"Come with me," says Dakake.

The chef takes him to N9NE's kitchen. "You have any strawberries?" Lee asks. "How about some pancakes?"

"I don't have any pancakes," Dakake says. "But I've got

some strawberries, and I could whip you up a little omelet quick."

"Oh, I would love that!" exclaims Lee.

From that day on, the two were great friends. Dakake would go to California and visit Lee in Beverly Hills every month or so. "His favorite, favorite, favorite dessert was cherry cheesecake Danish," Dakake reminisces. "I'd have my pastry chef make sheet trays, and I would take them to him in boxes and he'd pass them out to his staff."

Other celebrities are fans of N9NE as well. Dakake serves dinner to Bob Dylan in his room after a show. He delivers sprawling meals—two-pound lobster tails, double tomahawks, cold shellfish platters, "all that kind of fun stuff"—to Leonardo DiCaprio in his suite at the Bellagio. He serves steak paired with three-thousand-dollar bottles of vintage Château Margaux Bordeaux to Charlie Sheen. He whips up Colorado lamb and baked potato with sliced tomatoes for Hugh Hefner, who always arrives wearing his signature pajamas and captain's cap, accompanied by three beautiful blond Playmates. Hef comes to town regularly to stay at the Fantasy Tower, a new wing at the Palms featuring a Playboy Club and the Hugh Hefner Sky Villa, which rents for twenty-five thousand dollars a night.

Interspersed with the big names are the high rollers. The whales. The ones who are given everything Vegas has to offer, on the house. The ones who order two or three or four bottles of wine, at eight thousand dollars a pop. Some invite Dakake to join them at the blackjack or poker tables, where he watches them blow a million dollars, in cash, and then return to N9NE for steak as if nothing had happened. "If you're dropping a million," Dakake learns, "you got another million somewhere else." Some high rollers are sometimes accompanied by "high-class girls," women who charge ten thousand dollars a night for their company. "We never encouraged that at the Palms, but there was always a lot of pretty women," Dakake says. "It was a party hotel."

The phone rings again. The chef is summoned to Phil Maloof's personal penthouse suite atop the Fantasy Tower, where the bodyguard to the legendary rapper and entertainment mogul Jay-Z "is standing there to greet me," says Dakake. Jay-Z is having dinner at N9NE that night, and the bodyguard wants to make sure everything is in order. But instead of asking Dakake about the table or the food or the security, he poses an unexpected question.

"Is your cousin Chucky?" he asks. "Chucky Dakake, from Lincoln, Rhode Island?"

"Yeah," says Dakake, startled.

"I used to play baseball with him," the bodyguard says. "He was one of the best high school baseball players around."

On another night, Beyoncé is performing for a "buyout." Uber Eats has bought out the entire Palms concert arena for a private event. At the last minute, Dakake gets the word that Beyoncé and her crew need thirty vegan plates in twenty minutes—to go.

God, Dakake prays silently, *let me get this done for these people.*

The kitchen launches into a frenzy, with everyone cooking and boxing and putting the food into bags. Dakake takes everything out to the team of bodyguards and personal assistants, and spots Jay-Z with the couple's baby, Blue Ivy.

"Jay, here's your wife's food," Dakake tells him. "It's everything she asked for, and I got it done as fast as I could. Tell her thank you, much love, and hope to see both of you again."

"Why don't you tell her yourself?" Jay-Z says. "She's right behind you."

Dakake turns around and, sure enough, there she is: Beyoncé. His reward is a big hug, and a kiss on the cheek. "Chef B, thank you for everything," Beyoncé tells Dakake.

Another night, another big name: Carmelo Anthony, the Los Angeles Lakers basketball great, comes into N9NE. Over the years, Dakake has made a point of asking his celebrity guests to sign mementos for him: sports jerseys, dinner plates, every conceivable surface he can place in front of them. He knows he's living in a magical moment, and he wants something to remember it by. It's a kind of quid pro quo, a favor for all the service he provides, but the stars are happy to oblige.

On this particular evening he's got Anthony back in the kitchen, and he's asking him to autograph everything in sight when the basketball star notices the chef's pristine white office door.

"It's the perfect thing to sign," says Anthony. "And you're going to call it the Shakedown Door." Anthony scrawls his name across the door, and a tradition is born.

Eventually the door sports a silver plaque bearing a new name: the Shakedown Room. Before long, it's covered with the signatures of all the stars who pass through Dakake's kitchen: Nicolas Cage, Tom Brady, President Bill Clinton, Mike Tyson, Kobe Bryant. The door tells the story of its time—when the rich and famous all gathered together at a place called the Palms and its signature restaurant, N9NE. Las Vegas has always catered to celebrities, providing them with a luxurious escape from the demands of fame and fortune. But for a hard-partying resort like the Palms, stars were more than just honored guests—they *were* the party. Just by showing up, they provided living proof that the Palms was the place to be.

But sooner or later, every light in Las Vegas begins to dim, no matter how brightly it once burned. In 2011, the Maloofs sell off most of their interest in the Palms. A succession of new owners arrives: TPG, Leonard Green and Partners, and, later, the Fertitta family. The resort is eventually renovated from top to bottom. N9NE is gutted and re-created as Scotch 80 Prime, which opened in May 2018, its walls adorned with one hundred million dollars in personal Fertitta family art: Basquiats and Warhols and Damian Hirsts and more. "I mean, the artwork!" Dakake says. "Museums don't even have the artwork that was hanging in that restaurant."

Dakake stays on as executive chef for six months before resigning to move to the Caribbean to work in restaurant consulting for a friend. But Vegas soon calls him back again. "I'm a person of prayer, and I would pray, 'God, make me what you want me to be...But I would love to own my own restaurant before I hit fifty.' On October 29, 2020, my new restaurant opened. I had turned fifty on October 20."

This restaurant does more than showcase Dakake's culinary talents.

This one bears his name: Barry's Downtown Prime.

"The sign says 'Barry's,' baby, and I get a chill every time I see my name in red neon out front, and I thank Jesus every moment for it," he says of his new restaurant inside Circa, the first major new resort to open in downtown Las Vegas in forty years. Along with his partners, Yassine Lyoubi, Marco Cicione, and Donnie Rihn, he shares credit for the restaurant with his fiancée, Niki Taylor. They met while she was working weekends at the Rain in the Desert nightclub to put herself through acting school in Los Angeles, and she soon became his number one supporter.

The man who catered to celebrities and locals at N9NE is now a celebrity himself. But what makes him different from the city's other superstar chefs is that Dakake made his name here, in Vegas. He arrived in the city a survivor, and became a bona fide star.

"The city gave me life," Dakake says. "The city gave me hope. The city gave me heartache, some sadness—yes, all of that, too. But in the end, the city gave me happiness.

"Las Vegas," he says, "gave me my name. This is my home."

Chapter 18

THE GHOST OF ELVIS PRESLEY

CRUISING THE STRIP

JESSE GARON HAS a choice.

He's a nineteen-year-old kid going nowhere in Mesquite, Texas. He's listened to countless voices advising him on the importance of a good education. But he also knows about something called the Legends in Concert in Las Vegas and that it can pay eighteen hundred dollars a week, big money to a high school kid from a Dallas suburb.

All he has to do to audition for Legends is trade his country boy apparel for a white sequined jumpsuit, dye his hair black and pile it up into a pompadour with styling gel, curl his upper lip, and imitate his idol, someone to whom he feels such a spiritual connection that he refers to that person and himself as "we."

Meaning him and his alter ego, Elvis Presley.

Forget college. He is Elvis, now and forevermore. It is 1991, and Garon will soon have plastic surgery to make himself look even more like Elvis. He has changed his real name—which he never divulges—to "Jesse Garon," in homage to Elvis's twin brother, who died in the womb. Now, he is pulling out of Mesquite in his screaming pink Caddy, with a U-Haul trailer hitched to the back, filled with precisely one Elvis jumpsuit bearing a gold star on the back and all of his other worldly possessions.

"So, we put all our money together—fifteen hundred dollars—and we put a U-Haul behind our pink Cadillac and we hightailed it to Vegas and only broke down three times," Garon says of the fateful day he left his humble home.

There is no going back, he tells himself on the drive, in which he is dressed as Elvis. *We're a big loser if we have to even* think *about going back.*

He has an angel on his padded jumpsuit shoulders, and that angel's name is Elvis.

"Not to sound crazy, but there are two people in here," he explains. "One of them is Jesse, and the other me looks like Elvis."

A therapist will inform him that this whole "we" business is a sure sign of a split personality, but Garon doesn't care. All he cares about is the King. "I have no idea when I started calling myself 'we,' when all of that snuck in," he reflects. "One day someone just called me on it, asked, like, 'Why do you say 'we?'" I never even noticed when the hell I did it."

His Elvis résumé is paper thin: performing *Hound Dog* at a Dallas Ford dealership's Elvis impersonator contest, for which he won first prize: an all-expense-paid trip to Las Vegas. But Elvis is in his blood, which means that Vegas is, too.

Because Las Vegas, he says, "is the playground of the King of Rock and Roll."

Garon has the music turned up loud—playing "Viva Las Vegas," of course, plus "Suspicious Minds" and all of the other Elvis classics—as he follows the ghost of Elvis across Texas, through New Mexico and Arizona, and finally into Nevada and the "bright-light city" that will become both his new home and his new stage.

The King's ghost rides the hot winds of Las Vegas, his adopted hometown, second only to Memphis. His spirit stalks the streets, stages, restaurants, and wedding chapels, and the casinos where his titanic manager, Colonel Tom Parker, gambled while Elvis performed. His anthem to Sin City, "Viva Las Vegas," blasts from speakers and stages all over town.

Garon knows all of this, knows how Elvis first arrived in Vegas in April 1956 at age twenty-one, the young King and his band earning seventeen thousand dollars for a two-week gig with Freddy Martin and His Orchestra and the comedian Shecky Greene in the Venus Room at the New Frontier Hotel and Casino. "The Atomic Powered Singer," read the ads, which refer to Elvis as merely an "extra added attraction" to the lineup.

On opening night his show was something of a bust, going down "like a jug of corn liquor at a champagne party," according to one review. Another writer adds: "He curled his lips, swiveled his hips, and howled like a hound dog—but the crowd in the Venus Room at Las Vegas's New Frontier Hotel on April 23, 1956, couldn't have been less shook up."

But while Vegas initially left Elvis cold—"An audience like this don't show their appreciation the same way," he said. "They're eating when I come on"—he would soon become synonymous with the city, two diamonds in the rough destined for the global spotlight.

Jesse Garon also knows how Elvis returned in 1963 to film his most famous movie, *Viva Las Vegas,* during which the King and his crew worked and played all over town: drag racing in the Sahara's parking lot, cooling off in the swimming pool at the Flamingo, hanging out at the Sands and Hoover Dam and Mount Charleston. And on May 1, 1967, he married Priscilla Beaulieu at the new Aladdin hotel and casino in Vegas, where fans would later line up to bask in the space where he and Priscilla said "I do."

When Garon pulls into town, he practically falls to his knees before the Elvis statue at the former International Hotel (later the Las Vegas Hilton and now the Westgate

Las Vegas Resort and Casino). The statue, prominently displayed in the Westgate hotel's lobby, is constructed of bronze and depicts a larger-than-life Elvis. He wears his famous jumpsuit, with his guitar hanging in front of him. In his left hand he raises a microphone as his right reaches out toward his adoring crowd. His open palm faces the floor as if to offer a sacrament to the endless supplicants who, like Jesse Garon, have come to pay homage to the King.

Elvis and Barbra Streisand are both booked to open MGM movie mogul Kirk Kerkorian's International Hotel in 1969. As a headliner, Elvis drives the crowd wild. Knowing a gold mine when he sees one, Colonel Parker books Elvis for a planned summer festival at the hotel and return engagements in February.

Soon, Elvis is earning $125,000 a week in Vegas, with regular engagements at the International. Between 1969 and 1976, Elvis performs more than six hundred sell-out shows at the resort, according to one Las Vegas newspaper. Other estimates put the number even higher, closer to eight hundred or nine hundred.

It is here, before the statue of the King, that Garon embarks upon becoming a new King of Las Vegas, ready to step into the blue suede shoes and lavish Las Vegas lifestyle left behind when Elvis died at his home in Memphis, Graceland, at age forty-two, on August 16, 1977.

Garon's first Las Vegas residence, a $405-a-month apartment "in the middle of crack alley," is certainly no Graceland. Once Garon's here, however, the King smiles down upon him. Mere weeks after his arrival, he gets wind of a local Elvis lookalike contest at a bar called Arizona Charlie's. No less than one of Elvis's former bandleaders will be the judge. The prize: five hundred dollars. Garon climbs into his jumpsuit, gels up his hair, practices his lopsided grin in the mirror, and lets the King's spirit embrace him.

He is now no longer merely Jesse Garon.

He is Elvis.

Before the judge, he pours his entire heart and soul into the song.

He ties for first place and splits the five-hundred-dollar prize.

Now, he's ready to audition for Legends in Concert at the old Imperial Palace Hotel and Casino and, wonder of wonders, lands a spot in the lineup.

Then the city gives him another gift: a friend introduces him to the queen of the Las Vegas quickie wedding, Charolette Richards, who invites him to her famed Little White Wedding Chapel to audition for a job. It is 1992, and the movie *Honeymoon in Vegas* has revived the King's spirit in the city after Nicolas Cage's character parachutes from an airplane with a squadron of Elvis lookalikes—called the Flying Elvi—and gets hitched in a Las Vegas wedding chapel.

For most people, the movie is entertainment.

For Garon, it's a calling.

"That really kicked off the Elvis impersonator wedding," he says.

By then, though, Elvis lookalikes are leading weddings

for couples all over town, some more cocky than truly called. "Some of them think they are the only ones entitled to impersonate the King," Garon says.

But Garon has an important ally in Ms. Charolette, the Wedding Queen of the West. "She took a likin' to me and I took a likin' to her," he says. "Charolette gave me my start and I made her a lot of money." Soon Garon is performing seven or eight Elvis-themed weddings a day.

Fifteen minutes per wedding at most. Collect the fee. And move on to the next couple.

Next, Garon becomes the first *ordained* Elvis-impersonating reverend. Up to that point, ordination required a license from the governor, who required applicants to be part of a church congregation. Under pressure from the ACLU, which claimed separation of church and state, the statute was thrown out.

Garon becomes an early beneficiary.

"We finally got to be an ordained minister," he says. "That means we can actually file paperwork, sign paperwork, and charge a little bit more money."

By then, full-fledged Elvis fever has returned to Las Vegas, with various auctions of the King's items—for which Garon "saved every penny" to buy an authentic pair of sunglasses that the King wore during his Las Vegas days.

The cost: five thousand dollars.

Now, wearing the King's clothes, staring out through the King's glasses, and driving a pink Cadillac worthy of the King, Garon finds further proof that he is in the right town at the right time.

It is the year 2000, and Garon is looking for a new home.

A real estate agent takes him to Bel Air Drive, which Garon knows ranks high in Elvis Presley Las Vegas lore. The storied street winds through Las Vegas Country Club, where Elvis supposedly put up his crew, called his Memphis Mafia, in several houses while he was performing at the nearby International Hotel. The street is also the address of the Regency Towers, a high-rise condominium complex, which has served as a second, third, or temporary home to a host of other Las Vegas performers: comedian Rodney Dangerfield, singer-actress Debbie Reynolds ("a sweetheart," Garon says), Jackson family royalty La Toya Jackson, and comedian George Carlin.

The Bel Air Drive homeowner who forever reigns supreme is, of course, Elvis, who didn't even live there (he had a major-league suite at the International). "But I was told he bought four houses on Bel Air Drive, and gave or lent them to his friends," says Garon.

Garon knows all the folklore of the Bel Air Drive houses, with their backyard hot tubs and swimming pools. In these houses "the boys would get away from everything, from the girls, from their wives," he says. "It was a place to call their own."

Soon, they arrive at the Regency Towers. The real estate agent and Garon ride the elevator to the twenty-second floor and walk up to a condo, where a letter on the front door stops Garon in his Elvis-obsessed tracks:

The front door is decorated with a giant stainless-steel *K*.

Surely, this signifies the King, he thinks.

Actually, Garon is told that the *K* stands for *Kerkorian*—the condo's original owner, Kirk Kerkorian, the mogul who built the International Hotel and hired Elvis Presley to perform in its showroom, and who also had a large home on Bel Air Drive.

To Garon, however, it's another sign from above.

In this condominium, Garon will enshrine the ideology of "we," representing both himself and his alter ego in all their Las Vegas glory. First, he installs an Elvis-themed pinball machine. Then, a purple-leather-tufted throne worthy of the King. As Garon's own fame grows, he frames *Time* and *Fortune* magazine covers of himself as Elvis, along with an interior shot in *Playgirl* in which he posed nude with a painted-on Elvis jumpsuit. "We were the first Elvis impersonator to be in *Playgirl,* but we did it all for charity. Because if Elvis fans thought we were degrading his image in any way, man, they would eat me up. We were also the first to have a key to the city." The key was given to him by former mayor Oscar Goodman, who regularly rides in parades alongside his wife, current Vegas mayor Carolyn Goodman, with Garon at the wheel of his pink Cadillac.

But the ultimate testimonial is Garon's two Elvis closets, which store endless apparel from various episodes of

Elvis's life—which Garon imitates to startling perfection once he pulls on each costume. "We do all three: the young Elvis; the comeback Elvis, with the black leather; and then, of course, the jumpsuit Elvis."

Garon's residence also stands as a monument to the Las Vegas life of Elvis Presley, after the closing of the city's Elvis museum. Opened in November 1999, the Elvis-a-Rama Museum displayed local collector Chris Davidson's stash of more than two thousand pieces of Elvis memorabilia and an eighty-five-foot-long mural depicting the King's life and career. The museum was a vehicle for Davidson to show off his collection. But in 2004, thieves drove a stolen tow truck through the museum's back door, smashing three display cases and escaping with loot worth more than three hundred thousand dollars: Elvis's 1953 high school ring, solid gold ID bracelet and other precious jewelry, 1955 Hamilton wristwatch, and Las Vegas Hilton logo scarf.

ALL SHOOK UP: "THE KING'S" JEWELS STOLEN FROM LAS VEGAS ELVIS-A-RAMA MUSEUM announces the FBI's pun-filled public notice about the burglary. "Needless to say, fans are 'Crying in the Chapel.' The museum security staff says, 'I Got Stung.' 'Suspicious Minds' everywhere say it's 'Too Much.'"

More than a year and a half later, Elvis rises up in fury in the body of Duke Adams, a sixty-two-year-old local Elvis impersonator. While Adams waits in line at a pharmacy one day, a stranger, perhaps noticing the resemblance between Duke and the King, offers Adams a sweetheart deal on "items once owned by Elvis, including jewelry, clothing and the king's revolver," according to one account. Luckily, Adams remembers reading about the robbery and asks the thief to come by his office the next day—where the cops await. In 2006, Elvis Presley Enterprises, Inc., of Memphis, acquires what's left of the Las Vegas museum and promptly closes it.

The museum is gone, but for Garon, his home remains sacred ground in the adoration of the King.

In his condo, Garon begins his transformation. "The whole process takes about an hour," he says. First, the music: Elvis's greatest hits. Then the shower, to wash away traces of normalcy, along with the grit and grime. ("Nobody likes a stinky Elvis.") Then, the makeup, the hair and the lip, curled just right. He checks his look in a giant ornate mirror, underneath a vast crystal chandelier.

The transformation is startling.

Now, he is no longer a mere mortal, trying to make a living in Las Vegas.

Now, he is an embodiment of the King. And Las Vegas stands ready to pay homage.

Garon climbs into his pink 1960 Cadillac convertible and rolls out onto South Las Vegas Boulevard. In his chariot, Garon and his alter ego entertain the Elvis-needy multitudes in parades, weddings, and just plain sightings.

"I know he had Cadillacs," Garon says. "I just don't know if he had a 1960 pink Cadillac. But this is a classic that you would definitely think that Elvis *would* drive." (When the top is down, Garon "insists his Elvis hair is bulletproof up to 75 mph," notes *The Drive* magazine in a 2015 profile.)

Maybe he is driving to a wedding—in one year alone he performed ceremonies for six hundred fifty couples—or maybe he's heading over to the WELCOME TO FABULOUS LAS VEGAS sign, where hotly competitive Elvis impersonators in jumpsuits, black wigs, and sunglasses vie for the attention of tourists willing to pay to pose with them by the sign or to stroll the Strip with them as they sing the King's songs. Or maybe he'll attend a Las Vegas Elvis show. Though Cirque du Soleil's Elvis-themed show at the Aria Resort and Casino, *Viva Elvis,* has closed, Garon notes that "Planet Hollywood has *All Shook Up* and the Tropicana used to have an Elvis performance in the Legends show, which gave me my start."

Sometimes, Elvis even falls from the Vegas sky via the ten-member troupe of Elvis impersonators, the Flying Elvi first depicted in the movie *Honeymoon in Vegas,* who periodically parachute out of planes in wigs and full costume.

Elvis is in the air in Las Vegas, and on the ground, too. For a fee, Garon and his alter ego will take visitors on a tour through the Las Vegas landmarks where Elvis performed and partied, the restaurants and bars where Garon is treated like, well, a King.

Sometimes, he'll take visitors to the casino in the old International to conjure the torrid spirit of the manager who originally brought Elvis to Sin City, Colonel Tom Parker, who, unlike Elvis, never really left Las Vegas. According to legend, Colonel Parker continued gambling at the hotel, surrounded by the legacy he helped to create, until the day he died.

Elvis lives on, not only in the movies, music, and memories he left behind, but in the body of what the *Las Vegas Review-Journal* called the city's "go-to Elvis impressionist."

"I'll be honest, it can get tiring," Garon says of the city that expects him to be Elvis all the time. After more than three decades here, he sometimes forgets where Elvis ends and Garon begins. Once, he took three months off, dyed his hair blond, and did the things only Garon would do. But ultimately, he returned to his split personality and the paycheck and fame that it brings. "There's nothing like it, man. It's a good life. I have been very lucky. I get to do what I always wanted to do, and I haven't worked a day in my life."

Chapter 19

THE HABITAT OF
THE WHALES

THE COSMOPOLITAN RESERVE

THE CHOSEN HAVE been picked up in their hometown. Maybe it's Miami or Milwaukee, Macau or somewhere in the Middle East. Again, it doesn't matter where they're from, only where they're going. Because the moment they touch down in Las Vegas, either by commercial airline, their own plane, or one sent by the resort, the city begins throwing itself at their feet.

They are the breed of gambler Vegas bows to, the elusive individual whom every major hotel and casino dispatches emissaries around the globe to find, befriend, and seduce. The rarest of the rare, that minuscule percentage of humanity having the wherewithal—and the willingness—to gamble as much as a million dollars over a three-day weekend.

They are, in Vegas parlance, whales.

Which is why they are in this long black limo, being ferried to a place where the word *no* does not exist, where everything—the grandest suites, the greatest food, the finest spirits, whatever their whim in entertainment—comes absolutely free of charge. No matter what, Vegas has done its exhaustive research. Vegas knows *everything* about them. And their every wish is Vegas's command.

The limo rolls along, its windows so dark that the blazing neon of the Strip outside is barely visible. The tourists in T-shirts and flip-flops walk by, carrying their cocktails and slot machine coinage, oblivious to where the whales are going, a secret room within a secret world, a secret side of Vegas they'll never see—the megasuites on the very top five floors of the Cosmopolitan hotel and its even more exclusive private gambling salon: the Reserve.

The limo comes to a rest beneath a vast porte cochere, a large, clean, artfully lit, secluded arrival point where even the most privacy-obsessed Las Vegas legends—Elvis, Michael Jackson, Howard Hughes—would've felt right at home. As soon as the car doors swing open, an army descends: butlers, luggage handlers, stern security sentries wearing earpieces. Managers in business suits pass out business cards, while bellhops lug the Vuitton, Goyard, and Prada luggage, and butlers show the way to a private elevator.

Most whales are familiar with the other leading Las Vegas hotels, their opulent rooms and suites seeming merely to serve as blasting pads for the extravaganza down below. As the city's maestro Steve Wynn used to say on his in-house TV ads at the Mirage, "Hey, what are you doing in your room?"

But when they ascend to the Cosmopolitan's seventy-fifth floor, guided by the butlers to their suite, and those grand double doors swing open, it's almost impossible not to gasp. It's *huge,* and every inch of its thirty-five hundred square feet—as big a luxurious residence as is found in any major city—has been carefully planned to reflect the best by noted New York–based interior designer Daun Curry. There are two bedrooms, gigantic bathrooms and dressing areas, a white marble bathtub as big and deep as a pontoon boat, a kitchen, and something akin to a beauty salon, with an industrial-sized barber chair, shampoo basin, and sauna—more than enough space for family, paramours, and entourage. Its soaring windows look out upon a three-hundred-sixty-degree view of the Strip. Everything is oversized, but in some ways intimate: the opaque glass and gold leaf bar stocked with French wines and champagnes; the gargantuan Great Room, with its fifteen-foot ceilings, dining area, and entertainment center; the wraparound balconies, where two massive stone French Bulldogs, named Cowboy and Shelby, stare out on nothing less than the entirety of Las Vegas, from the Strip to the mountains.

Butlers unpack bags, some whisking away clothing to be pressed, while other attendants pour Taittinger Comtes de Champagne and other spirits. Various managers and factotums arrive to meet and greet as the desert sun slants into the suite, illuminating the fine art, gold leaf, mosaic tile walls, and leather banquettes and making the guest, for a split second, want to relax and indulge, take a long bath in that monstrous marble tub and kick back.

But wait. *What are you doing in your room?* This is, after all, the Cosmopolitan, the coolest hotel on the Strip. The hotel whose advertisements have sold it as "Just the Right Amount of Wrong," featuring hunky bare-legged bellmen delivering luggage to the hipsters and supermodels sprawling half naked on luxurious bed linens. A resort straight out of all those Vegas party movies, the Cosmopolitan opened in 2010 with a three-day party featuring celebrity guests entertained by the likes of Jay-Z and Coldplay. From there, the Cosmo continued to ratchet up the action, becoming, according to *Vegas* magazine, "the most interesting, innovative, youth-quaking enterprise on the Vegas Strip."

People say the only problem was that the party wasn't financially sustainable. "Deutsche Bank—which financed it first as a condominium tower (and got buried to the tune of an impossible-to-recoup $4.3 billion) and later as a casino—got stuck owning a gaming business it never wanted," *Vegas* reported. The Cosmopolitan had to find new ways to not only survive, but thrive.

At the top of the Cosmopolitan sits Bill McBeath, the Cosmopolitan's president and CEO from December 2014 to May 2022, who established the Reserve during his tenure at the new resort.

A serious, square-jawed Vegas veteran, he spent fifteen years working with Steve Wynn, first as CEO of Wynn's Treasure Island and then as president and COO of the Mirage and Bellagio resorts. McBeath is a "gambler's gambler," according to *Cigar Aficionado,* for whom wagering is both "hobby and passion." He's also an expert in what he calls "the math" of gaming, and how "every customer is a profit and loss silo."

In late 2014, shortly after the Blackstone Group purchased the Cosmopolitan from Germany's Deutsche Bank for $1.73 billion, the American private equity colossus hired McBeath from CityCenter (the sprawling hotel and casino complex that includes the Aria Resort and Casino and the Waldorf Astoria) to lead a reinvention. If Deutsche Bank was reluctant when it came to high-end gambling, as McBeath likes to say, he certainly wasn't. He invested his own money in the hotel, which, on first look, certainly couldn't be seen as a winner. The fabulously hip, cutting-edge monolith with a one-hundred-thousand-square-foot casino was committing a cardinal sin in the town that pushes everything to the limit: the Cosmopolitan was in possession of an underplayed hand.

"There is a tremendous amount of volatility in the high end," McBeath says. "The math obviously is designed to be in the house's favor." But the Cosmopolitan of old? "It struggled to attract high-end play. I recognized that it didn't have all of the amenities and assets to be competitive in the marketplace."

The Cosmopolitan had 3,005 rooms but only *four* premium suites, which meant the whales were migrating to other properties. Almost all of the major resorts had been wisely investing in gargantuan suites and VIP wings and towers for whale-style living and creating lavish private gambling salons for whale-sized play.

What did the Cosmopolitan have that the other megahotels didn't?

Space.

Sixty thousand square feet of empty space, says McBeath. "I was like, 'Oh, my gosh, this is the fifty-yard line of the Las Vegas Strip on top of the highest building with three-hundred-and-sixty-degree views of the valley with these incredible balconies.'" All of which stood...*empty!?*

Within ten months, twenty-one Boulevard Penthouses were created on the Cosmopolitan's top five floors.

But suites are for sleeping, and McBeath knew he needed something more, something else to maximize the hotel's profit center and turn the Cosmopolitan into a mint. He needed to create a habitat for the whales.

In the parlance of the new Las Vegas, he needed to

create private gaming, which would include a larger, high-limit, multiroom salon called the Talon Club. And, for the highest-limit, invitation-only players, the Reserve.

If he built it, McBeath knew, the whales would come.

Vegas didn't create private gaming, but as Vegas always does, it pushed the concept to the limit. "Our international sales and marketing team"—a stalwart team that scours the world for whales—"said, Mr. So-and-So would like to come but there's no private gaming," says McBeath.

Private gaming serves what McBeath calls "the very, very super-high-end and discerning customer" who doesn't feel comfortable being ogled by the masses in the public casino while pushing out a quarter million or so in chips onto the table and letting it ride.

This is where the whale hunters come in. Each resort and casino dispatches emissaries around the world to net the whales and bring them to Las Vegas.

Only a few thousand individuals worldwide qualify to gamble at this stratospheric level. These players don't run in packs; they have to be caught one at a time. "It's the type of person who says, 'I don't want a Ferrari and I don't want to jump out of an airplane,'" says a member of the Cosmopolitan's international marketing team. "They get a rush from gambling."

They have one other thing in common.

"Almost unlimited wealth," he says.

Now the whale, dutifully checked into the suite, is ready to do what they came to Las Vegas to do.

The whale makes a call, gives their name, and doesn't have to say another word.

Vegas already *knows*.

A VIP host or other casino executive answers the phone and says one word: yes. Everything immediately slips into gear. An "all hands on deck" alert goes out to a dozen or more individuals, all receiving the three words they've been waiting for the host to say:

"Activate the Reserve."

A mad rush of butlers, dealers, credit personnel, pit bosses, and hotel executives, fluent in the language and habits of the whale, heads to the seventy-first floor and into the Reserve. The cameras in the ceiling are immediately operational—viewed by unseen but all-knowing eyes from both Cosmopolitan security and the Nevada Gaming Commission. Forms are completed and credit checked to satisfy gaming commission regulations. And the credit desk is immediately open and ready to receive.

Within forty-five minutes, tops, the Reserve is ready for the arrival of the whale.

It could be morning. Or midnight. The whale might be dressed in a T-shirt. Or a tuxedo. One whale from the Far East even arrives in his pajamas. Attire doesn't matter. It's what's in the wallet that counts: a commitment to gamble as much as a million dollars. They might have that money as a line of credit, in a suitcase, or even—as one gambler did—in hundred-dollar bills in a paper sack.

The gambler exits the elevator on the seventy-first floor and walks through a portal and up to a door marked THE RESERVE, every move being observed by a coterie of cameras. A VIP envoy punches a button that communicates with hotel surveillance. Once the gambler is inspected and approved, a buzzer sounds, the door swings open, and the whale enters the ultimate den of Roll 'Em. Designed by Adam Tihany, the Reserve is twenty-three hundred square feet of elegance, with windows providing the same ethereal view to Vegas eternity as the suites. Two smartly attired twin gambling salons—tables set with the games of choice, baccarat being the most popular here—adjoin a bar and reception area.

It feels like a London gentlemen's club from the 1920s—or something that might've been found on the *Titanic*, a glorious ship able to deliver its passengers to heaven or hell on the same starry night.

Dealers, managers, and more immediately descend, greeting, coddling, preparing the whale for the moment at hand. The devoted butler and new best friend stands behind the bar, a wonder of rare woods, polished steel, and gleaming bottles and goblets, offering the world.

There are menus available from any of the Cosmopolitan's array of restaurants, from which food will be swiftly delivered and served. In the mood for designer spaghetti from a landmark New York City Italian emporium? Sushi and New Age Asian American fare? A tomahawk bone-in rib eye? Paella? Or a 4 a.m. breakfast? One word, or nod, and the food will magically appear.

The gambler will be here for a while. Day might stretch into night and then day again. But first, cocktails. The solicitous butler offers a limitless choice. Perhaps a glass of M or Reflexion, top scotches from Macallan, the venerable Highland producer of single-malt whiskeys. Or the rarest of the rare, Rémy Martin Louis XIII Black Pearl Cognac—which starts at thirty-nine thousand a bottle, but is absolutely free to whales.

It's a quick walk into one of the two gaming salons, where the dealers look like they've been waiting forever, bidding good days or good evenings in the gambler's native tongue: English, Arabic, French, Italian, Spanish, Mandarin, Cantonese...And then the gambler takes a seat, pushes the chips out on the table, prays to a deity, and places a bet.

Chapter 20

THE HUSTLER

THE WILD SIDE OF TOWN

AFTER MIDNIGHT, ANOTHER Las Vegas dawns.

The neon lights of infinite gentlemen's clubs are blazing, along with infinite gentlemen flocking to these clubs in search of frolic and fun.

Midnight is when Sam checks in for his eight-hour shift. The general manager of a huge gentlemen's club in a town filled with them, Sam oversees as many as two hundred dancers and wall-to-wall crowds. The club has multiple bars, stages, and private rooms. There are special events and themed lunch and dinner menus. A fleet of limos and SUVs ferries the eager multitudes to its doors without charge. And it's open twenty-four hours a day, three hundred sixty-five days a year.

"But there's no point in rushing because everything's

open twenty-four seven," Sam says. "The locals in Las Vegas, we go out at midnight." Between midnight and 4 a.m., he says, is when "the bulk of our people come in."

A veteran of the Las Vegas night, Sam began as a limo driver before graduating to gentlemen's clubs. Now, as a general manager, he has seen it all—and knows it all—and what he knows most is this: "Everything in Las Vegas revolves around money."

"Because there's so many ways to make money in Vegas," he says, and then pauses. There is something that goes hand in hand with the jackpot: "Appearances. No matter where you go in Vegas, everyone is attractive. From the front desk at the hotel to the valet parkers out front. I'm in my forties but I look like I'm in my thirties. Because you live a different life out here."

To live the Vegas dream, you have to look the part. In Vegas, the tabernacle of worship is the gym. "And the wellness clinic," says Sam. "Employers here want people to be attractive, pretty, outgoing. Hence the day-pool parties in the summertime. The nightclubs here are taking in millions upon millions of dollars. We did a renovation of our club for a couple million. We're talking thirty-million-dollar buildings."

His meaning is clear: beautiful people are required to staff the beautiful buildings.

Especially when they are taking their clothes off.

"Because you're selling fantasy," Sam continues. "The fantasy of the Vegas experience. Coming to town and getting the girl. Or winning the jackpot. Or just pretending to be someone you're not."

Sam is an expert on the Las Vegas fantasy, which cuts both good and bad. It can be good, in the way the city can enrich the poor and heal the infirm. Or it can be bad, in the way Vegas can suck a visitor dry.

"In a strip club, everyone is trying to take advantage of everyone else," Sam says. "Every girl is trying to get as much money as she can from the guy, and every guy is trying to see how much he can do and how much he can get from the woman. As the staff you're in the middle: 'Did you take his money? Give it back.' And, 'Sir, prostitution is illegal in this town.'

"Everybody thinks prostitution is legal in Las Vegas because they've seen it portrayed that way on television. But it's illegal. Even though, if you go to any casino and walk by the center bar and there's a girl there by herself, chances are she's a prostitute."

In a prime corner of one of the mainstream high-end resort casinos, beneath the all-seeing eyes in the sky, a young woman, Dixie, sits at a slot machine. She's not playing—she's working. She wears a barely-there blouse paired with designer jeans, stiletto heels, and a come-hither smile directed at the endless parade of men passing by.

It doesn't take long for one of them to proposition her.

"What's a guy like me gotta do to get some time with a girl like you?" he asks.

"Well," Dixie replies in her sweet Southern drawl, "I'm sure we could figure something out."

The man awaits an answer.

She throws out a number. "One thousand dollars."

Dixie doesn't typically advertise her wares in the resorts on Las Vegas Boulevard. She walks a different street: the information superhighway, where she is open for business twenty-four seven via escort ads and social media. "I'm fully exposing myself on the internet," she says. "Anybody can find me there, if you know my name or my number."

Dixie is a foot soldier in the vast army of individuals who ply their trade in the city, where prostitution is illegal but ever present, from the streetwalkers hustling on the Strip to the ladies of the evening strolling through the casinos to the porn stars, models, A-list exotic dancers, and high-priced professionals who are ferried by limousine to the city's richest enclaves, where they entertain clients behind doors firmly closed to the public.

The calls come at all hours.

Needy. Lonely. Amorous. Winners and losers. High rollers and low. Minnows and whales. All seeking the same thing.

Not just sex.

Companionship disguised as sex.

When Dixie's phone lights up with a text, email, or DM, she knows it's showtime. Her network, as she calls it, has netted her another client, hopefully a whale.

The network is more than just internet ads and Instagram accounts. It's a web of strategically placed individuals with whom Dixie and other high-end professionals are deeply entwined: an array that, she says, includes nightclub personnel and limo drivers and personal butlers at the premier accommodations exclusive to the high-rolling gamblers and visiting celebrities. These are the matchmakers of Las Vegas, says Dixie, the ones who pair men at play with women at work; the ones who make it easier for women like Dixie to find top-tier clients. "They take half the work out of it for you," she says.

Most of these individuals insist that it doesn't happen that way. Prostitution is illegal, they point out, and butlers and hosts and other employees don't want to risk losing good jobs. But Dixie has her own personal experience in the matter, and she isn't afraid to talk about it.

When an emissary calls from one of the city's most exclusive resorts, Dixie says, she quickly does the math. "You have to gamble a quarter million dollars to even stay there," she says. "You have your own butler. And if the butler is smart, he'll have a few contacts for lovely ladies he can call when his patron is lonely" and in need of some comfort after suffering a losing streak, or celebrating a win.

"That's when the butler says, 'Let me call my friend,'" Dixie says. "And he calls me and says, 'Hey, I've got a guy who just lost a quarter million and he wants a lady for the night.' And I say, 'Okay, cool. Tell him it's five thousand dollars.'" She knows that's pocket change for a high roller.

And, she adds, the butler knows she'll tip him 20 percent of the five grand.

Within minutes, Dixie is dressed and on her way to the rendezvous. It's a system that works to everyone's benefit, she says. "If you grease the wheels," she says, "then everybody wants to participate."

It happens almost every day, from dusk to dawn and every hour in between. Sometimes Dixie takes her own car. Sometimes she's picked up by a rideshare or limo driver. But once she arrives, it's usually the same. "The over-the-top luxury I've been exposed to in this city is like no other place in the world," Dixie says. "Four-bedroom accommodations. Fountain in the foyer. Private pool and hot tub. Tapestries that cost more than my home. Anything that money can buy."

Inside the VIP accommodation is a man more than willing to pay by the hour, day, night, week, month, or lifetime for a woman who can make him feel alive and powerful—more than the dice, the cards, the five-star restaurants, or the backstage passes—and, however fleetingly, loved.

"I'm in the higher end," says another escort, Mia. "Eight thousand dollars for twelve hours. I just booked a week for fifty thousand dollars. I don't do hour appointments. It's all about the experience for me. From start to finish. I'm a travel companion, a girlfriend experience. And I'm certified as a love, sex, and relationship coach. So I'm a licensed therapist, too."

Men—and frequently couples—take women like Mia

everywhere: by limo, via commercial and private air, by cruise ship and superyacht. "I've gone on luxury African safaris, to the Swiss Alps, France, Germany, China, Singapore, Korea," she says. "People call me a modern-day geisha."

She's introduced as a friend or work colleague and once, accompanying a client to the floor of the New York Stock Exchange, "as a PR representative." No one but her client knows she's a working girl, whose luggage is packed with designer clothing and "a whole lot of sex toys, which has made many a TSA officer's day when they see the toys over their security scanners."

Women like Mia can have hundreds of thousands of followers on social media sites like Instagram, but their talent is making each client feel as if they are there for him alone. "Everybody wants to feel loved, wanted, seen. 'I exist!'" says Mia. "'So I'm going to hire a girl to make me feel like that for a while.'"

Although the clients arrive in a variety of ways, each is carefully vetted to keep the women safe. If they can't offer verifiable identification, they won't get any further than the initial contact.

This year, Mia could earn half a million dollars. "I know girls who make eighty thousand to one hundred thousand dollars a month," she says.

And she hopes to keep working. "We all work together to keep the city moving as a Vegas experience. Because what is Las Vegas without sex?"

♣

Selling sex is big business in Las Vegas. From the lamp-post flyers on the Strip to the galaxy of online ads, sex is the commodity that earned Vegas its nickname, Sin City. The city's growth is due, in large part, to its sex industry. It took off in 1931, when women of the night began moving to the area in droves to keep pace with the influx of labor-ers constructing the Hoover Dam, some fifty miles away. While prostitution (and serving liquor) were crimes in Boulder City, the town erected to serve the dam's workers, they were legal at that time in Las Vegas, which already had its own red-light district, called Block 16. Thus, it can be said that Las Vegas was born not of cards, but of call girls.

Vegas cracked down on Block 16 in 1941. Decades later, as legalized brothels sprang up across Nevada, Las Vegas leaders persuaded the state legislature to keep pros-titution illegal in the state's big cities. But the sex industry, from escorting to exotic dancing, continues to proliferate. By 2012, some twelve thousand exotic dancers were regis-tered in Vegas, according to one study, with an estimated twenty-five hundred working on any given night in the city's strip clubs. "Advertisements for escort services are everywhere in Las Vegas: on billboards, inside taxicabs... and on handbills available up and down the strip," accord-ing to Jack Sheehan's book *Skin City: Uncovering the Las Vegas Sex Industry*. In 2009, the *Las Vegas Review-Journal* published an article called WORKING GIRLS, featuring police mug shots of the city's "50 most prolific prostitutes," one of whom had been arrested eighteen times in a single year.

Over the years there have been attempts to legalize prostitution in the city. In 2003, mayor Oscar Goodman unsuccessfully pushed for establishing a red-light district downtown. "Anybody who thinks prostitution isn't taking place in Las Vegas hotel rooms and back alleys is willfully ignorant," he says. "I thought it was deserving of rational, unbiased discussion. But because of the conservative nature of the constituency, they didn't even want to talk about it." But the profession endures because of the money.

Exotic dancing can be so lucrative that a money management course was once conducted by a former dancer named Sabrina Markey "as part of her Strippers 101 curriculum," Sheehan writes in *Skin City*, quoting Ms. Markey: "Exotic dancers kept many Las Vegas retail stores afloat following the recession brought on by 9/11. If there's one thing these girls do better than dance, it's shop."

Dancing in a strip club is what first brought Dixie to Vegas. She started off dancing in Atlanta, where she grew up. One night when she was off work, she went out clubbing, and was approached on the dance floor by what she calls a "highly educated Southern gentleman." He told her that he worked in the entertainment industry. He promised to "take me out of the club life," she recalls. "That was the dream he sold me. He swept me off my feet."

They began dating, and soon she was traveling first class with him all over the world, staying in the most expensive hotels, rubbing elbows with celebrities, experiencing the best of everything. She soon realized that the entertainment industry was only one of her boyfriend's business endeavors. His work, she came to realize, encompassed "the things of the night. All things promiscuous, all things taboo."

After six months of traveling, there was only one place left for them to go—to what Dixie calls "the mecca of adult entertainment." As their plane banked in the dark desert sky over Las Vegas and the immense castles along the Strip came into view, Dixie had one thought: *I'm home.*

For a while, she and her Southern prince continued to live the dream. They stayed in the "swankiest suites on the Strip," dined in the best restaurants, attended the all-star concerts. But it wasn't long before his money disappeared, and along with it, her dream of escaping the strip club life. "I've given you a luxury life for six months, and I've fallen on hard times," her boyfriend told her. "I need you to pick up the slack."

"We had run through all of his money, so now it was kind of all on me," Dixie says. "That's when I learned how to hustle."

Which is how she found herself returning to her old profession. One afternoon Dixie pulled out an old costume and auditioned at one of Las Vegas's supersize gentlemen's clubs.

Walking in, Dixie was overwhelmed. The club is more stadium than strip club: sprawling across thousands of square feet, it features copious bars, stages, and VIP rooms for the movie stars and celebrity athletes and high rollers who like to party in private. Dixie felt a twinge of fear. "There were three hundred women clocked in on any given night," she says. "The most gorgeous women from all over the world—Australia, London, Thailand, you name it. Which is overwhelming as hell for a little small-town girl. I was out of my element."

Then her Southern pride kicked in. *I'm an outstanding performer from Atlanta,* she told herself. *We breed some of the best dancers in the country!* Removing her clothes to expose her costume—essentially a bra and a G-string—she strutted onto one of the club's secondary stages, removed her top, and began dancing. She had one chance at a job—one song, one routine. The manager in charge of the club's auditions was watching, along with the afternoon crowd, judging whether Dixie was worthy of joining the club's all-star lineup.

She nailed it.

Hired on the spot, she reported for duty that very evening. Before hitting the stage, she was advised of the ground rules. Show up at 8 p.m. Clock in upon arrival and pay your approximately hundred-dollar fee—the club's cut of her nightly earnings. No touching the patrons, no going home with them, no soliciting sex. Everything she earned, after tipping out the various support personnel, was hers to keep. She could clock out whenever she wanted, which for Dixie meant the moment she earned her nightly net of one thousand dollars.

Before long, Dixie had enough cash to leave the boyfriend and get her own place. To make a little more money on the side, she asked a girlfriend who was working as an escort to teach her the ropes. She learned some of the jargon: *in calls,* for example, meant hosting a client in her apartment, and *out calls* meant going to meet him at his hotel.

The income was decent, but not enough to quit her job at the gentlemen's club. Until one night, when Dixie and her friend decided to attend the Mixed Martial Arts Awards at the Hard Rock Hotel. There, among the celebrity crowd, was a bona fide TV star who took one look at Dixie and was instantly, well…

"Infatuated," she says. "A month later he calls me out of the blue. It was his birthday." Dixie was so surprised, she didn't know what to do. So she decided to wing it—making naughty small talk, sending him sexy photos, letting him lead the way.

The flirting went on for weeks. Then one day, there was a knock on her door. A FedEx messenger handed her a package. Inside was five thousand dollars in cold, hard cash.

What did she have to do for the money? Pretty much anything the TV star wanted in terms of "companionship." But five thousand dollars was just the start. "He became what one would call a sugar daddy for a number of years for me," she says. "He figured out that it's not necessary to go to a strip club and find the golden ticket. There were other ways to go about it. And I figured out how to be a sugar baby." Which she defines as "a young female who receives some type of monetary reward for her companionship." At long last she was able to leave the strip club life behind. Now she was in business for herself.

Which, Dixie discovered, requires knowing *everything* about the Las Vegas scene. She learned how not to be awestruck by celebrity, because "you see celebrities here all the time." She learned how to gamble, because that's what the clients do. She learned how to speak with anyone about pretty much anything, because the preamble is as important as what follows. She learned how to manage her money, and manage her time, and screen out the creeps.

"How do I screen them? I give them options on what they can provide to verify that they have good intentions for me. A guy who sends me his ID or his LinkedIn information or his Facebook, he's probably not going to harm me. That eliminates people with bad intentions, showing me verification of your profession. I'm not going to risk getting raped or murdered or dismembered and thrown in the desert."

Most of all, Dixie learned not to "freelance"—not to sell herself in public places.

"No sir! No sir! *Never.*"

Which she learned the hard way, as she sat by the slot machine at the casino that evening.

She was out freelancing that day. Dressed "real fashionable. Edgy. *Fashionably* edgy. But obviously looking available."

The outfit works, like it always does. As the man propositions her in the casino, she adds up his attributes, her mind faster than any calculator: "nice shoes, nice belt, clean cut, well put together." A good bet for a quick grand.

So she names her price: one thousand dollars.

"Sold," he says.

But instead of whisking her off to a high-roller suite, or even the back seat of his car, he pauses. That's when Dixie feels a hand on her shoulder. She turns around to find an undercover detective flashing his badge.

"You're under arrest, sugar," he tells her.

"For what?" she asks.

"For soliciting prostitution."

"That was my first lesson," observes Dixie. "My second lesson came years later. Same casino. It's like I got a bad omen there or something. I spoke to the wrong person for too long. Honestly, that's what I was arrested for. When he mentioned sex for money, I declined. But he did mention it, and in the state of Nevada, the fact that I continued the conversation was enough to get arrested for soliciting. Undercovers are really big out here. They're serious about cracking down on prostitution. So twice I got popped for the same thing—talking."

As the two cops arrest her by the slot machines, she tries to protest. "I'm not soliciting prostitution," she tells them.

"You can explain that to the judge," they shoot back. "Don't give us any headache and this can go real smooth."

They walk her through the casino and wait until they're out of the public eye to put the cuffs on her, which taught her an unforgettable legal lesson about soliciting in Las Vegas.

"If you agree to receive money in exchange for any kind of sexual act, you're guilty," she says.

Chapter 21

HERE COMES THE SUN

CIRCA RESORT AND CASINO, AND THE WYNN

JUST AFTER MIDNIGHT in the monumental Circa Resort and Casino, the newest major resort and casino to open in downtown Las Vegas in forty years, the resort's co-owner holds an impromptu meeting with several of his executives at Mega Bar.

"Ha ha, I'm at Mega Bar," Derek Stevens texts shortly before midnight. Stevens, a big man in a blue sportscoat, is a Vegas sensation, a throwback in an age of corporate ownership to the days when a single figurehead stamped his personality on a resort—in his case, the first adults-only casino resort: the $1 billion, 35-story, 777-room Circa Resort and Casino. It was designed around the things the fifty-five-year-old Stevens, who is from Detroit, loves, including maximizing the midnight hour.

True to Stevens's bigger-is-better philosophy, Mega Bar is no mere bar. At one hundred sixty-five feet, it's the longest bar in Nevada, and Stevens sits squarely at its center, with members of his executive team and staff around him as the music blares, the wheels spin, and go-go-dancing dealers dance on tables.

Around Stevens sit a receptionist, a VIP host, one of Circa's builders, and others—all equal with the boss at the bar.

"Where else are you going to meet the owner of a major Las Vegas resort in a bar at midnight?" says one.

"Work hard, play hard," says Stevens. "I don't drink Monday, Tuesday, Wednesday, only Thursday, Friday, Saturday."

It's a Friday, so he's drinking and greeting his fellow celebrants, all of whom are as in love with the town as Stevens, who attended the riotous 1993 boxing match between Evander Holyfield and Riddick Bowe at Caesars Palace, in which the parachutist James "Fan Man" Miller flew into the arena, crashed his paraglider into the side of the boxing ring, "and completely changed the momentum of the fight," says Stevens, who had, at that moment, already decided that someday, some way, he would make his home here.

In 2008, after buying the Las Vegas 51s minor league baseball team (now the Aviators), Derek Stevens and his younger brother, Greg, bought into the downtown Golden Gate Hotel and Casino, eventually becoming majority owners. A succession of resorts, casinos, and other enterprises followed—many stoked by ideas hatched at bars like Mega Bar in Circa and in Stevens's previous Vegas resorts, where he and his team devised some of their best ideas. "We come up with a lot of marketing ideas late at night," he says.

Like when rapper Kanye West tweeted in 2016 that he was fifty-three million dollars in debt and suggested Facebook founder Mark Zuckerberg invest a billion in his "ideas," and Stevens tweeted back that if Kanye performed in his Downtown Las Vegas Events Center, he'd keep only the beverage revenue and let the rapper keep the box office take. Or when Stevens released a video on YouTube of an executive directors' board meeting at his downtown hotel and casino, the D Las Vegas, in which he and his team lounged over cocktails in a boardroom filled with burlesque dancers (male and female), jugglers, and Coney D, a costumed hot dog mascot.

"He just loves the people," one Circa executive says of Stevens. "It's a pretty normal night. He sits here, greets the customers, and talks to everybody who wants to talk. Very approachable."

"I'm not sure what he's drinking," someone adds. "He's normally a Captain Morgan and Diet Coke guy."

Tonight it's Jack Daniels and Coke, Marlboros, and a prime seat at Mega Bar.

"We targeted Circa to people who are enthusiastic for life, young at heart," says Stevens. "I've always said that we have to be honored when someone from, say, Michigan, Georgia, or Ohio comes and gives us forty-eight or seventy-two hours of their life. We have to be cognizant that a lot went into their showing up. Their trip started when they coordinated their flights or flew in the grandparents to watch the kids. And arranged for junior's soccer and baseball practices and their daughter's this and that."

He stares out at the nonstop action swirling around him.

"We have the responsibility to give them the time of their life," he says. "An experience that you can't get on Main Street USA.

"There's not a lot of consultants here," he adds. "It's, well, myself.

"I like betting on sports," he continues. "My wife likes going to swimming pools. And when I've got big bets on Sundays and we're out at a pool somewhere and I've got eight games going, well…Me and my buddies always said, 'Boy! If we ever have a chance to build a great outdoor venue we're gonna build one that gives us the ability to watch all the games at once.'"

The result is something called Stadium Swim.

"People said, 'So you're gonna build the best pool in downtown Las Vegas.' I said, 'Wrong and wrong. I'm not building a pool. I'm building a Stadium Swim. The world's first outdoor aqua-theater watch party. It's not just a pool. It's a venue. An attraction for all of Las Vegas.'"

Stadium Swim is an extravagant rooftop pool complex, which Circa's website not-so-humbly calls "the best pool in history," accessible by "the longest escalator in the state of Nevada," leading to the resort's fourth and fifth floor, where six massive pools are open to the sky on three levels beneath a mammoth one-hundred-forty-three-foot screen, showing a multitude of sporting events. Up to four thousand guests a day pay fees ranging from twenty dollars to as much as ten thousand dollars, at certain times of the year, for an "owner's suite," which accommodates up to twenty-five guests.

"Then, Circa Sports," Stevens says, referring to what is billed as "the largest betting experience in the world," a three-level sports betting theater where up to one thousand guests can bet on a variety of games and sporting events playing out on an enormous wall-to-wall high definition screen that takes a team of ten to operate, visible to patrons dining in three restaurants and drinking in several bars just behind and beneath the Circa casino.

"In the last thirty years, sportsbook designs in Vegas have all been minimalist," says Stevens. "I said, 'We're going the other way. I wanna have the world's biggest sportsbook, and I want it to not just be a large screen, but I want three stories. I want it tiered. I want it as a theater.'

"And they said, 'Well, where's your nightclub going to be?' and I go, 'No, you're missing it. I'm not putting a nightclub in here.' And they go, 'Well, where're you gonna put your showroom?' I go, 'Missing the point. The sportsbook *is* our theater.'"

Even Circa's eight-story, 982-car parking garage is amped to the outer limits. Garage Mahal, as it's known, is billed as "a literal work of art" by Circa's website. "Take in art installations by featured artists on our two corner video walls as you take your car in and out," the website says. It's not merely a parking lot, it's a "parking experience."

"I also want everybody to feel very friendly, and that they're in a very friendly home," says Stevens. "Where there's a lot of high-fiving and a lot of hugging. Some places may put some people off because maybe it's just not that friendly or it's too highfalutin' or something like that. So, we've done a lot of things to make sure that's not the case here."

He and his team stay at Mega Bar until long after midnight.

But while Stevens and his executives are greeting the soon-to-be dawning new Las Vegas day, across town in the Wynn Las Vegas casino a dealer named Bill Luna is bidding goodbye to the casino life he's known for thirty years.

Five days a week, Bill Luna drives thirty minutes from his home in the town of Sunrise Manor to the golden tower of the Wynn resort and casino. He parks his Acura in the customer garage and walks into the resort's basement. Called "the back of the house," it's a forever bustling city one floor beneath the casino, where eleven thousand employees punch in and out during the endless working days and nights.

In the Dealer's Lounge, Luna changes out of his shorts and flip-flops into all-navy slacks, shirt, and vest and black shoes—and from an ordinary life into an extraordinary one, as one of the casino's hundreds of card, roulette wheel, and craps dealers.

The game he deals is Ultimate Texas Hold 'Em, casino style, with a running jackpot that ranges from two hundred fifty thousand to four hundred fifty thousand dollars, but he knows that's only the format: his real game is relating to his customers.

Once he's fully dressed and ready to go, he swipes his Wynn security badge, punches in to the electronic time clock, takes the escalator upstairs, and steps out onto the casino floor.

Luna arrived at the Wynn "when the joint first opened," he likes to say. Prior to Vegas, he spent ten years building submarines for General Dynamics and thirteen years selling Subarus in Mystic, Connecticut—then another thirteen years at his "dream job" dealing blackjack and baccarat at the Foxwoods Resort Casino in Ledyard, Connecticut, before hearing the siren call that led him and his fiancée, Shelley, to set out for the land of chance.

"Steve Wynn," Luna remembers someone telling him. "Building a new place in Vegas called the Wynn."

Coincidentally, two weeks later Bill and Shelley flew out to Las Vegas for the first time, to see Luna's favorite entertainer, Boz Scaggs, perform in concert. They were mesmerized by the volcano at the Mirage, the live bands at the House of Blues, the fiery pirate show at Treasure Island, the erupting fountains at the Bellagio. The heat, the glitz, the glamour. Three days later, back in cold, gray Providence, Rhode Island, watching her soon-to-be husband digging their car out of the snow at the airport, Shelley gave Luna his marching orders:

"I don't wanna live here anymore," she said.

He and Shelley applied online for casino jobs at the Wynn. In-person interviews commenced. They had to submit hair samples to be tested for any evidence of drug use. And finally, the words: *you're hired.*

They started on, of all days, April Fool's Day, 2005.

Now, Bill Luna's a veteran. By the time he clocks in for his shift at the Wynn, the lights of the Strip are blazing full blast. At the Peppermill, that venerable neon-lit restaurant and lounge, open twenty-four hours on weekends, where the night owls sit on booths of red leather beneath faux cherry trees. At Drai's After Hours, thumping with electronic dance music, where bottle service can run five figures as the late-night crowd parties in what the club calls its "13,000+ square feet of intimate lounge space." At the twenty-four-hour wedding chapels where couples with their cars' brights on drive up for their quickie ceremonies. And of course, at every resort and casino up and down the Strip, the cards perpetually flying, Lady Luck hovering, bestowing either blessing or curse.

Bill Luna walks onto the floor like he owns the joint, preparing to take his place at his designated Ultimate Texas Hold 'Em table, where his predecessor, the dealer who's worked the previous eight-hour shift, is as eager to go home as Luna is ready to go on.

"This is Bill," says the departing dealer. "I'm sure he'll take good care of you. Thank you all."

She claps her hands and turns her palms up, to show

the eyes-in-the-sky security squad that they are empty of chips or cash.

Then, Luna takes his place in the pit, and does what he does best: he begins talking.

"How's everybody doing? Where ya from? How long ya been here? When you goin' home?"

The gamblers stare back, some smiling, some frowning, some sober, some not.

"You gotta make them comfortable," Luna explains. "It's the way you run your game."

He plays them as they play him, teasing them with the cards and with his stories, accentuating the good, playing down the bad, trying his best to manage their moods: "You gotta make 'em feel like you're on their side."

He never knows who will sit before him as he deals the cards that can make or break a Vegas vacation. Maybe it will be the late queen's jeweler, just in from London "with a crowd of Brits, all wearing two-hundred-thousand-dollar watches, firing money all over the place" via "markers" (a casino-issued short-term line of credit, resembling a check to be signed by the gambler) for twenty grand and higher. Or the British royal who never divulges his last name, playing two hundred fifty thousand dollars a hand. Could be an Arab prince, a corporate CEO, a billionaire's pilot on a few hours' leave. Or a group of LA gang members milling around the table, with a SWAT team in the distance ready to pounce. Luna hopes there's a few "King Georges," what dealers call the big tippers who throw down five hundred or one thousand dollars or, once, even more than one hundred thousand dollars for Lady Luck's emissary standing before them.

"Turkey, Spain, Argentina, Brazil, Mexico, Canada, Italy…you name it, they come," he says.

Luna is a star in a city of superstars, a dealer in high demand for an eager clientele.

And now it's showtime, another shift and another endless stream of dollars in the city where the lights blaze, the dice roll, the wheels turn, and the cards turn over, twenty-four hours a day, seven days a week.

Only this isn't daytime.

It's the dark of night: 4 a.m.

Luna has begun his last night on the graveyard shift.

In the town without time, in the casinos without clocks, in "the game world," as it's called, the hours of the day are regulated only by what drives everything in Las Vegas: money. "We consider end of day when we count the money, somewhere between three and five o'clock in the morning," says a casino supervisor at one of the major resorts.

At 4 a.m., in casinos across the city, from the lowliest joints to the MGM Grand, the nightly ritual of the money counting begins, when the floor is quiet and only a few gamblers, the real players, are scattered about. The reason for the 4 a.m. count? So the games aren't interrupted at peak hours: "We don't want to disrupt the customers or interrupt their mojo," says the supervisor.

The collection of the drop boxes begins. Black metal containers a bit bigger than a shoebox, the drop boxes are retrieved from every table, filled with bills and markers, sometimes in twenties, sometimes fifties and hundreds, deposited over the previous twenty-four hours through a slot into a box.

As the swing shift dealers prepare to head home at 4 a.m., a casino supervisor and a member of the security team arrives with a huge rolling cart. At each table, the supervisor counts the chips in the rack on the table. Once the game has been "counted," security pulls the box and loads it onto the rack. The old drop box, heavy with markers and cash, locks automatically and goes into the secure cart. A new, empty drop box goes in its place.

The supervisor does the same for the next table, and the next, and the one after that, until each table's winnings have been collected. Finally, the cart, heavy with drop boxes, rolls to the "soft count" room, meaning the cash room. Under bright lights and heavy surveillance, each drop box is opened and the fortune inside run through an electric currency counter once, then again. By 7 a.m., the night audit is usually done, and the casino's win/loss ratio is calculated.

The dealer's tips get counted, too, by the "toke committee," whose representatives collect up each dealer's "toke box"—a small metal box on every table. Prior to the early 1980s, dealers kept their own tips. Now, after the gratuity chips or cash is added up, it's taken to the cashier's cage to be deposited in the bank, then equally divided up by the dealers on each shift.

The count will be done by sunrise.

However, this is still deepest night: 4 a.m., the beginning of the graveyard shift.

Along with the night owls come the cleaning crews, thousands strong. Rolling across the marble casino floors in a brigade of industrial vacuums, brooms, mops, polishers, the crews fan out across the endless marble halls to deep clean and perfume the air with a variety of scents—from the Venetian's "Arancia" to the Cosmopolitan's "Desert Breeze"—so no evidence remains of the crowds that roared through only hours before.

The full-time floral department sweeps through: watering, pruning, replanting fresh flowers and greenery.

The crews do their best to stay far from the tables. Because everything is geared toward the players, even at this ungodly hour, in a carefully controlled environment where everything is engineered—"intentionally," says the supervisor—to keep the players at the tables.

The high-end restaurants have long closed, the last at 11 p.m. And while all-night clubs rage in one quadrant of many of the resorts, the guests going to sleep have been shepherded to rooms in other areas or towers, free from the noise below. "We never want to have you come to Vegas and think that you had a miserable time or had trouble sleeping," says the supervisor.

Those stumbling into the casinos from these late-night clubs are on something of an assembly line, their ebb and flow carefully "staged." "Everyone knows that Vegas is built on partying," says the supervisor. But there's a time, around 4 a.m., when the party people must depart so the gamblers still awake can concentrate on their cards instead of the crazies.

"The East Coast people used to getting up at 7 a.m. on the East Coast are now on West Coast time, and they're up at four or five in the morning," the supervisor says. "They want to come out in their workout clothes and get a coffee, and maybe play a few hands, and they don't want to see the people that have been up for nine hours at a nightclub."

For others, midnight is morning. "The Asians, some of our biggest gamblers, don't change their sleeping patterns when they come to the US," says the supervisor. "They are fifteen hours ahead of us. So, it isn't unusual for them to play most of the night and go to bed when they would normally go to bed at home. So we try to get the nightclub people to bed or to their hotels without offering them a lot."

Because no resort wants the inebriated stumbling through the same spaces as the late-night gamblers, many resorts provide the perfect vehicle to get them off the floor and into cabs or rideshare services. "We would have wheelchairs ready to wheel the people out rather than let them fall or be hurt," says the supervisor.

And because no casino wants their gamblers to see a line of wheelchair-exiting partiers, some resorts erect a wall, behind which the wheelchairs can unobtrusively roll.

Nevertheless, everything is available no matter the hour, especially in the high-limit areas.

"We can get food to you anytime you want and bring it to you right at the table," says the supervisor, all of which is unseen by the masses on the main floor. It's a postmidnight feast: everything from Beluga caviar for the early-bird Americans and Europeans to congee—Chinese rice porridge—for the Asians. The request is made to a dealer, cocktail waitress, or pit boss, and a side table appears at the gaming table, the food and drink delivered—all without the gambler having to take a moment's break.

The dealers move with the players: one hour on, twenty minutes off. If they're assigned to a table with no players, a supervisor will execute a "tap out," a light tap on the shoulder, followed by a direction to another table where they are needed.

"You have to be nimble," says the supervisor.

At last, at around 5:30 a.m., comes the sun. The resorts are clean. The air is fresh and scented. No evidence of the previous night's debauchery remains. "It all looks like a brand-new day," says the supervisor. A new day ready for the coffee bar and gymnasium brigades, the convention-eers and the newlyweds, the minnows and the whales, inhaling the newly perfumed air and reveling in the pris-tine surroundings.

Las Vegas is reborn.

At around 6 a.m., Tony descends from his suite into the Wynn casino.

He has precisely two hours to indulge in his passion: playing Ultimate Texas Hold 'Em at the table that, even at this hour, when most tables lay empty, is usually packed, due to the magnetism of the dealer, Bill Luna.

Wearing his workout clothes, Tony first sat down at Luna's table at six o'clock one morning in 2008, looking "like nobody special," Luna recalls thinking, until the stranger spoke.

"Gimme a marker for ten grand," Luna remembers him saying.

"Where ya from?" the dealer asks, as he always does.

"Los Angeles," the gambler replies.

And his story gradually pours out.

Tony has what he calls "an excuse" to come to Vegas. An immensely successful businessman, he has amassed a fortune in his occupation. But when he sits down at the gambling table, all evidence of the mogul vanishes.

He's not gambling for the money. He's already got more than enough. But almost nothing matches the thrill of sitting before Luna and awaiting the deliverance of those blessed—or cursed—cards. The reverential quiet in the normally noisy space. The air devoid of cigarette smoke. The casino floor minus the hordes that will thunder through it a few hours' hence.

At this hour the casino almost feels holy.

This is what Tony loves about gambling on the grave-yard shift. Most of all, he loves the maximized time. "The reality is I'm working, so there's a reason why I'm in town," he says. "Other than a dinner, I don't really have much time to spare."

Yet time doesn't seem to matter once the dealing begins.

"It's a game, and while I can't win enough to change my life, who can resist a game?" he asks.

Luna notices something after one of his first deals.

The cards come raining down. Tony turns them over.

A straight flush.

"I look over and he's jumping up and down in the middle of the aisle, literally yelling, 'Yippie! Yahoo!'" says Luna. "And I'm like, 'What the hell's going on with this guy?'"

Luna is accustomed to players getting excited when they win, but this is at a whole different level. "He's a fourteen-year-old wrapped up in a sixty-year-old body," he says, "jumping up and down and playing table max like he's playing five dollars a hand. When he's playing fifteen hundred to three thousand dollars per."

From that point on, they are a team: Tony coming in to play before changing from sweatsuit to business suit to begin his Las Vegas business day; Luna silently hoping the cards come up a winner—first because they're friends, and secondly, because he just loves to witness the enthusiasm.

Tony travels to Vegas every other week on business. He always grabs a cup of coffee in the lobby, then heads straight to Luna's table around 6 a.m. for two hours of uninterrupted play. Then he spends an hour in the gym and goes off to work, then catches the flight back home.

One Sunday at 6 a.m., Tony casually mentions to Luna that he has an early plane to catch. Yet he keeps enthusiastically gambling. Once it gets to be 10 a.m., Luna can't hold it in anymore.

"Aren't you going to miss your plane?" asks Luna.

"Don't worry, they'll wait for me," says Tony, and Luna immediately understands. *The guy's flying private.*

Tony and the other regulars at Luna's table have formed something of a gambling family. There's the late great Charlie from Houston, a ten-hour-a-day player. "He was the foremost authority on oil and gas and a poker savant, who flew to Vegas every weekend to play Ultimate Texas Hold 'Em with me," says Luna. There's the delightful young couple from Manchester, England, who, having made a fortune in investments, sit for hours at Luna's table for the fun, the stories, the laughs, and the camaraderie. A wealthy import-export entrepreneur and his wife show up regularly to play with their best friends, an internationally famous soap star and her husband. One of the Wynn casino's top slot players takes a break from the machines to revel with the crowd at Luna's table. And there's always the poor guy who insists on "sticking by a system," says Luna, even if it means he always loses, at fifteen hundred dollars a hand.

Professional golfers, former NFL coaches, money managers, and movie stars pass by as night turns to dawn. And Luna will never forget one sterling early morning when, he says, Elaine Wynn's nephew rolls through the casino with two VIP guests in tow: former secretary of state Henry

Kissinger and his wife, Nancy. "Bring Doctor Kissinger over and I'll teach him to play Ultimate Texas Hold 'Em!" Luna exclaims. After a fifteen-minute lesson, Kissinger plays precisely one hand. "He wins, says goodbye, and off he goes."

"Bill has a cantankerous, East Coast way about him," says Tony, "which makes playing with him interesting. I always say, 'He's kind of an asshole, but he's my asshole, and I love him.'"

Other than the cards, Tony comes for "the laughs," and the departure from the stereotypical Las Vegas party scene—the night owls passing in the early-morning hours, adrift and drunk. "It's six in the morning and they haven't been to bed yet."

He calls them the "zombies."

"Because that's what I'd look like if I stayed up all night, too."

Later in the morning, some of the restaurants open for breakfast, but Luna's shift won't be over until noon, when the day shift begins, and the fresh crew of dealers takes over. The zombies creep home or to their rooms. The players trade in their chips for cash.

But before Luna's regulars return to their everyday lives, to their heartland towns or big cities, they pay homage to the dealer who has given them so much. Because after twenty-eight years in the casino business, Luna is retiring, and the players at his Ultimate Texas Hold 'Em table are throwing him a goodbye party. Right in the Wynn casino, during the graveyard shift, with blessings from management. Complete with toasts. Balloons. Testi-monials. And a bottle of Billecart-Salmon Brut Rosé cham-pagne, purchased by Luna's most enthusiastic player, Tony.

"King of the hill, Bill," says a regular in a video one of the gamblers takes of this momentous occasion, as Luna prepares for his final deal.

"The last hand," mourns another.

"Oh, Bill, don't get me going!" a woman at the table shrieks.

"Gimme something *special*!" shouts Tony, the biggest noisemaker.

The chips rise, the cards come raining down, and when it's done, Luna has ended his storied career. Cham-pagne is hoisted high.

One Las Vegas career ends, while a brand-new Las Vegas day begins.

Chapter 22

THE VALLEY
OF FIRE

THE MOJAVE DESERT

THE BIG BIRD rises at dawn from the Las Vegas airport, saluting the sun.

"Everybody buckled up?" asks the Maverick Helicopters pilot, who has flown through the war in Iraq. "Because here we go!"

There are seven passengers aboard the helicopter. Four women and their best friend, who is celebrating her fortieth birthday with a girls' weekend in Vegas. A former Chippendale's dancer, who is videotaping the morning's excursion. And, sitting next to the pilot, Chundrea Gardner, now simply known as Dray, a dexterous fifty-five-year-old yoga instructor who grew up on the streets of South Central Los Angeles. As the helicopter leaves the Strip behind, the passengers gaze through its glass bottom as Las Vegas reveals its greatest wonder of all, just a twenty-minute flight away: the Valley of Fire, forty-six thousand acres of vast outcroppings in the Mojave Desert, majestic pillars and arches that seem to have been sculpted from the sandstone, blazing pink, orange, and red in the fiery dawn. The valley is considered a sacred place, inhabited for at least eleven thousand years by a succession of Indigenous peoples, from the Basketmakers and the Ancestral Puebloans to the Paiutes, who left behind ancient petroglyphs chiseled into the stone walls.

Now, the five women in spandex are arriving in this sacred valley, to practice a discipline that is both ancient and new: yoga. Or, as this adventure is called, HeliYoga.

The helicopter touches down in true Vegas fashion: a dramatic landing on a tiny spit of reddish-pink rock, surrounded by nothing but deep-blue sky. "Let's set up," says Dray.

Climbing out of the chopper, the soft rock crunching beneath their feet, the women work their way over to a blazing-red mesa, just large enough to accommodate their yoga mats. They feel lucky to be among the few granted access to this magical spot—and the woman leading the group feels the luckiest of all. Her name is Nikolai, and today is her birthday. A jewelry designer from Hawaii, she specializes in creating works out of jade, a gemstone believed to bring good luck. She felt luck shining on her back home, the moment she read about HeliYoga in a travel magazine. And now, for a fee of around four thousand dollars, luck has delivered her and her friends to what feels like the top of the world.

Nikolai and her friends have spent the last few days in some of the best resorts in the world—the Delano, the Bellagio, the Wynn. But nothing compares to this. As the sun rises to their left, the women are breathless, both from their sense of awe and from the altitude, almost three thousand feet above sea level. Dray hands each of them a pair of wireless headphones. Silence, he tells them, is integral to his practice, which he calls Silent Savasana. Through the headphones, he can offer them instructions softly, without raising his voice.

"Yoga is the ultimate act of self-love," he begins, as they sit on their mats. "The most important relationship you have in this lifetime is the one you have with yourself. You are your most important piece of work. As we embark upon this journey, there is no comparing, no competing. Just do your best to be your best."

The women take a deep breath, followed by a long, slow exhale.

"Yoga isn't about expectations," Dray continues. "Expectations lead to heartbreak and misery. We are all on the same road, just in different distances. Love yourself enough to struggle. But most importantly, love yourself."

Another breath. Another exhale.

"Let's begin."

Dray knows about beginnings, knows the rigors of the rock-bottom climb from the depths of despair. Today he's a testament to the power of self-improvement, his wisdom and serenity inspiring the multitudes—"concert numbers," as he puts it—who flock to the yoga sessions he leads at the Las Vegas resorts. But only a decade before, the god of Las Vegas yoga desperately needed healing himself. It's the story of a less-than-celestial arrival in Sin City, or as Dray calls it, Zen City, and how yoga saved his life and set him on his path to enlightenment.

It begins in 1991. Dray is twenty-three, still going by his given name, Chundrea Gardner. He lives in South Central Los Angeles, which presents him with a choice: "life or death." He knows that if he stays, chances are very high that he will fall victim to the violence that has confronted him his entire life. His hands have been broken seven times—"once by police, once in football, and five times in fights." A shooting happens while he's at a nightclub, bullets flying overhead as he tries to help save other patrons. "The life expectancy for a black man in South Central Los Angeles is twenty-five," he says. His mind blazes with six words: *get out while you still can.*

"In Africa, you had to kill a lion to become a man," he later reflects. "There weren't any lions in South Central Los Angeles. So I decided to get on the I-15 and move to Las Vegas so I could stand alone and be a man!"

He has one thousand dollars in his pocket and his possessions packed into his battered old Nissan. Five hours of driving later, he pulls into the Strip and he knows he has arrived.

I'm never leaving, he says to himself. *Somehow, some way, I'm gonna leave my footprint on this town.*

He spends his first night in a mammoth red-and-white circus tent—the hotel and casino extravaganza known as Circus Circus. "Twenty-five bucks for a room," he says. "Ninety-nine-cent drinks and twenty-five-cent hot dogs. Shit was amazing."

When he awakens the next morning, the fact that he doesn't know a soul in town sinks in. But his head is filled with affirmations. *I'm gonna make this happen. Sink or swim. Drop me off anywhere and I'm gonna survive.*

For starters, he drops his clunky name, Chundrea Gardner. From now on, he'll be known simply as Dray. A single name only, as befits a star in Las Vegas: Elvis, Wayne, Cher, Céline, Penn and Teller. In the city of opportunity, he quickly finds a job. The first: pot washer at the Palace Station hotel and casino. This being Vegas, he isn't washing just any pots, but sauté pans. With lightning-fast chefs preparing delicacies on the pans the equally fast Dray is cleaning. "You had to move *fast*. I was dealing with hot-ass skillets!"

Next comes telemarketing. Bartending. VIP host. Bodyguard. DJ. Musician. For a time, he runs a "condominium on wheels, the first rolling party bus in Las Vegas, with a stripper pole and room for ten." Soon he's selling real estate, wearing Versace and Armani and bringing in hundreds of thousands of dollars a year, a family man with a wife and daughter. He has survived South Central, and conquered Las Vegas.

Until his back brings him back down to earth.

It's been bothering him since his bartending days, the pain shooting down like a switchblade. Finally, his doctor sends him for an MRI, which shows a cyst on his spine, pushing down on his vertebrae, the result of bone rubbing on bone after years of abuse: "football, jiu jitsu, wrestling, car accidents, motorcycle accidents, street fights." The cyst is growing, and his doctor insists on immediate back surgery—otherwise, the condition will worsen and Dray will be left unable to walk. The nerve damage causes him seizures, which leave him feeling like he's "been hit by a truck for three weeks." His future looks dim, a lifetime of hospitals and misery. Forget about real estate, forget about walking, much less leaving a footprint on Las Vegas.

Then a friend who has been diagnosed with hypertension is told that yoga might help. He asks Dray if he'd like to accompany him to a yoga studio. Only to observe, of course—there's no way Dray could actually strike a yoga pose, given the crippling pain in his back.

"What the hell," Dray tells his friend. "I've got nothin' else to do."

When he arrives at the first yoga studio he has ever seen in his life—Bikram Yoga West, the Las Vegas temple of the popular discipline of intense yoga in a room heated to one hundred five degrees—Dray can't even walk inside. "I was using a cane and wearing a diaper," he says. "I was crawling on my chest like I was in a war and there was sniper fire blasting over me."

The room is *hot*. Hotter than outside, and Vegas on this

day is Death Valley hot. Watching as his friend and the other students do downward dog and warrior poses, Dray is overcome with a sense of loss. "I sat in the back and I cried," he says. One of the yoga instructors notices and comes over to encourage him.

Give it a try, she suggests. *You don't have to do the whole pose. Just do something—anything. Just give it your best, whatever that is.*

In the heat, Dray begins to move. An inch or two feels like a mile to him. But he does it. Then he comes back "the next day and the next day and the next day." To bathe in the heat, and to do his best to move. In that room, hot as any biblical desert, he makes a deal with God. "If you help me move again," he vows, "I will dedicate my life to this purpose and this calling."

Within two weeks, the cane is gone. Within a year, he's enrolled in an intensive yoga program, performing the most challenging poses day after day, for thirty days straight. He makes good on his promise. He gives away the clothes from his previous life, the Versace and Armani, and joins a program to become a yoga teacher. He wants to share the miracle that Las Vegas has handed him, as it has so many others before him. The power to start over again.

Dray becomes certified in a variety of disciplines, but his style is entirely his own. Drawing on his experience as a Vegas musician and DJ, he equips his students with wireless headphones, enabling him to speak with them directly, his voice inside their heads. He intersperses his words with music—not the soothing New Age sounds usually associated with yoga, but Sinatra, Al Green, Prince, David Bowie, the Notorious B.I.G.—"to help people get away from thinking and help them relax."

His classes become not merely a sensation; they become a movement, the crowds at Dray's yoga events as large, he says, as those that pack the city's biggest showrooms. He takes over the mammoth swimming pools at almost all the Las Vegas resorts—the MGM Grand, Caesars Palace, Mandalay Bay, the Palazzo at the Venetian, Tao, Red Rock Casino and Spa—bringing bliss to places where booze normally reigns. And numbers, being the currency of Las Vegas, attract attention. One day Dray gets a call from Maverick Helicopters, the biggest helicopter operator in Las Vegas. The company ferries passengers in its fleet of nearly fifty helicopters day and night, to NASCAR races and Coachella and, its most popular destination, the Grand Canyon—a four-hour visit to the canyon and back, more than thirty flights a day.

"Would you be interested in doing something that has never been done before?" the company representative asks Dray.

"Absolutely," replies the man who was told he would never walk again. "That's what I specialize in."

"Let's combine our visions," the representative suggests. "We have the helicopters. You're the most popular yoga instructor in the city. Let's see if we can do some yoga classes in spots only accessible to us."

There is a place, Dray learns, of breathtaking natural wonder only twenty minutes away from the city. A state park whose glories rival those of the Grand Canyon. You can't drive or hike to the tops of its mesas or land a plane there. Its wild interior is accessible only by helicopter. It's called the Valley of Fire, and its beauty is so other-worldly that it stood in for the planet Mars in the Arnold Schwarzenegger movie *Total Recall,* its red rocks glowing with the power of rebirth and renewal. When Maverick first flies Dray to the valley, fifty-five miles northeast of the city, he is awestruck.

"This is paradise," he says. "Like being on another planet."

Dray scopes out the rocky terrain, finding the best site for a yoga session: a flat plane on a high ridge overlooking the entire valley. Soon yoga enthusiasts from all over the world are flocking to join Maverick Helicopters and Dray on the HeliYoga excursions. Bridal parties. Bachelorette parties. Young staffers from an international cosmetics company. A group of social media influencers posting their Valley of Fire experience to their seven million followers. And engagements, proposals coming after the yoga is done. "She opens her eyes," Dray says, "and he's on his mat on his knees with the ring."

Now, atop the mesa, Dray leads Nikolai and her four friends through a series of poses. "Love yourself enough to struggle," he tells them. "Everybody wants to buy the Rolex and the Maserati and the new Lamborghini. But they don't love themselves. You gotta say, *I* am the Lambo! *I* am the Rolex! All that shit that everybody's trying to buy, and they don't realize that they *are* all of that."

The miracle of his healing has taught Dray what matters most in life. "Vegas, they say, is the entertainment capital of the world," he tells the women as the sun rises. "But a healthy *you* is also an entertainment capital, and it is your responsibility to heal. You've traveled from glitz and glamour to the present. You are here. No yesterday. No tomorrow. *Now.*"

As the women follow Dray's voice, practicing poses and focusing on their breathing, the photographer Jason Harper films their every move. Like Dray, he came to Vegas to make his mark, landing a spot as a backup dancer in the world's most famous all-male strip show: Chippendale's. Overnight, he was performing before an audience of six hundred screaming women to thundering songs like "Save a Horse (Ride a Cowboy)." Then one day, it was time to shoot the behind-the-scenes video for the annual Chippendale's calendar, and the videographer who had handled the job for years couldn't do it. So Harper jumped behind the camera and found his future. "I fell in love with photography," he says. He has spent the weekend filming Nikolai and her friends, documenting all the highlights of her birthday getaway: the fabulous restaurants, the luxury spas, the endless nights of partying. And now, as their final day breaks, the pinnacle experience: the helicopter yoga adventure in the Valley of Fire.

After seventy-five minutes of pure bliss, the yoga session comes to a close. Dray instructs the women to lie on their backs beneath the magnificent sky as he leads them through Savasana, the final relaxation meditation.

Breathe, he tells the five women, breathe deeply. Take in the majestic Mojave Desert air, and don't let it go too quickly; it's not just oxygen, it's *everything*. "Anything that survives the longest breathes the slowest, and those that expire quickest have the fastest breath," he tells them over their headsets. "So there is a connection between our breath and our life. If we change our breathing, we can change our life. We can expand our life and destroy our stress levels. *Breathe*. In and out, through your nose. We worry more about the shell than the soul. Self-love is the greatest gift you can give humanity. But until you heal the wounds, you're gonna bleed. Be the light that you want to see in the world and be the blessing that you want your life to become. It starts with you."

Then Dray clasps his hands before him. "Namaste," he says softly.

When the women open their eyes, they feel refreshed and reborn. They rise up on their yoga mats and revel one last time in the ancient landscape that stretches before them, almost as far as the eye can see. Before a final champagne toast, before the helicopter flight back across the desert and the Strip, they salute the brand-new day. They salute nature itself, the majestic Valley of Fire, now painted in even more vibrant and otherworldly colors by the risen sun. Then they board the helicopter and take off, flying over the city twinkling in the distance, the festival of electric lights and gambling, spectacle and escape, a bacchanal unrivaled in the world or time immemorial. They salute the place that brought them to a moment they will remember the rest of their lives.

They salute the glory of Las Vegas, Nevada.

ACKNOWLEDGMENTS

For their valuable assistance, insights and expertise, the authors wish to thank everyone quoted or mentioned by name in this book, which could not have been written without them.

Additionally, we would like to thank: Lauren Addante, Chris Baldizan, R.J. Cipriani, Catherine Cole, Chris Cole, Anne Dongois, Debbie Faint, Roberto Garcia, Michael Gaughan, Bruce Gelb, Scott Ghertner, Taylor Goldberg, Samantha Grimes, Michael Gruber, Erik Himel, Pete Kepes, Jeff Ma, Erin Nappi, Debi Nutton, Ann Paladie, Philip Plastina, Joseph Rajchel, David Roger, Brooke Sanchez, David Schwartz, Corey Ware, Susan White, Gina Wilborn, George M. Wilson IV, Debra and Roland Wright, as well as the early morning crew at the Fountains of Bellagio (including Arnold Cabrera, Adam Rohleder, and Loni Singer), Jenn Michaels of MGM Resorts, Shakala Alvaranga and Geoff Schumacher at the Mob Museum, and Aaron Berger and Emily Fellmer of the Neon Museum.

Special thanks to the *Las Vegas Review-Journal* and

the *Las Vegas Sun,* whose archives are a repository of the illustrious city's history, and the other publications and sources quoted in this book.

And thank you also to Eric Bates, Richard "Rip" Beyman, Laura Blocker, Erica Commisso, Grazie Christie, Barbara Davis, Lottie Jackson, Mary Jordan, David Karp, Brad Krevoy, Wayne Lawson, Jon Leckie, Justin McGown, Jan Miller of Dupree Miller and Associates, Marc and Jane Nathanson, John Pelosi, Jeff Rich, Bill Robinson, and everyone on the outstanding Little, Brown editorial and production teams.

ABOUT THE AUTHORS

James Patterson is one of the best-known and biggest-selling writers of all time. Among his creations are some of the world's most popular series, including Alex Cross, the Women's Murder Club, Michael Bennett and the Private novels. He has written many other number one bestsellers including collaborations with President Bill Clinton and Dolly Parton, stand-alone thrillers and non-fiction. James has donated millions in grants to independent bookshops and has been the most borrowed adult author in UK libraries for the past fourteen years in a row. He lives in Florida with his family.

Mark Seal is the author of numerous non-fiction books, including *Wildflower,* about the incredible life and brutal murder of Kenyan naturalist and filmmaker Joan Root; *The Man in the Rockefeller Suit,* about the life and crimes of the serial con artist who called himself Clark Rockefeller; and *Leave the Gun, Take the Cannoli: The Epic Story of the Making of The Godfather.* A contributing editor at *Vanity Fair* since 2003, he has twice been a National Magazine Awards finalist.

Discover the next thrilling instalment in James
Patterson's globally bestselling Alex Cross series . . .

Alex
CROSS
Must Die

OUT NOW

Also By James Patterson

ALEX CROSS NOVELS

Along Came a Spider • Kiss the Girls • Jack and Jill • Cat and Mouse • Pop Goes the Weasel • Roses are Red • Violets are Blue • Four Blind Mice • The Big Bad Wolf • London Bridges • Mary, Mary • Cross • Double Cross • Cross Country • Alex Cross's Trial (*with Richard DiLallo*) • I, Alex Cross • Cross Fire • Kill Alex Cross • Merry Christmas, Alex Cross • Alex Cross, Run • Cross My Heart • Hope to Die • Cross Justice • Cross the Line • The People vs. Alex Cross • Target: Alex Cross • Criss Cross • Deadly Cross • Fear No Evil • Triple Cross • Alex Cross Must Die

THE WOMEN'S MURDER CLUB SERIES

1st to Die (*with Andrew Gross*) • 2nd Chance (*with Andrew Gross*) • 3rd Degree (*with Andrew Gross*) • 4th of July (*with Maxine Paetro*) • The 5th Horseman (*with Maxine Paetro*) • The 6th Target (*with Maxine Paetro*) • 7th Heaven (*with Maxine Paetro*) • 8th Confession (*with Maxine Paetro*) • 9th Judgement (*with Maxine Paetro*) • 10th Anniversary (*with Maxine Paetro*) • 11th Hour (*with Maxine Paetro*) • 12th of Never (*with Maxine Paetro*) • Unlucky 13 (*with Maxine Paetro*) • 14th Deadly Sin (*with Maxine Paetro*) • 15th Affair (*with Maxine Paetro*) • 16th Seduction (*with Maxine Paetro*) • 17th Suspect (*with Maxine Paetro*) • 18th Abduction (*with Maxine Paetro*) • 19th Christmas (*with Maxine Paetro*) • 20th Victim (*with Maxine Paetro*) • 21st Birthday (*with Maxine Paetro*) • 22 Seconds (*with Maxine Paetro*) • 23rd Midnight (*with Maxine Paetro*)

DETECTIVE MICHAEL BENNETT SERIES

Step on a Crack (*with Michael Ledwidge*) • Run for Your Life (*with Michael Ledwidge*) • Worst Case (*with Michael Ledwidge*) • Tick Tock (*with Michael Ledwidge*) • I, Michael Bennett (*with Michael Ledwidge*) • Gone (*with Michael Ledwidge*) • Burn (*with Michael Ledwidge*) • Alert (*with Michael Ledwidge*) • Bullseye (*with Michael*

Ledwidge) • Haunted (*with James O. Born*) • Ambush (*with James O. Born*) • Blindside (*with James O. Born*) • The Russian (*with James O. Born*) • Shattered (*with James O. Born*) • Obsessed (*with James O. Born*)

PRIVATE NOVELS

Private (*with Maxine Paetro*) • Private London (*with Mark Pearson*) • Private Games (*with Mark Sullivan*) • Private: No. 1 Suspect (*with Maxine Paetro*) • Private Berlin (*with Mark Sullivan*) • Private Down Under (*with Michael White*) • Private L.A. (*with Mark Sullivan*) • Private India (*with Ashwin Sanghi*) • Private Vegas (*with Maxine Paetro*) • Private Sydney (*with Kathryn Fox*) • Private Paris (*with Mark Sullivan*) • The Games (*with Mark Sullivan*) • Private Delhi (*with Ashwin Sanghi*) • Private Princess (*with Rees Jones*) • Private Moscow (*with Adam Hamdy*) • Private Rogue (*with Adam Hamdy*) • Private Beijing (*with Adam Hamdy*) • Private Rome (*with Adam Hamdy*)

NYPD RED SERIES

NYPD Red (*with Marshall Karp*) • NYPD Red 2 (*with Marshall Karp*) • NYPD Red 3 (*with Marshall Karp*) • NYPD Red 4 (*with Marshall Karp*) • NYPD Red 5 (*with Marshall Karp*) • NYPD Red 6 (*with Marshall Karp*)

DETECTIVE HARRIET BLUE SERIES

Never Never (*with Candice Fox*) • Fifty Fifty (*with Candice Fox*) • Liar Liar (*with Candice Fox*) • Hush Hush (*with Candice Fox*)

INSTINCT SERIES

Instinct (*with Howard Roughan, previously published as* Murder Games) • Killer Instinct (*with Howard Roughan*) • Steal (*with Howard Roughan*)

THE BLACK BOOK SERIES

The Black Book (*with David Ellis*) • The Red Book (*with David Ellis*) • Escape (*with David Ellis*)

STAND-ALONE THRILLERS

The Thomas Berryman Number • Hide and Seek • Black Market • The Midnight Club • Sail (*with Howard Roughan*) • Swimsuit (*with Maxine Paetro*) • Don't Blink (*with Howard Roughan*) • Postcard Killers (*with Liza Marklund*) • Toys (*with Neil McMahon*) • Now You See Her (*with Michael Ledwidge*) • Kill Me If You Can (*with Marshall Karp*) • Guilty Wives (*with David Ellis*) • Zoo (*with Michael Ledwidge*) • Second Honeymoon (*with Howard Roughan*) • Mistress (*with David Ellis*) • Invisible (*with David Ellis*) • Truth or Die (*with Howard Roughan*) • Murder House (*with David Ellis*) • The Store (*with Richard DiLallo*) • Texas Ranger (*with Andrew Bourelle*) • The President is Missing (*with Bill Clinton*) • Revenge (*with Andrew Holmes*) • Juror No. 3 (*with Nancy Allen*) • The First Lady (*with Brendan DuBois*) • The Chef (*with Max DiLallo*) • Out of Sight (*with Brendan DuBois*) • Unsolved (*with David Ellis*) • The Inn (*with Candice Fox*) • Lost (*with James O. Born*) • Texas Outlaw (*with Andrew Bourelle*) • The Summer House (*with Brendan DuBois*) • 1st Case (*with Chris Tebbetts*) • Cajun Justice (*with Tucker Axum*)• The Midwife Murders (*with Richard DiLallo*) • The Coast-to-Coast Murders (*with J.D. Barker*) • Three Women Disappear (*with Shan Serafin*) • The President's Daughter (*with Bill Clinton*) • The Shadow (*with Brian Sitts*) • The Noise (*with J.D. Barker*) • 2 Sisters Detective Agency (*with Candice Fox*) • Jailhouse Lawyer (*with Nancy Allen*) • The Horsewoman (*with Mike Lupica*) • Run Rose Run (*with Dolly Parton*) • Death of the Black Widow (*with J.D. Barker*) • The Ninth Month (*with Richard DiLallo*) • The Girl in the Castle (*with Emily Raymond*) • Blowback (*with Brendan DuBois*) • The Twelve Topsy-Turvy, Very Messy Days of Christmas (*with Tad Safran*) • The Perfect Assassin (*with Brian Sitts*) • House of Wolves (*with Mike Lupica*) • Countdown (*with Brendan DuBois*) • Cross Down (*with Brendan DuBois*) • Circle of Death (*with Brian Sitts*) • Lion & Lamb (with *Duane Swierczynski*) • 12 Months to Live (*with Mike Lupica*)

NON-FICTION

Torn Apart (*with Hal and Cory Friedman*) • The Murder of King Tut (*with Martin Dugard*) • All-American Murder (*with Alex Abramovich and Mike Harvkey*) • The Kennedy Curse (*with Cynthia Fagen*) • The Last Days of John Lennon (*with Casey Sherman and Dave Wedge*) • Walk in My Combat Boots (*with Matt*

Eversmann and Chris Mooney) • ER Nurses (*with Matt Eversmann*) • James Patterson by James Patterson: The Stories of My Life • Diana, William and Harry (*with Chris Mooney*) • American Cops (*with Matt Eversmann*)

MURDER IS FOREVER TRUE CRIME

Murder, Interrupted (*with Alex Abramovich and Christopher Charles*) • Home Sweet Murder (*with Andrew Bourelle and Scott Slaven*) • Murder Beyond the Grave (*with Andrew Bourelle and Christopher Charles*) • Murder Thy Neighbour (*with Andrew Bourelle and Max DiLallo*) • Murder of Innocence (*with Max DiLallo and Andrew Bourelle*) • Till Murder Do Us Part (*with Andrew Bourelle and Max DiLallo*)

COLLECTIONS

Triple Threat (*with Max DiLallo and Andrew Bourelle*) • Kill or Be Killed (*with Maxine Paetro, Rees Jones, Shan Serafin and Emily Raymond*) • The Moores are Missing (*with Loren D. Estleman, Sam Hawken and Ed Chatterton*) • The Family Lawyer (*with Robert Rotstein, Christopher Charles and Rachel Howzell Hall*) • Murder in Paradise (*with Doug Allyn, Connor Hyde and Duane Swierczynski*) • The House Next Door (*with Susan DiLallo, Max DiLallo and Brendan DuBois*) • 13-Minute Murder (*with Shan Serafin, Christopher Farnsworth and Scott Slaven*) • The River Murders (*with James O. Born*) • The Palm Beach Murders (*with James O. Born, Duane Swierczynski and Tim Arnold*) • Paris Detective • 3 Days to Live • 23 ½ Lies (*with Maxine Paetro*)

For more information about James Patterson's novels, visit www.penguin.co.uk.

.